DAILY TALKS
WITH
GOD

NOELLE BONJOUR

WESTBOW
PRESS®
A DIVISION OF THOMAS NELSON
& ZONDERVAN

WestBow Press books may be ordered through booksellers or by contacting:

WestBow Press
A Division of Thomas Nelson & Zondervan
1663 Liberty Drive
Bloomington, IN 47403
www.westbowpress.com
1 (866) 928-1240

Scripture quotations marked NIV are taken from the Holy Bible, New
International Version®. NIV®. Copyright © 1973, 1978, 1984 by International
Bible Society. Used by permission of Zondervan. All rights reserved. [Biblica]

ISBN: 978-1-9736-2423-3 (sc)
ISBN: 978-1-9736-2424-0 (hc)
ISBN: 978-1-9736-2422-6 (e)

Library of Congress Control Number: 2018903753

Print information available on the last page.

WestBow Press rev. date: 03/29/2018

For Sarah, who challenged me to this project in the first place
and for Philip and Ben, who provided inspiration
for me when it was otherwise eluding me.

Introduction

I started out writing daily devotions as a Lenten discipline, as I found myself seeking a better way to grow in my faith. I learned many things through that first Lent of writing devotions, and my faith did indeed grow and mature in ways it never had before. I was spending time every day with God's Holy Word, with the spiritual food I didn't even realize my soul was craving.

Devotions are an important part of the spiritual lives of many Christians. It doesn't matter if a person starts or ends their day with a devotion. What matters is that we Christians spend time daily with our God. We all have that hunger that only God can satisfy.

Everything a person needs for a little daily meditation can be found on the following pages. Each day begins with a Bible verse or short passage, taken from the New International Version. Then comes the meditation on the passage and a concluding prayer.

My hope is that these daily meditations enrich the spiritual lives of the readers as much as they enriched my life as the author.

God bless,
Noelle

January 1

In the beginning was the Word, and the Word
was with God, and the Word was God.

—John 1:1

John is my favorite Gospel. There is nothing ordinary about this book. Even the way it begins is unique. Rather than beginning with the birth of Jesus, or even the birth of John the Baptist, this Gospel goes back to the beginning of everything. "Let's start at the very beginning."

The Gospel of John is full of details (which is probably why I, a detail-oriented person, enjoy it so much). And John begins with two very powerful details. First, Jesus is God's Word, the promise spoken through the ages of the Old Testament. Second, Jesus is one with God and always has been.

So, as we begin our new year, full of promise and plans, let's pause to remember the ultimate promise and the ultimate plan—Jesus, the Word made flesh. No matter where our year's journey takes us, Jesus will always journey with us. He is God's Word, with God from the beginning and with us now.

Word of God, thank You for coming to the earth to fulfill the promise of salvation for all of mankind. As I journey through this new year, please walk with me and remind me of Your constant presence. Amen.

January 2

If I have the gift of prophecy and can fathom all
mysteries and all knowledge, and if I have a faith
that can move mountains, but do not have love,
I am nothing.

—1 Corinthians 13:2

While this entire passage is usually read at weddings, this
verse is really something that we need to be aware of on a daily
basis.

We all have talents. Some people use their talents to get
ahead in life. They want fortune and glory, so to speak. Others
can use the same talents without any recognition, helping others
because it is the right thing to do.

Did you ever watch the TV show *Extreme Makeover: Home
Edition*? How does that compare to Habitat for Humanity? Both
have helped many very deserving families. Yet, *Extreme Makeover:
Home Edition* only helped people as long as the show was popular
and had high enough ratings. Habitat for Humanity continues
to help people, powered by people whose only desire is to help.

No matter how beneficial an act is, unless it is done out of
love, it is done for the wrong reason.

Lord of love, guide my actions and teach me how to use the
talents You gave me to help others, not for personal gain but out
of love for Your creation. In Jesus' name I pray. Amen.

January 3

But when you give to the needy, do not let your left hand know what your right hand is doing, so that your giving may be in secret. Then your Father, who sees what is done in secret, will reward you.

—Matthew 6:3–4

This follows along the same lines as yesterday's verse. Make sure you are doing the right thing for the right reason. But there is more to these verses than simply doing something without recognition.

Jesus did not say "if you give to the needy." No, He said "when." Jesus was making a point of saying that we should be helping those around us.

With that distinction, Jesus reiterates the purpose behind doing acts of charity. We are not to be giving to the needy for personal recognition, but instead, we should be helping those around us because it is the Christian thing to do. We are to be working in secret out of love. Then God will reward us, which is a much better reward than anything this world could offer us!

Father who sees in secret, show me how to help those around me in ways that only You will see. Let me do my acts of giving out of love, giving You and You alone the glory for my actions. In Jesus' name, amen.

January 4

Jesus replied, "'Love the Lord your God with all your heart and with all your soul and with all your mind.' This is the first and greatest commandment."

—Matthew 22:37–38

"I love you, but...." Have you ever had someone say this to you? Those first three words are quite powerful as they are. However, that fourth word has the power to tear down what the first three built up. "I love you, but you are such a dork." Or "I love you, but I'll love you more if you do something for me." All the good that was done by being told you are loved can disappear in a moment when followed by an insult (even a playful insult) or a condition.

Knowing how you feel about it, think about how God feels when receiving an "I love you, but...." We may not come right out and say it. However, our actions can speak it just as loudly as our voices. "God, I love You, but I don't want to worship You today." "God, I love You, but I'll love You more if You give me what I ask for."

When asked what the greatest commandment was, Jesus responded that we are to love God with our entire being—heart, soul, and mind. No "buts" about it!

O Lord my God, I love You. I love You with all of my heart and soul and mind. For Jesus' sake, please forgive me when I fail to show You how much I love You. Amen.

January 5

The Lord says: "These people come near to Me with their mouth and honor Me with their lips, but their hearts are far from Me. Their worship of Me is based on merely human rules they have been taught."

—Isaiah 29:13

Unless I am sitting down to eat with my parents, I usually do not say "table grace" before I eat anymore. That's not to say I do not pray before meals. I just do not recite prayers except when with my parents or at church.

My reason for that is simple—too often, when reciting a prayer, I find myself *saying* it, not actually *praying* it. So, to make sure I am truly praying, I do not recite prayers I memorized years ago. I pray by telling God what is on my mind or in my heart at that moment.

God knows when we are just going through the motions, singing hymns or reciting prayers because that's "what we do." Yet that is not what God wants. So let's break away from doing things because that's how we've been taught to worship God. Instead, let's allow our hearts to lead our worship. That's what God really wants—our hearts.

Forgive me, Lord, when my adherence to human rules and traditions detracts from my worship of You. Remind me anew every day to draw close to You, not with my lips alone but also with my heart. Amen.

January 6

> After Jesus was born in Bethlehem in Judea, during the time of King Herod, Magi from the east came to Jerusalem and asked, "Where is the one who has been born king of the Jews? We saw His star when it rose and have come to worship Him."
>
> —Matthew 2:1–2

Matthew is the only Gospel that tells us about the wise men, one of the biggest errors of most nativity scenes. The Magi were never at the stable. In this story, the Magi enter a house. Also, Jesus was potentially two years old by this point, when you consider the age of the children King Herod killed when he was trying to kill Jesus.

Okay, so Jesus wasn't a baby in a stable when the Magi came. It's okay that they couldn't be there to worship Jesus right away, as the shepherds were. All that matters is that the Magi saw the star and did come.

It also does not matter when we come to Jesus. The important thing is that we recognize Jesus for who He is and come to Him. Take heed of His star shining in your life. Then, come and worship your King.

Dearest Jesus, King of not just the Jews but of all creation, shine in my life and guide me to You. Like the Magi, I want to come worship You. Amen.

January 7

In the same way, let your light shine before others, that they may see your good deeds and glorify your Father in heaven.

—Matthew 5:16

"You may be the only Bible some people read." I am very partial to that saying because it drives home a very valid point.

The Gideons have distributed over two billion Bibles to date, according to their website. While I know that many of them have been used, I'd be willing to bet that quite a few have gone unopened. Just because you hand someone a Bible does not mean he or she is going to read it. However, when you truly live your faith, showing what you believe through the way you speak and act, you become a Bible that people around you cannot help but "read."

And you don't have to do anything big. You don't have to stand on street corners and hand out Bibles like the Gideons or walk door-to-door in neighborhoods like the Jehovah's Witnesses. There's nothing wrong with being that bold. But remember that the little things, like not being afraid to pray in public or referring to God in a way that is not swearing, can make all the difference in someone's life.

Heavenly Father, help me be a light that glorifies You and leads the lost back to You. Amen.

January 8

He hurls down His hail like pebbles. Who can
withstand His icy blast?

—Psalm 147:17

Having lived in South Dakota most of my adult life and
having spent many Christmases in South Dakota as a child, I
am very familiar with trying to stay warm amid the icy blast of
winter. While South Dakota winters are not necessarily as bad
as they are stereotyped to be, they can be downright frigid at
times! There is nothing more comforting than coming back to
the warmth of the house after feeding my outside animals on a
cold winter day.

Even if we don't live in the "frozen north," we can experience
the icy blast of storms that life throws at us. And whether it is
a storm produced by Mother Nature or life's circumstances, we
can feel helpless in trying to withstand the blasts coming at us.

That's where today's verse comes in handy. It reminds us
to return to the Lord our God. We need to step away from the
storm pounding away at us and seek the comfort found in the
warmth of God's love. Alone, we cannot withstand the icy blasts.
Only with God's help will we survive every storm that comes
our way.

Lord, You and You alone can give me the strength needed to
weather the storms of this world. When I begin to falter under
the blows, bring me back to Your warmth and love. In Jesus'
name I pray. Amen.

January 9

For our struggle is not against flesh and blood,
but against the rulers, against the authorities,
against the powers of this dark world and against
the spiritual forces of evil in the heavenly realms.
—Ephesians 6:12

I remember an episode of *The West Wing* where the White House staff are dealing with several problems at once and one staff member tells another, "You're fighting the wrong battle." She felt her coworker was simply picking more fights to compensate for the fights he didn't feel he could win.

We, like the Ephesians being addressed in Paul's letter, are in a similar situation. We have many problems facing us, many struggles to address. Paul wanted to make sure the Ephesians were fighting the right battle. We today still need to make sure we are addressing the correct struggle.

There are times when we might feel overwhelmed by the forces of evil and by all the darkness in this world. The feeling of being overwhelmed may lead us to want to pick a different battle. Instead, we need to stay strong in our faith in the Lord and hold to His truths. We can win this struggle, with God's help.

God, grant me the strength to endure the struggles against the evil and darkness in this world. Help me cling to Your righteousness and Your light. Amen.

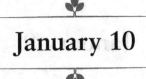

January 10

Give, and it will be given to you. A good measure, pressed down, shaken together and running over, will be poured into your lap. For with the measure you use, it will be measured to you.

—Luke 6:38

Many televangelists would like us to believe that if we send them money, we will come into even greater money. Apparently, if I send $1,000 to some guy preaching on TV, my third cousin twice removed is going to leave me $1,000,000 in his will. People can use this verse to back those beliefs.

Now, I'm no biblical scholar, but I do not believe that is what Jesus is saying in this verse. After all, Jesus says nothing about a time frame on when blessings shall be returned to us. The "good measure" we will receive may not come during our time on earth.

However, that should not stop us from doing good works. I am not saying we should donate to every televangelist that comes along. What I am saying is that we should help others and not expect the instant gratification society tells us we should. Instead, we should give of ourselves for others and wait patiently for our eternal reward from God.

Jesus, teach me how to give of myself for others, not to receive instant gratification but rather to receive Your heavenly reward. Amen.

January 11

For your ways are in full view of the Lord, and
He examines all your paths.

—Proverbs 5:21

There is a lot of comfort in this verse. My grandmother did not like the song "They Call the Wind Maria" because of one line: "And now I'm lost...not even God can find me." Grandma knew that it was not possible to ever be out of God's sight. But I know too well how it can feel like you're lost from even God.

It's at those times when this verse is especially comforting. Regardless of where we may find ourselves, God knows exactly where we are. We are never out of His sight.

Not only that, but God is also fully aware of the path we are on, the path we should be on, and what path is needed to get us where we belong. Just like with GPS units in our cars, if we take a wrong turn in life, God can "recalculate" to help us get going in the right direction again. So no matter how lost we feel, we truly are never so lost that not even God can find us.

Thank you, Lord, for examining my paths and always keeping me in Your view. When I feel that I am lost, even from You, please comfort me and guide me back to you. In Jesus' name, amen.

January 12

Love does no harm to a neighbor. Therefore love
is the fulfillment of the law.

—Romans 13:10

In the New International Version of the Bible, which is the translation I've used for this book, the word "love" appears 551 times in the entire Bible. Compare that to some other words. "Faith" shows up only 270 times. "Believe" shows up 160 times. Believe it or not, "forgive" only appears in the NIV Bible 74 times. I think that alone shows how important love is.

If you have faith in God, if you truly believe in Him, then you are going to love Him. If you act out of love toward your neighbors, then you have no need to be forgiven. The Ten Commandments can even be summed up into just two commandments: love God with all of your heart, soul, and mind, and love your neighbor as yourself.

The best definition of love that I have ever heard is that love means putting someone else's needs ahead of your own. That's what led Jesus to the cross. When you act out of love, you will not hurt anyone. You will not break God's law.

Loving Father, teach me how to love as You do, how to put other's needs ahead of my own. In Jesus' name I pray. Amen.

January 13

You will seek Me and find Me when you seek
Me with all your heart.

—Jeremiah 29:13

My motto for doing anything is "if something is worth
doing, then it is worth doing well." I do not believe in making
half-hearted attempts at anything. Even when dusting my house
(which I detest doing), I put my entire being into it. I don't just
dust around things. I will actually move every knickknack,
every model horse, every thing where I am dusting.

God does not want us coming to Him half-heartedly either.
If we seek out God only when we want something from Him,
then it is like we are dusting the open spaces. If we are unwilling
to admit our mistakes to God and actively seek His forgiveness,
then it is like we are dusting around knickknacks.

It's not that God will not accept us unless we give our whole
heart to Him. But if we come to God half-heartedly, we will not
receive the full peace we seek. It's only when we seek God with
the intention of surrendering our entire being to Him that we
will find the full peace of God.

Forgive me, dear God, when I fail to seek You with my whole
heart. Let me surrender myself to You, without any reservations,
so that I may find the full peace that only You can offer. Amen.

January 14

Then He called the crowd to Him along with His disciples and said: "Whoever wants to be My disciple must deny themselves and take up their cross and follow Me."

—Mark 8:34

At the start of the 2014 professional baseball season, I decided to pick a team to support. For personal reasons, I chose the Kansas City Royals. I didn't care that they weren't doing so well at that time.

Toward the end of the regular baseball season, when the Royals were bound for the playoffs, I was browsing in a sports store. I overheard another customer asking an employee about Kansas City Royals shirts. The employee admitted that there had not been much demand for them. The customer responded, "But they're winning now!"

Every sport has those "fair weather fans"—those fans who have loyalty only to the team with the best record. Jesus does not want us to be His "fair weather fans." To follow Jesus means to bear a cross, to take the struggles in stride, even when that means we get ridiculed or even persecuted for our faith. Christ's ultimate victory will be that much sweeter for those of us who held our faith, no matter what.

Jesus, I do not want to be a "fair weather disciple." Help me to stay true to You, especially when it involves bearing a cross. Amen.

January 15

I thank my God every time I remember you.
—Philippians 1:3

I have about a 30-minute commute to work in the morning. I love that drive because it gives me a chance to think. This morning, I found myself thinking about previous jobs I've had and the bosses that had come with those jobs. Then I started thinking about my current boss and the fact that part of what makes my job now so wonderful is the boss that I have. And at that moment, I thanked God for my boss.

Our lives are full of blessings, but too often the blessings we think about—and thank God for—are the material blessings. We thank God for the roof over our head, or the car we drive, or the paycheck we receive.

But when do we thank God for the people in our lives? Mother's Day? Father's Day? We should be grateful for the human blessings in our lives every day, not just on holidays.

Think about your friends, your family. If tomorrow the only people left in your life were the ones you thanked God for today, would you still be so blessed?

God, I thank You for every person You have placed in my life as a blessing to me. You have given me people to help me through difficult times and to celebrate with me in good times. Thank You for enriching my life with those people. Amen.

January 16

Be kind and compassionate to one another, forgiving each other, just as in Christ God forgave you.

—Ephesians 4:32

A couple weeks ago, I ordered a custom ring from a jewelry store. It was to have the March and May birthstones mounted on yellow gold. Shortly before it was scheduled to arrive at the store for me to pick it up, I got a call from the store manager, wanting to confirm that the ring was supposed to be white gold.

She had incorrectly entered the information, so the shop incorrectly made the ring. They were going to have to start all over, delaying when the ring would be available. My response to the manager's apology was simple. I told her that mistakes happen.

Only God is perfect, and through Christ, God forgives us for all of our mistakes. Therefore, I do not believe God is asking too much of us by expecting us to forgive each other's imperfections. Forgiveness comes easier when we choose to regard each other with kindness and compassion. Just remember how you like to be treated when you make mistakes.

Thank You, dear God, for Your forgiveness. Please help me learn how to forgive others as You have forgiven me. Let me show kindness and compassion to others, especially when they somehow wrong me. In Jesus' name I pray. Amen.

January 17

And He has given us this command: Anyone who loves God must also love their brother and sister.

—1 John 4:21

This verse is an interesting paraphrase of the command that Jesus gave His disciples. John 15:12 says, "My command is this: Love each other as I have loved you." The writer of 1 John took a few liberties with the wording of Jesus' command. Or did he?

Think about this for a moment. When you love someone, will you not do everything you can to make that person happy? I'm sure most of us can think of at least one instance where we did something simply because we knew it would please a loved one. We just cannot help ourselves. That's what love does to us.

Our love toward God is that same way. If we truly love God, we should want to do whatever it takes to please God. And what would please God more than seeing His children loving each other as He loves us? Our love for God should make us want to love our brothers and sisters in Christ. It should be something we just cannot help. We should have that deep down need to love others.

Lord, I love You. Let my love for You consume me to the point that I cannot help but love everyone around me. In Jesus' name, amen.

January 18

"Meaningless! Meaningless!" says the Teacher. "Utterly meaningless! Everything is meaningless."

—Ecclesiastes 1:2

Have you ever felt like nothing you did mattered? Have you ever wondered why you are working so hard to no avail? Have you ever wanted to give up because you felt everything was meaningless?

One of my friends, a chiropractor, told me about some of the struggles he faced when starting his practice. He got so frustrated with patients wanting him to "fix" them, even though they would not do any stretches on their own to help their own problems. My friend actually closed his clinic, ready to walk away for good. However, he found acceptance, returned to work, and is still in practice today.

We may feel that our work is in vain, that everything we do is meaningless. We are not alone in those feelings. Rather than giving up, we simply need to turn to God. As long as we are doing God's calling, whether at our job, in our church, or at home, our work is not meaningless. It has a purpose to God, and God's validation is the only one we need.

Heavenly Father, when I feel that I am working in vain and that everything I do is meaningless, remind me that my toils have purpose to You. Then give me the strength to carry on in my tasks. Amen.

January 19

And we know that in all things God works for the good of those who love Him, who have been called according to His purpose.

—Romans 8:28

"Everything happens for a reason." While meant to be words of comfort, they can seem to be quite cruel. That statement can be interpreted as meaning that God even intends the bad things in our lives to happen to us. It's not really comforting to think that God wanted our loved one to die prematurely or that God wanted us to lose our job.

Something that is more comforting to say would be, "God will find a way to use this for good." Maybe the premature death of your loved one will bring you closer to those other people you still have in your life. Maybe that lost job will be replaced by a job more befitting of your talents.

Remember that God does indeed work for the good of those who love Him. Be open to God's purpose. Let Him use your life's circumstances, good or bad, for His ultimate good.

Lord, take my life and everything in it. Use all that happens to me for good, according to Your purpose. And when I fail to see what good can come of a situation, remind me that You can use any bad circumstance for good. Amen.

January 20

Cast all your anxiety on Him because He cares for you.

—1 Peter 5:7

I am all too familiar with sleepless nights brought on by worries or concerns. All too often I have found myself lying awake in bed, staring at the ceiling, listening to the heavy breathing of the dog sleeping beside me, but unable to quiet my thoughts so I could also fall asleep. My sleepless nights are usually the results of too big of bills coupled with too small of paychecks.

One important thing to note about what Peter says is that he tells us to cast all of our anxiety on God. Not some of it, not most of it. ALL of it. If I am worried about my financial situation, or anything else for that matter, and I pray to God simply to share my anxiety with Him, I do not get to sleep any sooner. Because I still am holding on to what has me worried, I am not at peace.

We need to let go of our anxiety. Don't just tell God about what's bothering you. Rather, put Him in the driver's seat of your life. But when you let Him take the wheel, don't be a backseat driver. Get that much-needed sleep, resting assured that God cares for you.

Lord, when I'm worried and cannot sleep, help me to give all of my anxiety to You, withholding none of it. I know You care about me and will take care of my situations much better than I could by myself. Amen.

January 21

Do you give the horse its strength or clothe its neck with a flowing mane? Do you make it leap like a locust, striking terror with its proud snorting?

—Job 39:19–20

As a horse lover, I am particularly fond of this passage in Job as it is poetic in its description of horses. But to say this passage is about the horse is to overlook these two verses at the beginning of the passage.

God is talking to Job, who is dealing with one disaster after another. More importantly, God is trying to get Job to realize who really has the power and control. Job liked to think that he did, but this is just one of many passages where God asks Job who really does these things.

I have a unique relationship with my horses, allowing me to do things with them that others dare not even try. However, I must beware that I do not get cocky or careless. Like Job, I do not give the horse its strength. I must still respect my horses for their size and strength, and I must remember that only God has absolute control of my horses…and of everything else in my life.

God, protect me from the cockiness that comes from thinking I am in control. Remind me that in all things, only You have absolute control. Forgive me when I forget that Your hands are way more capable than my own and that You should be in control of my life. Amen.

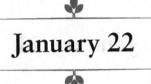

January 22

But Jesus answered, "No more of this!" And He
touched the man's ear and healed him.

—Luke 22:51

Jesus healed many people by simply touching them. That is
something we cannot do. Or can we?

By scientific definitions, the skin is the largest organ of the
human body. And it is full of nerves, making the skin highly
sensitive to touch. Consequently, a simple touch can do so much
more than we give it credit for.

Studies have been done on the various benefits of physical
contact. Reported benefits range from decreased stress to
greater trust between individuals, from stronger immune system
to lower violence. Basically, physical contact improves a person's
overall wellbeing.

So don't underestimate the power you have in your touch.
Go ahead and lay a hand on a person's shoulder. Give someone
a handshake or a high-five. Or engage even more of the large
organ we call skin, and give someone a hug! You might be
surprised at what all you can heal—in others and in yourself—
just with a touch.

Jesus, You healed many people with a touch. Give me the
courage to cross the invisible barriers that separate me from
others so that I, too, may heal people with a touch. Amen.

January 23

Trust in the Lord with all your heart and lean not on your own understanding; in all your ways submit to Him, and He will make your paths straight.

—Proverbs 3:5–6

Imagine for a moment that you are on a cross-country journey, to an unknown destination. The only navigation you are permitted to use are map insets, and you will only be given them periodically along the journey. Would you go on that journey?

How about if someone who did know the way was doing the driving and all you had to do was go along for the ride? Would you go then?

Essentially, we are all on that journey as we make our way through this world and this life. If we are wise, we will choose to let God do the driving while we just enjoy the ride. That is what we do when we trust God. He knows things that we do not, the way we need to go to successfully arrive at our final destination.

Comparing our understanding of this life to what God knows is like comparing a map inset to an entire world atlas. We have but a small picture of our world, but God sees it all. Doesn't it just make sense to trust the one who sees the big picture?

Lord God, You know how to get me where I need to be. Teach me to always trust You and to not rely on my own knowledge or experience. Amen.

January 24

On the contrary, those parts of the body that
seem to be weaker are indispensable.
—1 Corinthians 12:22

I am hopelessly right-handed. I do both heavy lifting (like carrying dog food bags) and fine motor tasks (like unlocking doors) on my right side. Sometimes I wonder why I even have a left hand!

But then I think about how much I enjoy playing guitar. My left hand is vital to playing my guitar because without it, I couldn't hold down strings to create the chords. My left hand is also crucial to my playing my alto clarinet, an instrument I love so much that I refer to it as my "baby." And when it comes right down to it, even simple things like getting dressed or washing my hair would be difficult without my left hand.

That is exactly what the apostle Paul is trying to explain in this passage, only in reference to the body of Christ. We might feel that certain people are not as important for one reason or another. However, no matter what their role in the church may be, every single person is important to the function of the body of Christ. Every person is indispensable, and we need to remember that.

Christ, all of us in Your church form Your body, and every single one of us is important to You. Help me to always treat my fellow members with the respect due to them for simply being part of Your church. Amen.

January 25

> My dear children, I write this to you so that you
> will not sin. But if anybody does sin, we have
> an advocate with the Father—Jesus Christ, the
> Righteous One.
>
> —1 John 2:1

Most vehicles these days are equipped with airbags as a standard safety device. Airbags are just one of those features that a person would hope they never have to use. However, it doesn't take much imagination to think about the injuries that may be sustained in an accident if the person, be they driver or passenger, does not have the protection of an airbag.

Jesus is essentially our spiritual airbag. We are not supposed to sin. But no matter how hard we try, we will slip up. All it takes is one little thought, and we are right back to being a sinner. However, Jesus steps in and prevents our sin from causing us permanent damage.

When He died on the cross, Jesus interceded for us, shielding us from the eternal pain and suffering that we deserve for our sins. Just as airbags can leave bruises on vehicle occupants, we may still feel some effects of our sin. But as long as we accept Christ as our Savior, He will always shield us from the deadly consequences of our sin.

Jesus, thank You for being my advocate and saving me from my sin. I promise to try my hardest to not sin, resting in the assurance of Your forgiveness when I do mess up. Amen.

January 26

...though he may stumble, he will not fall, for the Lord upholds him with His hand.

—Psalm 37:24

While I have undoubtedly heard this verse before, it really stood out with me when I heard it quoted in my pastor's puppet show one Sunday morning. This particular puppet show was about coping with loss. My pastor's puppet shows are always the children's message, but we adults can relate to them too. In this show, one puppet is coping with his team's loss of a game.

But the Sunday my pastor did this show was the Sunday before the one-year anniversary of my beloved Arabian horse's death. Naturally, my mind was focused on a different type of loss. When, through tears, I told my pastor about the loss I was remembering, he admitted that the adults in the congregation would probably think of "loss" differently than the kids would.

I'm glad I saw this puppet show. As I remember finding my horse on the ground and falling to my knees beside her, I can also remember that God upheld me through that terrible time. I am also comforted knowing that He will continue to uphold me every time I stumble on grief caused by a bittersweet memory.

Dear God, thank You for upholding us whenever grief causes us to stumble. Amen.

January 27

"Neither this man nor his parents sinned," said Jesus, "but this happened so that the works of God might be displayed in him."

—John 9:3

Ah, yes. The age-old belief that bad things are always a punishment. The man in question in this verse had been born blind. Someone must have sinned to cause this blindness. So, who sinned? Whose fault is it?

But Jesus points His disciples in a different direction. Not all bad things are punishments for sin. Rather, they are a way for God's glory to be revealed. Jesus used this man's blindness to show that Jesus really was sent from God. Jesus couldn't give sight to someone who could already see. Blindness, a bad thing, was needed.

When bad things happen, we often ask, "Why?" What we should be asking is, "How will God use this?" Then we can follow that up with a question asked of God: "How can I help?" Jesus used the man's blindness to display the power of God. We, too, can be instruments God uses to display His works. In times of trials, let's stop focusing on blame. Like Jesus encouraged the disciples to do, let's turn our focus to God's glory.

Lord, I know that every bad thing that happens to me can be used to reveal Your glory. Help me to focus on You, rather than the bad things in my life. Amen.

January 28

What, then, shall we say in response to these things? If God is for us, who can be against us?
—Romans 8:31

Bullying is a common problem in our schools today. But I am noticing that bullying is also a problem among adults. As a daughter of a teacher in a small school district, I was bullied a lot. I just didn't realize that my classmates were actually bullying me. And I am becoming increasingly aware of adults around me who are also bullies.

We teach our children that the way to deal with a bully is to stand up to the bullies. Yet, it's been my experience that we adults just keep backing down, believing that it's not worth it. "Just let it go" seems to be an ongoing theme among adult bullying.

Maybe that theme comes from the fact that as adults, we want to avoid confrontations. We want to keep the peace. But this verse in Romans should give us the courage to stand our ground and face our bullies. If God is for us, who really can be against us? Nobody!

So, as we teach our children to handle their bullies, let's practice what we preach. Remembering that God is for us, let's stand up to the adult bullies too. After all, "God plus one is always a majority."

Lord God, grant me the strength to stand up to bullies, resting in the assurance that You are on my side. Amen.

January 29

He says, "Be still, and know that I am God;
I will be exalted among the nations, I will be
exalted in the earth."

—Psalm 46:10

There is a woman, a member of an area Christian singing group, who was inspired to write a song entitled "Be Still." She wrote it after a friend of hers described experiencing so much stress that he felt like his world was just spinning around him. The song brought a simple message—be still and know that God is with you.

One Tuesday morning, following the most stressful Monday I have ever had, that song just popped into my head. Monday's stresses weren't gone on Tuesday. I still had a lot of things to cope with, but I know that God made that song come to my mind to bring that same message to me.

Being still is something that many of us find challenging. We are so accustomed to running nonstop that we can't even slow down. Yet, when our lives seem to be spinning out of control, when we feel it most necessary to keep moving, is when we most need to heed the words of this psalm. Be still. Know that God is God. More importantly, *let* God be God.

Dear God, when my life seems to be spinning out of control, help me to let go of everything else and cling only to You. Teach me how to be still so I can feel Your peace wash over me. In Jesus' name, amen.

January 30

Above all, you must understand that no prophecy of Scripture came about by the prophet's own interpretation of things. For prophecy never had its origin in the human will, but prophets, though human, spoke from God as they were carried along by the Holy Spirit.

—2 Peter 1:20–21

"We do not interpret Scripture. Scripture interprets us." These words were spoken to me by a pastor friend I had met for coffee. I had told him about how sometimes I just cannot write a devotion on a particular verse because I simply do not feel anything from it. He responded with these words of wisdom.

Since that conversation, I find myself looking at the Bible differently. This pastor was right, and these verses from Peter's second letter support that view. The Bible is not open to our interpretation. Rather, the Bible *is* the interpreter.

When you read the Bible, listen to what the Scriptures are saying. When they speak to you, remember that it is not you interpreting what you have read. It is the Holy Spirit interpreting you. And if a verse does not speak to you, don't force any understanding to come. The Holy Spirit may not want to use those verses with you.

Holy Spirit, speak to me through the Scriptures. Allow me to be interpreted by what I read in the Bible. Amen.

January 31

Fools find no pleasure in understanding, but delight in airing their own opinions.

—Proverbs 18:2

In January, many churches have annual meetings to see where they stand after a year has ended and to determine what needs to be done in the year to come. Budgets need to balanced. Council and various committee members need to be elected.

I, for one, dread church annual meetings. It never seems to fail that at least one person will bring up something that the majority of us fail to see as a concern. But that one person keeps making the same statements over and over again, as though whipping a dead horse. They talk and talk and talk and do not listen to what anyone else says on the matter.

Like this verse in Proverbs states, some people do not care about hearing others, only in making themselves heard. It remains my hope, however, that I never catch myself airing my own opinions without trying to understand what others are saying also.

Father in heaven, give me patience with those people who do not seek understanding but just want to make themselves heard. And please keep me open to hear and listen and understand those who are talking to me. Amen.

February 1

But in your hearts revere Christ as Lord. Always be prepared to give an answer to everyone who asks you to give the reason for the hope that you have. But do this with gentleness and respect.

—1 Peter 3:15

My car's license plates have started some interesting conversations. They simply say JHN1513. John 15:13 is my favorite Bible verse, so when I decided to put personalized plates on my car, I knew I was going to try to find a way to represent that verse.

Some people who have seen my license plates simply compliment me on them. Others ask me what that verse says. Regardless of how the conversations begin, the result is always the same—I share my faith with another person.

The first time this happened, I was caught off guard. I would have done well to remember these words from Peter's first letter! Now I learned to be prepared to talk about my license plates and about my faith. We should all be ready like that.

Lord Jesus, help me to always be ready to share my faith in You, whenever and wherever the situation arises. In Your holy name, amen.

February 2

There is a time for everything, and a season for
every activity under the heavens.

—Ecclesiastes 3:1

In the passage of Ecclesiastes that starts with this verse,
quite a list is given of activities to which there is a season. If I
would add anything to that list, I would add something about
there being a time to offer help and a time to accept help.

I am a very helpful person by nature. I am always quick to
volunteer myself to come to the aid of another person, but when
I herniated a disc in my low back, it was no longer a time for
me offer to help. Rather, it was the time for me to ask for help.

There really is a time for everything. It can be frustrating
to wait for the times to shift, like for me waiting for the time to
heal and the time to once again offer help. However, there is also
comfort in this verse, in this passage. There is indeed a time to
weep, but there is that time to laugh. There is a time to mourn,
but there is also a time to dance. Through that disc herniation, I
experienced the time to tear, but I also experienced the time to
mend. Those times will always come. We just have to be patient
and wait for them.

God, You created everything to happen in its due time. Help
me to trust in Your timing and to patiently wait for the seasons
to change. Amen.

February 3

To answer before listening—that is folly and shame.

—Proverbs 18:13

One of my friends on Facebook once shared a meme that said, "The biggest communication problem is we do not listen to understand. We listen to reply." And that is very true.

Whenever someone jumps into a conversation with something to say without letting the other person finish their thought first, the person jumping in tends to say something that is really irrelevant. And many times the person who was still speaking ends up irritated, saying, "Will you let me finish?"

Listening is an important skill. All animals have the ability and the desire to listen. After all, listening will allow predators to hear food coming and prey to hear a threat coming. Listening saves lives.

We humans may not necessarily have the need to listen to save our lives, but listening does show those around us that we care. It may be February, but it's never too late to make a new resolution. Maybe you can resolve to listen more and to listen for the right reasons.

Heavenly Father, teach me to listen to those around me to understand what they are saying, not just to reply to it. In Jesus' name, amen.

February 4

Do not be anxious about anything, but in every situation, by prayer and petition, with thanksgiving, present your requests to God. And the peace of God, which transcends all understanding, will guard your hearts and minds in Christ Jesus.

—Philippians 4:6–7

It was the morning of our Sunday school Christmas program. I was playing my guitar to accompany the kids' singing. I was very stressed that morning because, even though I had chosen the Christmas carols the kids would be singing, I still struggled with some of the chord changes.

Finally, overcome with so much anxiety that I wanted to cry, I secluded myself in a quiet place at church to pray. All I prayed was, "God, the Christmas program is now in Your very capable hands." At that point, I was much calmer. I was at peace.

God is so much bigger than all of us. He can handle everything we throw at Him. When we turn our anxieties over to God, the result is always the same. He takes our worry and gives us His peace.

God, take my worries, my cares, my anxieties. I leave everything in Your hands, which are so much more capable than my own. Grant me Your peace. In Jesus' name I pray. Amen.

February 5

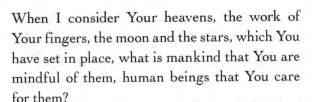

When I consider Your heavens, the work of Your fingers, the moon and the stars, which You have set in place, what is mankind that You are mindful of them, human beings that You care for them?

—Psalm 8:3–4

What have I done to deserve this? Ever find yourself so blessed that you start asking this question? Obviously the psalmist understood the feeling of being blessed beyond merit.

I especially find myself questioning my blessings when I consider my friends and family, both human and animal. There is so much love in my life. I'm just one human, and one that makes a great many mistakes. What have I done to deserve their love? What have I done to deserve God putting these loved ones in my life?

The point is, we don't deserve our blessings. We don't deserve the love God has for us. We can't earn God's favor. The care that God has for us reflects His compassion, not our merit.

What have we done to deserve this? Nothing. God is just that good.

Thank You, God, for blessing me in ways I do not deserve. May I always be as grateful as You are caring. Amen.

February 6

And I will do whatever you ask in My name,
so that the Father may be glorified in the Son.
You may ask Me for anything in My name, and
I will do it.

—John 14:13–14

This is something I have struggled with over the years. Why did Jesus say that He would give us anything we ask for in His name and yet so many of our prayers seem to go unanswered? I wrestle with these verses especially every time I think back to 1990.

In May of 1990, I lost my maternal grandfather to cancer. When he received his diagnosis, the entire family had been praying for his healing. Even friends of the family were praying for Grandpa's healing. But it didn't happen.

Or did it? Yes, Grandpa died of cancer. But through that bodily death, Grandpa was returned to health because in Heaven, there is no cancer. We wanted Grandpa to live, and he does live with Jesus. What better way to bring glory to the Father than to have Jesus make Grandpa, and all of us, fit to live with God forever?

Dear Jesus, as I pray for what I want, help me to see that whatever Your answer is, it is the best way to glorify the Father. In Your name I pray. Amen.

February 7

Each of you should use whatever gift you have
received to serve others, as faithful stewards of
God's grace in its various forms.

—1 Peter 4:10

God has given every one of us a gift, something that we
can excel at doing. Too many people think about gifts as being
athletic or musical talents. But that is a very narrow view of
God-given gifts.

We all have at least one gift (most of us have several),
and we are called to use them. This verse from Peter's first
letter reiterates what Jesus said with the parable of the three
servants given talents (see Matthew 25:14–30). Having gifts is
not enough. We must use them.

I, for example, seem to have a gift for writing. I don't
just mean writing devotions or stories. I am not very good at
consoling someone in person, but I can provide amazing comfort
to people when I email them or write letters to them. I don't
understand it, but I have accepted it and embraced it. I can
write, and I use my writing to serve others.

What can you do?

God, thank You for giving me talents. Teach me how to use them
to honor You and in service to others. In Jesus' name, amen.

February 8

Praise be to the God and Father of our Lord Jesus Christ, the Father of compassion and the God of all comfort, who comforts us in all our troubles, so that we can comfort those in any trouble with the comfort we ourselves receive from God.

—2 Corinthians 1:3–4

We love because God first loved us. With love comes the ability and the desire to comfort those in need. Therefore, Paul is stating the obvious when he gives God the credit for the comfort we give others. Or is it really that obvious?

How many times would you say you have experienced comfort given to you directly from God? Compare that to the number of times you have been comforted by another human being. If you're like me, you would say that you are more often comforted by humans than by God. Yet who taught humans how to comfort?

Comfort, like everything else in our lives, is a gift from God. Sometimes we receive the gift directly from God, but there are also times when God gives us His gifts through another person. And, as Paul says, praise be to God for all He gives us!

God of all comfort, thank You for comforting me in my times of trouble, be it directly from You or through others in my life. Amen.

February 9

For the word of God is alive and active. Sharper than any double-edged sword, it penetrates even to dividing soul and spirit, joints and marrow; it judges the thoughts and attitudes of the heart.
—Hebrews 4:12

A double-edged sword's danger comes from the fact that one side is doing what you want it to while the other side is staring back at you, able to do serious damage if you make a mistake. Because of that, it tends to be used to describe anything that can work against you just as easily as it can work for you.

The Bible, God's living Word, is a prime example of a double-edged sword. When He was on earth, Jesus chastened people by pointing out their wrongdoings. The same Jesus provided grace and forgiveness by dying on the cross.

Today Jesus is still capable of pointing out our mistakes, which, of course, is not in our favor! The Bible brings us words of condemnation. Yet Jesus still provides us grace and forgiveness, through the same Holy Scriptures. Thanks be to God for both sides of His Word!

Lord, Your Holy Word is indeed alive, casting judgment on me, and at the same time, offering grace and forgiveness. Thank You for Your Word, in the Bible and in the flesh of Jesus Christ. Amen.

February 10

I can do all this through Him who gives me strength.

—Philippians 4:13

This verse is commonly taken out of context. In the preceding couple of verses, Paul talks about being content with what he has, regardless of how much or how little that is. So, technically, verse 13 is saying that Paul can be content through God giving him strength.

Verse 13 is a wonderful verse to pull out of context. Even though it can take on several different meanings when used by itself, all of those meanings are still valid points. We can indeed do anything through God, who gives us strength. Whether we are aspiring to a lofty goal or trying to endure a challenge, or, like Paul, simply striving to be content with what we will be able to accomplish because of the strength we receive from God.

However, let's not forget the context in which Paul wrote this sentence. Let's also use the strength God gives us to be content in times of plenty and in times of need. That, too, can be accomplished through God.

God, grant me the strength to not only achieve the goals for which I am striving and to endure whatever challenges I face, but also to always be content with what I have, even when I find myself in need. In Jesus' name I pray. Amen.

February 11

Have confidence in your leaders and submit to
their authority, because they keep watch over
you as those who must give an account. Do this
so that their work will be a joy, not a burden, for
that would be of no benefit to you.

—Hebrews 13:17

I once saw a post on Facebook that was titled "Pray for Your
Pastor." That post went on to share many heartbreaking statistics
about pastors. The statistics that I found most troubling were
the frighteningly high number of pastors who report battling
depression, feeling discouraged, or who have no close friends.

Pastors have a hard job. Even part-time pastors are on call
24 hours a day, 7 days a week. Everything they do is under
constant scrutiny. Their leisure time, if they even get any, is not
even their own. And they have more responsibilities than most
of us ever realize.

It's okay to not agree with your pastor. It's okay to not like
your pastor. But if you have ever worked in a job where you were
unappreciated, you can understand why you should still support
your pastor. Your pastor does not ever get to walk away from the
job. Help pastors out by doing your part to make their calling
a blessing, rather than a curse. They'll be able to help you that
much more. And, of course, pray for your pastor.

Lord, I pray for my pastor and for all pastors. Give them the
strength to carry out their challenging call. Amen.

February 12

My Father, who has given them to Me, is greater than all; no one can snatch them out of My Father's hand.

—John 10:29

"No one can snatch them out of My Father's hand." What amazing comfort is found in that statement! Jesus is referring to His "sheep"—those who believe in Him and follow Him. That means Jesus is not speaking of some vague "them." Jesus is speaking of us!

So the Father has given us into Jesus' care. There we will live forever. We are safe and secure with Jesus because the Father won't have it any other way. And the Father is greater than anyone and anything in all of creation. Jesus' words here are the ultimate truth. It's not just that no one *will* snatch us away from God. It really is that no one *can*!

That thought is so reassuring. No matter what happens in this life, no matter who I meet or what I do, I will always be in God's care. I belong to God the Father and to God the Son.

We are the sheep of the Good Shepherd, and we are always safe and secure in His fold. Nothing will change that because nothing *can* change that.

Father, You are the greatest of all. Thank You for the assurance that we will always be with You because there is not anything that can ever tear us away from You. Amen.

February 13

If your brother or sister sins against you, rebuke
them; and if they repent, forgive them.
—Luke 17:3b

The church is the body of Christ, so it is a divine institution.
Unfortunately, there is a human aspect to the church also. And
with that human aspect comes conflict.

A pastor I know once shared some wonderful words of
wisdom with his confirmation students. He told them that, at
some point in their lives, the church would hurt them. Because
the church is comprised of humans, it will hurt them eventually.
With that knowledge, the students could plan ahead for how
they would react. They could choose to run away, or they could
use the inevitable pain to express and receive forgiveness.

Jesus knew that we humans will have conflicts, even as His
church. That's why He addressed the topic of conflict with His
disciples. He wanted them—and us—to know how He would
have us handle conflict.

We cannot control what others say or do, but we can decide in
advance how we ourselves will deal with conflict. Just because
conflict is inevitable does not mean it must also be detrimental.

Jesus, when faced with conflict in the church, help me to respond
with love and forgiveness. Amen.

February 14

Greater love has no one than this: to lay down one's life for one's friends.

—John 15:13

Valentine's Day is a holiday to celebrate love. Today's society tends to put more emphasis on the romantic love. However, I would like to look at a different type of love.

The love I want to raise up today, the love mentioned in today's verse, is what the Greeks called *agape*, or selfless love. It's love that is extended to everyone, whether blood relation or complete stranger.

Agape is the love that law enforcement officers have for everyone, causing them to be willing to die in the line of duty. It is also the love that military members have for their country, enabling them to fight to the death on the frontline.

This is the love that Christ showed on the cross, when He died for everyone. And *agape* is the love that we as Christians are called to extend to one another. So today and every day, let's celebrate *agape* and remember the selfless love of Christ.

Lord Jesus, thank You for Your selfless love. Thank You for giving the ultimate sacrifice out of love. Teach me how to truly embrace *agape* love and to love everyone around me. In Your holy name, amen.

February 15

[K]eep your tongue from evil and your lips from
telling lies.

—Psalm 34:13

A professor once called a student up to the front of the class
to help with a demonstration. The professor handed the student
a ceramic plate and told the student to drop it on the floor.
When the student did so, the plate shattered. The professor then
instructed the student to apologize to the plate. The student did
so. Then the professor pointed out that the plate was still broken.

From the first time I read this story, I loved it. Yes, we
as Christians are called to forgive others just as God has
forgiven us. But the professor wanted to illustrate how seeking
forgiveness does not automatically undo the damage caused by
the sin. Whether the damage was caused by words spoken or
actions done, an apology does not automatically fix everything.

The illustration of the plate is something we should all
remember. We should seek forgiveness when we do wrong, but
we should strive to not do wrong in the first place. Remember
that once it's dropped, the plate remains broken.

God, keep me aware of what I say and do. Help me avoid sinning
in the first place, rather than having to seek forgiveness after the
damage is done. Amen.

February 16

Though the fig tree does not bud and there are no grapes on the vines, though the olive crop fails and the fields produce no food, though there are no sheep in the pen and no cattle in the stalls, yet I will rejoice in the Lord, I will be joyful in God my Savior.

—Habakkuk 3:17–18

I am an optimist. In most situations, I can find an aspect that is good. Essentially, I always try to remind myself that the situation could be worse.

Yet I have experienced times when I become afraid to think about how a situation could get worse because it seems to be falling apart around me. I think, "At least this thing hasn't happened yet," only to have that particular thing happen. It can be tough to maintain optimism when Murphy's Law seems to be at work.

However, this lesser-known prophet appears to be the ultimate optimist. He is basically saying that he will still rejoice in God even when there is absolutely no apparent reason to do so. The prophet is neither looking at what else could go wrong nor at what is still going right. He is looking to God, plain and simple. And that is what we should also do. When we shift our focus to God, we won't even notice how bad things are.

God, when things get rough, help me turn my attention to You. Let me praise You because You are my Lord and Savior! Amen.

February 17

[A]nd my spirit rejoices in God my Savior.
—Luke 1:47

Have you ever felt such great joy that you could hardly contain yourself? This verse comes from "The Magnificat," also known as "Mary's Song." Mary was so elated about being chosen to be the Messiah's earthly mother that she essentially broke into song when telling Elizabeth.

There are many ways to express joy. Some dance. Some sing. Some shout from rooftops. There really is no wrong way to express one's joy. You could even post it on Facebook or tweet about it on Twitter!

However, I do believe we all need to take a lesson from Mary. In expressing her great joy, she acknowledged God first and foremost. She gave God all the credit for her joy.

The next time you feel so much joy that you cannot keep it to yourself, go ahead and let it out. Share it with those around you. But let your first shout be of praise to the Lord!

Dearest Lord, my soul does indeed proclaim Your greatness, and my spirit does rejoice in You. Thank You for all the joy You have brought to my life! In Jesus' name I pray. Amen.

February 18

Jesus wept.

—John 11:35

This is the shortest verse in the entire Bible. This verse takes place in the context of Jesus being surrounded by mourners who were grieving the death of someone who had also been Jesus' friend.

I do not believe Jesus actually wept out of grief. After all, Jesus knew He was going to raise Lazarus from the dead. I believe Jesus wept because He understood the pain and grief Mary, Martha, and the other mourners were experiencing. Jesus was human. He had emotions.

I personally am very emotional. I love people, especially friends and family, deeply and strongly. Thus, when someone I care about is hurting, I feel their pain in ways I cannot explain. One consequence of being this emotional is that I can cry at the drop of a hat.

There is a general belief that "big girls and boys" don't cry. Only "big babies" cry. That is *not* true! Jesus cried! And if it was okay for Jesus to weep, then it's okay for us to weep also. I think Jesus Himself proves that crying is not a sign of weakness. Rather, it's a sign of being too strong for too long.

Dearest Jesus, when something in life makes me want to cry, hold me close to You. Let me cry on Your shoulder. Amen.

February 19

The apostles said to the Lord, "Increase our faith!"

—Luke 17:5

There is a local paint store that has a lighted sign they use to advertise their services. The sign will change from the service (such as guidance for remodeling) to the employee who specializes in that area of service. Today as I drove by that business, I missed the service being highlighted but looked at the sign in time to see the employee who will help. What I saw was, "Ask for Faith!"

That is exactly what the disciples did in today's verse. They asked Jesus for faith, specifically for more faith. Have you ever found yourself with that same request? Jesus' answer to the apostles was essentially that faith the size of a mustard seed is enough to move mountains. It's not the amount of faith that matters. It's that a person has faith.

When you feel your faith is inadequate, take heart. A little faith goes a long way. However, if you feel like your faith is missing entirely, go ahead and pray about it. Ask for faith!

Heavenly Father, when I feel like my faith is lacking, please remind me that the tiniest amount of faith can still accomplish amazing things. And when I feel like my faith has gone entirely, please send Your Holy Spirit to renew my lacking faith. In Jesus' name, amen.

February 20

Peace I leave with you; My peace I give you. I do not give to you as the world gives. Do not let your hearts be troubled and do not be afraid.
—John 14:27

The world is not a peaceful place. I don't mean that the world is full of war and violence, although it certainly is. But the world's lack of peace shows up on a smaller scale too, in the conflicts between individuals.

I have had my fair share of conflicts with other people on an individual basis. However, the most frustrating conflicts for me are the ones where nothing changes, despite the disagreements. I can waste a lot of energy fighting personal battles that I cannot win.

And it's during those conflicts when I am especially in need of the peace that only Christ can give. I do not simply need peace in the form of the absence of conflict. I also need the peace of heart and mind. That is the peace that you just cannot find in this world. God alone can provide the peace that is true serenity.

Today, I would like to close with one of few prayers that I have memorized and still recite. Part of a longer prayer written by Reinhold Niebuhr, it is commonly known as the "serenity prayer."

God, grant me the serenity to accept the things I cannot change; courage to change the things I can; and wisdom to know the difference. Amen.

February 21

"In your anger do not sin": Do not let the sun go down while you are still angry, and do not give the devil a foothold.

—Ephesians 4:26–27

This is advice commonly given to newlyweds. "Don't go to bed angry." However, this is not just good advice for married couples. Everyone should take this to heart.

Being angry is hard work, and yet, nothing is ever accomplished by anger. When we are angry, we do not tend to think before speaking. We simply react. And that is how we can sin in our anger. The longer we are angry, the more likely we are to sin. Thus, we should move on from anger as quickly as possible.

It is okay to be angry. Even Jesus got angry. Jesus was quite angry when He turned the tables in the temple! But we need to make sure that we do not let our anger take control of us.

When we get angry, we still need to keep our focus on God. God will lead us from anger to forgiveness. God will help us withstand the devil's attempt to get us.

Gracious God, when I get angry, please help me keep my focus on You. Help me let go of my anger and grudges and embrace forgiveness. In Jesus' name I pray. Amen.

February 22

Truly I tell you, anyone who will not receive the kingdom of God like a little child will never enter it.

—Mark 10:15

The Gospel writers felt this was important, as this is one story that appears in multiple Gospels. Jesus obviously valued children. And when we stop to think about it, we adults can learn a lot from children.

When hearing a child tell someone about a new friend, how does the child describe that friend? I personally have heard children give the name of their friend and maybe where they met this friend. I have never heard a child describe a friend using skin color, or age, or really any physical characteristic other than gender. And even the gender will usually be mentioned in passing or simply by the use of pronouns.

Children just don't seem to care about the physical aspects of a person. They care about what's inside. Children are not born knowing how to hate. It's something they learn. Even the rivalry between the genders is something that children learn. Differences don't matter to a child, and they shouldn't to us adults either.

Thank You, God, for the children in my midst. Remind me that I have as much to learn from them as I have to teach them, and grant that I only teach them things that will benefit them. In Jesus' name, amen.

February 23

A person may think their own ways are right,
but the Lord weighs the heart.

—Proverbs 21:2

This is probably the ultimate disagreement—what a person thinks is right versus what God knows is right. Disagreements end one of two ways. Either they end in a stalemate, where both parties "agree to disagree," or they end when one party finally admits to being wrong.

Of course, nobody likes being wrong. I know one person who is so adamant about being right that she assumes her word is the truth until someone else can prove her wrong. Even though she is proven wrong a lot, she still always insists that she is right, even if she has no proof of her own to back her claim.

When we do have a disagreement with someone, we really shouldn't try to figure out who is right and who is wrong. We humans are just not that good at knowing who is truly right. Rather, we should pray about our disagreements, not that the other party come to see things our way, but that both parties come to see things God's way. After all, God's way is the only truly right way!

Lord, when my ways conflict with someone else, please bring us both to see things from Your perspective. Show me Your way, the only right way. Amen.

February 24

Very truly I tell you, whoever believes in Me will do the works I have been doing, and they will do even greater things than these, because I am going to the Father.

—John 14:12

Jesus spoke these words the night He was betrayed. That means He had already given sight to a blind man, healed countless people of various afflictions, and had even raised people from death. Those are some pretty great works!

While Jesus' disciples went on to heal the sick and raise the dead, how many of us can do that today? Can we heal the sick or raise the dead with a word or a touch?

Actually, we can. A kind word or a caring touch, even a simple hug, can heal someone's broken spirit. In some cases, such words and deeds can bring a person back from the brink of suicide. Ever hear the story about the high school kid who unknowingly stopped a classmate from committing suicide simply by helping the classmate carry his books home? As believers in Christ, we do have the power to help those around us, and many times we won't even know that we did. Jesus knew His power, but we have no idea of ours!

Jesus, through You, I do have the power to heal the sick and raise the dead with just a word. Help me to use that power for the good of those around me. In Your name, amen.

February 25

Watch and pray so that you will not fall into temptation. The spirit is willing, but the flesh is weak.

—Matthew 26:41

Whenever I hear this verse, I think about Lent. Many people, in many denominations, take on Lenten disciplines. For people who give up something they really like for Lent, this can be a long church season, filled with temptations. Personally, I used to give up my one true addiction—chocolate! That was always especially hard for me as I was surrounded by Easter candies and Girl Scout cookies. Oh, those thin mint cookies!

When we take on a Lenten discipline, we do so because we want to strengthen our relationship with God. It may take the form of a ritual fast, giving up something we enjoy, or by taking on something extra to make us a better person. In either case, our spirit is very willing. Yet our flesh is weak, and most, if not all of us, are tempted at some point to abandon our Lenten discipline.

So what should we do when we face that temptation? The same thing Jesus told His disciples to do: pray.

Lord God, whenever I am faced with temptation, whether in my Lenten discipline or another time, please give me the strength to persevere. Amen.

February 26

Carry each other's burdens, and in this way you
will fulfill the law of Christ.

—Galatians 6:2

"Trust me when I say I know life throws many curveballs,
and it is tough, *very* tough. But that is when you lean on others
for support." One of my very good friends said these words to
me to encourage me to lean on others when life was getting me
down.

That is something I struggle with. I am great at helping
others carry their burdens, but I don't like to burden others with
my problems. I seem to think that I must keep myself strong for
others, and so I cannot show any weakness myself.

While the apostle Paul may have been encouraging the
Galatians to be willing to carry others' burdens, I also see
this verse as encouragement to allow burdens to be carried.
Leaning on someone in difficult times isn't actually burdening
that other person. As a frequent support person, I can say that
with certainty. It isn't a sign of weakness to let someone else
carry your burdens. Sharing each other's struggles is a Christian
thing to do!

Lord, teach me how to carry the burdens of others and how to
let others help me carry mine. In Jesus' name I pray. Amen.

February 27

Blessed are those who mourn, for they will be comforted.

—Matthew 5:4

This verse is part of Jesus' Beatitudes. It is one of several strange blessings that Jesus talks about. Every single "blessed" He says is something that none of us thinks about as being a blessing. However, this is not such a strange blessing when you look at Jesus' reasoning behind His statement: "...for they shall be comforted."

Grief is unique to each person. When we mourn, we can feel very alone. However, I cannot name a single time when I have mourned and there was no one to offer comfort. Whether I was mourning the death of a family member, friend, or a beloved animal, I have always been comforted. Even years later, when a memory stirs up the grief again, someone is always there to comfort me.

Jesus isn't saying that mourning is a blessing, but rather that comfort is. We should not fight grief. We should let it come. After all, if we do not mourn, we cannot be comforted. And there is blessing in being comforted.

Lord, thank You for providing me comfort when I mourn. It is a blessing that I do not deserve but am deeply grateful for. Amen.

February 28

The righteous lead blameless lives; blessed are their children after them.

—Proverbs 20:7

For several years, I have been lucky enough to lead Sunday school music at my church. Those kids can be a handful at times. But even on those Sundays when the kids really try my patience, I never regret working with the children of my congregation.

Most of the kids are in Sunday school every week. Their parents faithfully bring them to church and Sunday school. The parents are faithful, and their children are indeed blessed because of it.

These children are learning about God. They are learning about how much God loves them and about how they can turn to God in good times and in bad times. The lessons that the kids learn in Sunday school will help them throughout their entire lives.

Eventually these kids will grow up. Having been raised by faithful parents, if these kids have children of their own, they will most likely also be faithful parents, like their parents before them. Faithfulness and righteousness do tend to get passed on from one generation to the next. Righteous parents do have blessed children.

Heavenly Father, thank You for faithful parents. Please continue to bless their children. In Jesus' name, amen.

February 29

The Lord is my strength and my shield; my heart
trusts in Him, and He helps me. My heart leaps
for joy, and with my song I will praise Him.

—Psalm 28:7

Today is "Leap Day"—the day used to catch our calendar
up with the earth's revolution around the sun. Since it actually
takes the earth 365 1/4 days to revolve around the sun, every
fourth year we get an extra day.

The psalmist in today's verse doesn't need a special "Leap
Day." His reason for leaping has nothing to do with the earth's
position in regards to the sun. Rather, he says his heart leaps for
joy. This joy comes from trusting the Lord for help.

When was the last time you thought about the strength and
help that comes from God? Did your heart leap for joy? Did
your body join your heart in leaping?

We should make every day a "Leap Day." Every day we
should embrace the joy that comes from knowing God. We
should let that joy make our heart leap. And there's nothing that
says that we can't let our entire being leap for joy.

Thank You, Lord, for being my strength and shield. To know
You is to know true joy, the joy that makes my heart leap. Like
the psalmist, I will praise You! Amen.

March 1

Jesus said to her, "I am the resurrection and the life. The one who believes in Me will live, even though they die; and whoever lives by believing in Me will never die. Do you believe this?"
—John 11:25-26

It can be difficult to know what to say to someone who is grieving. Expressions of sympathy can come across sounding cold or insensitive. Most people, unsure of what to say, simply say "I'm sorry."

What Jesus said in today's verses was directed at Martha, who had recently buried her brother Lazarus. Jesus knew Martha was grieving, and He had His own words of comfort for her. They were words of hope and of a promise that death is not the end.

At this point in my life, I have lost both sets of grandparents, as well as several "honorary" grandparents and a cherished friend. Sometimes my grief is renewed when I think about the things I wish I'd said to these loved ones before they died, but Jesus' words to Martha provide hope for me also. My loved ones were strong in their faith and helped shape my faith. I will see them again, and I will have another chance to tell them how much they mean to me!

Jesus, thank You for the promise that death is not final. I look forward to being reunited with my loved ones in You. Amen.

March 2

God has said, "Never will I leave you; never will I forsake you."

—Hebrews 13:5b

I can count on one hand the number of close friends I have, those with whom I can share anything and everything. That's not to say those are the only friends I have, but they are the closest. They are the ones I rely on the most. I tend to go more for quality than quantity in my friendships.

Of course, the problem with such a philosophy of friendship is that there may be occasions when everyone in that small handful of close friends is unavailable. We all have separate lives, and although usually at least one friend is available to me, there have been times when I cannot reach out to any of them. And if I happen to encounter a rough patch in my life during one of those times, I can be left feeling very alone.

It was during one of those times when one of my very close friends finally got back to me and reminded me of this Bible verse, pointing out that no matter how alone I may feel, I am never truly alone. What a great comfort that was during such a rough week!

Dear God, remind us that You are always with us, even when we feel completely alone. You will never leave us or forsake us. Amen.

March 3

The name of the Lord is a fortified tower; the righteous run to it and are safe.

—Proverbs 18:10

One of my favorite Dakota Road songs is called "The Lord is My Defense." It lists a number of times when a person may struggle, like when haunted by a memory or when even friends just don't understand. But during all those times, "the Lord is my defense."

The chorus contains the line, "Here no harm can come to me." And that is very true. We may face hardships, trials, tribulations. Call them what you will, but life is not a bed of roses.

However, when we run to God, we find safety from the dangers. We find comfort from the griefs. We find understanding, acceptance, and love.

The best part is that we do not have to go any place in particular to find this refuge. We can find it at church, but we can also find it at home, out in nature, in our daily commute. All we have to do is call upon the name of the Lord. His name is the fortified tower, which can be found wherever we are!

Lord, Your name is a fortified tower. You are my defense. With You, I am safe and secure. Thank You for the protection You alone can give me. Amen.

March 4

But I know where you are.

—Isaiah 37:28a

She was 93 years old. She suffered from dementia, which was progressively getting worse with each passing year, and lived in a nursing home. One day when her daughter and son-in-law came to visit her, she got very excited. "You found me!" she exclaimed. Her daughter replied, "I know where you are." She asked her daughter, "How can you know where I am when I don't even know where I am?"

"I know where you are." There are many times in life when we might feel lost, but God always knows where we are. God can always find us.

Whether we feel lost due to grief, desperation, or frustration at life not going as we'd planned, God knows exactly where we are. Not only does God know where we are, but He will also come to us.

God will not leave us lost in our confusion. He will show us the way He wants us to go. All we have to do is call out to Him when we feel lost. Then we just wait for God to come to us and guide us back where we belong.

God, when I feel lost and alone, help me to be still. Help me hear You assure me that You always have and always will know where I am. Amen.

March 5

"Men of Galilee," they said, "why do you stand there looking into the sky? This same Jesus, who has been taken from you into heaven, will come back in the same way you have seen Him go into heaven." Then the apostles returned to Jerusalem from the hill called the Mount of Olives, a Sabbath day's walk from the city.

—Acts 1:11–12

The apostles had spent three years with Jesus. Now the time had come for Jesus to return to heaven. The apostles needed to transition from being students of Jesus to teachers about Jesus. They couldn't stand there, looking up at the sky, wishing Jesus hadn't left. This was the end, but it was also the beginning.

We all face endings like that. People move around in life. Sometimes we're the ones moving away. Sometimes we're the ones being left behind.

Either way, things cannot stay the same. Jesus needed to leave so the apostles would spread their wings. We, too, need endings in order to have beginnings that allow us to take flight ourselves. That is important to note—no ending is final. It's simply a transition to a new beginning.

Lord, when You bring me to the end of a chapter of my life, help me to embrace it as the beginning of the next chapter. Amen.

March 6

Jesus looked at them and said, "With man this is impossible, but with God all things are possible."
—Matthew 19:26

"Who can be saved?" the disciples had asked. This was Jesus' response. We humans cannot save ourselves. There is nothing we can say or do to earn our spot in heaven.

Luckily for us, though, nothing is impossible for God. God had a plan that would redeem a fallen humanity. Through Jesus, God made the impossible possible.

The act of making us worthy for heaven is not the only impossible feat that God has made possible. We are unable to make ourselves worthy for heaven, but we are also unable to believe in Jesus on our own. God sent Jesus to die on the cross to pay the price for our sins, which we could never pay ourselves. And then God sends the Holy Spirit to bring us the ability to believe in Jesus.

Audrey Hepburn once said, "Nothing is impossible. The word itself says 'I'm possible'!" That is most certainly true of God. Everything is indeed possible for God.

God, with You all things are possible. Thank You for sending Jesus to redeem me and the Holy Spirit to give me faith. Amen.

March 7

For where two or three gather in My name, there
I am with them.

—Matthew 18:20

When my two dogs and my parents' dog get together, it can
be very difficult to ignore them. That is especially true when one
of the dogs decides they need to go outside. If the dog needing
to go out is ignored long enough, that dog will enlist the help of
the other two dogs. Before long, all three dogs are asking to go
outside, and that is very difficult to ignore.

Although God does not necessarily ignore us, we gather
together to worship and pray for the same reason my parents'
and my dog join forces on requests to go outside. Voices united
are stronger than individual voices.

However, it is not left up to us alone to add strength to our
voices. It only takes two or three gathered in Jesus' name for
Jesus to add His voice to ours. That does not mean that large
groups should not gather to worship and pray together. It simply
means we do not have to concern ourselves with having a large
enough group. Two or three is all it takes, although more is
always acceptable!

Jesus, You have promised that You will be among two or three
gathered in Your name. Thank You for coming among us. Amen.

March 8

"Should you not fear Me?" declares the LORD. "Should you not tremble in My presence? I made the sand a boundary for the sea, an everlasting barrier it cannot cross. The waves may roll, but they cannot prevail; they may roar, but they cannot cross it."

—Jeremiah 5:22

For most of my childhood, I was terrified of thunderstorms because of the lightning. I learned at a very young age that lightning can kill. Even inside my house, I did not feel safe from lightning. But eventually I came to understand that I did not need to fear lightning as much as I needed to respect it.

The New Living Translation begins today's verse slightly differently: "Have you no respect for Me?" Yes, we should fear God. But we should not have the crippling fear that can almost be considered a phobia. Rather, the fear we should have toward God is more a reverence, an acknowledgment of and respect for God's power.

God's power is more than we can possibly fathom, and it is wise for us to have a respectful fear of that power. That alone should be reason enough to never put God to the test!

God, I fear You; I respect You. Please forgive me when I fail to show You the fear and respect due Your holy name. Amen.

March 9

Whoever does God's will is My brother and sister and mother.

—Mark 3:35

"Blood is thicker than water." That phrase is often used to explain why someone is fiercely loyal to their family. For some people, family is everything.

However, I have a friend with whom I am so close that we refer to each other as sisters. We are not blood relatives, but the relationship we have makes kinship irrelevant. And, according to Jesus' words, this friend and I are sisters because we are both Christians.

Blood is not thicker than the waters of baptism. When we are baptized, we are adopted into God's family. That makes us as much brothers and sisters as those of us born to the same parents. We all have the same heavenly Father.

The context of today's verse has Jesus responding to people trying to pull Him away from a crowd because His blood relatives have come. Jesus won't leave, however, because His spiritual family is just as important. We need to remember this lesson. It is not about our kinship with others. It's about who serves God.

Lord Jesus, You have said that all who do God's will are Your family. Remind me of that, and help me to treat my fellow believers as the brothers and sisters that they are. Amen.

March 10

The thief comes only to steal and kill and destroy;
I have come that they may have life, and have it
to the full.

—John 10:10

Since I am not a biblical scholar, I can only speculate as to who Jesus meant by "the thief." The thief could very easily mean Satan, but it could refer to anyone or anything that prevent us from living life to the fullest.

In fact, we can sabotage our own chances of having life to the full. Whenever we try to run our lives rather than let God control our lives, the results are always the same. Our worries, concerns, and self-absorbed behaviors take away from our quality of life.

However, when we let Jesus take control, we find peace of mind, body, and spirit. We find joy that we cannot contain within ourselves. Everything is better when we surrender to the Lord. And then we truly do have life and have it to the full!

So take a moment to look at your life. What is preventing you from living life to the fullest? Is Satan stealing away your happiness? Or are you sabotaging yourself? Step back. Let Jesus take control.

Jesus, through You only can I have life to the full. Help me surrender myself to you so that I do not destroy myself. Let me find my fullest peace and joy in You. Amen.

March 11

I wait for the Lord, my whole being waits, and
in His word I put my hope.

—Psalm 130:5

Waiting can be hard! As a child, I remember having to wait
for special days, like Christmas or my birthday, and getting
more and more antsy with each passing day. The night before
was always the worst!

I am no better at waiting as an adult. One year for my
birthday, a friend of mine gave me two tickets to the Gala of
the Royal Horses, a dream come true for me, given my love of
horses! The thing was, my birthday was in May and the show
wasn't until June. With each passing day, I was again becoming
increasingly antsy. When the day of the show rolled around, I
was so excited I could barely sit still or hold a thought in my
head!

When we are experiencing difficult times, we wait for God
to bring us through. We hope in His promise that He will never
leave us, but waiting for the Lord to help us can be difficult, even
frustrating. And yet, just as when we are waiting for a special
day or event, there is nothing we can do to speed along God's
saving grace. All we can do is wait. Wait and hope.

Lord, waiting is a part of life. Grant me the strength to endure
whatever waiting I must with patience and hope. In Jesus' name
I pray. Amen.

March 12

Your love has given me great joy and encouragement, because you, brother, have refreshed the hearts of the Lord's people.

—Philemon 1:7

This verse in Paul's letter to Philemon reminds me of something one of my pastors once said in a sermon. This pastor was explaining the importance of coming to church because our presence can be just the encouragement that someone else needs. He went on to say that even he has received encouragement from seeing everyone out in the pews.

There are many examples of how what we say or do can have a positive effect on everyone around us. We don't know what Philemon was doing to "refresh the hearts" of those around him. What we do know is that whatever he was doing, he did out of love for God's people. And that alone gave Paul, who was sitting in prison, great joy and encouragement.

Don't be bashful in what you do. No matter how big or small the action, remember that you might just be the encouragement that someone else needs. You can lift other people up simply by being a loving child of God.

God, help me to love those around me so that I may serve others in whatever way they need. Let me give of myself, even when I do not realize what I am giving or to whom. Amen.

March 13

My God, my God, why have You forsaken me?
Why are You so far from saving me, so far from
my cries of anguish?

—Psalm 22:1

"My God, my God, why have You forsaken me?" For most of my childhood, I associated these words with Jesus' crucifixion. After all, I would only hear them when I'd hear the Passion story. They were words of agony spoken by the Son of God, who had gone from being welcomed into Jerusalem as a king to being executed as a criminal less than a week later.

I was surprised when I first learned that these particular words of Jesus actually are found in a psalm. They are not just the words of the Son of God feeling abandoned by His Heavenly Father. They are also the words of a mortal experiencing his own utter despair.

There have been times in my life when I, like the psalmist, have cried out these words of utter despair. I have had struggles that left me feeling so hopelessly alone that even friends and family were not there anymore, let alone God. But it was at those times when I was most comforted by the fact that Jesus, not just the psalmist, had cried out these words of agony. That meant I wasn't ever truly alone because Jesus did know how I felt.

Dearest Jesus, when I walk through my darkest times, remind me that You also experienced utter despair and that You will never forsake me. In Your name, amen.

March 14

Sarah said, "God has brought me laughter, and everyone who hears about this will laugh with me."

—Genesis 21:6

"Laughter is the best medicine." Ever wonder why people will encourage patients in the hospital to laugh, but heaven forbid someone laugh at church?

Laughing is good for you! Laughter relaxes your whole body, boosts your immune system, and triggers the release of endorphins, just to name a few of its health benefits. Laughter has mental and emotional benefits as well, including things like stress relief.

Too many people feel that there is no room for laughter in church. Most pictures of Jesus depict Him as completely serious. I have seen one or two pictures where Jesus has a hint of a smile. My favorite picture of Jesus, however, shows Him laughing.

We were created in God's image, and God created us to have a sense of humor. Therefore, a logical conclusion is that God has a sense of humor. True, we all have different senses of humor. We don't all find the exact same things to be funny. But wouldn't it be nice if we all, rather than get offended if the pastor tells jokes in a sermon, embraced humor, in its many forms, for what it is—a gift from God?

God, let me laugh! Let Your joy inside me overflow and come out of me in the form of laughter! Amen.

March 15

Don't let anyone look down on you because you
are young, but set an example for the believers in
speech, in conduct, in love, in faith and in purity.
—1 Timothy 4:12

There is more than one way to look at this verse. The apostle
Paul was writing to Timothy, who was young in age. However,
we can also look at this as meaning being young in faith or new
to a particular congregation.

When I was 25 years old, I became president of the women's
group at the church to which I belonged at the time. I was met
with a lot of resistance to my proposed mild changes because
"that's just not the way things were done."

When I transferred membership to a smaller church closer
to my acreage, I was asked to serve on the church council. I met
resistance while on the council because I had not grown up in
that church. Therefore, at least in the minds of some members,
I didn't know what I was talking about.

But every time I encounter resistance, I remember this verse.
It reminds me that I should not let what others think of me
become the way I think of myself. The only opinion that matters
is God's, and He loves us.

Thank You, God, for loving me. When others try to tear me
down, please help me resist and build me back up when needed.
Amen.

March 16

Who is wise and understanding among you? Let
them show it by their good life, by deeds done in
the humility that comes from wisdom.

—James 3:13

Growing up around horses and "horse people," I noticed
something. The people who really knew a lot about horses were
the ones who were slower to offer advice. In fact, most would
wait until someone asked for their advice. However, the people
who were quick to tell me how I should handle my horse were
the ones who really didn't know that much.

In my adult life, I find the same thing to be true, and not just
about horses. The people who are truly wise about any topic are
never quick to talk about it. Rather, they act about it.

More often than not, a person giving unsolicited advice
doesn't understand the entire situation but still thinks they can
solve all problems. A wise person is also humble enough to
realize that they do not know everything. Therefore, they do
what works for them. Then, if someone asks, the wise person will
give advice in the form of "this is what I did," rather than "this
is what you should do." True wisdom is always accompanied by
humility and understanding.

Lord, teach me Your wisdom, but also grant me Your
understanding and humility. Amen.

March 17

Despite their fear of the peoples around them, they built the altar on its foundation and sacrificed burnt offerings on it to the Lord, both the morning and evening sacrifices.

—Ezra 3:3

The Israelites had just returned from exile and had a lot of rebuilding to do. And their land was not all theirs any longer. They were surrounded by peoples who had different beliefs, and the Israelites weren't sure how these other groups of people would handle Jewish rituals. They were afraid of these other groups.

But notice that the Israelites did not let their fear stop them. They still rebuilt the altar, and they still offered their burnt sacrifices on the altar. In fact, they sacrificed twice a day, as their rituals said they should.

How many of us fail to do religious rituals out of fear of others? Do we pray at restaurants, or are we too afraid of what others may think of us? Do we turn down invitations to social events because they conflict with worship services, or are we too afraid of being ridiculed for being Christian?

The Israelites were afraid, but they did not let that fear stop them. And neither should we. When we put God first in our lives, nothing can hold us back, not even fear.

Lord God, help me to keep putting You first in my life and not to be controlled by my fear of others. Amen.

March 18

Whatever you have learned or received or heard
from me, or seen in me—put it into practice. And
the God of peace will be with you.

—Philippians 4:9

Ever hear that someone "missed it by eighteen inches"? That
is sometimes said of someone who has gotten faith into their
head but not into their heart. Eighteen inches—the distance
between your brain and your heart—can make all the difference.

In his letter to the Philippians, Paul wants to make sure
they don't "miss it by eighteen inches." It is not enough to learn,
receive, hear, or see. Actions are also needed.

When we learn something, we usually say we understand it.
Understanding is done with the brain. It is important that we
understand our faith. But when we live our faith—that is, when
we put our beliefs, our ideals, our convictions into practice—we
have our faith in our heart.

Don't "miss it by eighteen inches." Take what you understand
in your head and live it through your heart. Put your faith into
practice.

God, take the faith I have in my head and put it in my heart.
Show me how to live out my faith, and help me guide others into
putting faith into practice. Let none of Your followers "miss it
by eighteen inches." Amen.

March 19

The Lord will be king over the whole earth. On that day there will be one Lord, and His name the only name.

—Zechariah 14:9

One day, a friend of mine and I were talking about how businesses do so much subcontracting these days that stores don't even know where their products come from. Therefore, boycotting a store for something like their use of sweatshops really isn't effective because the store may not even be aware of who is ultimately producing their merchandise. This friend of mine then made the comment about how the world was messed up beyond repair.

My friend made a pretty accurate statement about the nature of the world. That's why this verse in Zechariah is so encouraging. Yes, the world is terribly messed up now, and there is not much we humans can do to fix it. But someday, the Lord will take complete control of the earth. The Lord will fix what we broke.

When that day comes, there will no longer be the false gods of money and power. The Lord will be recognized as the one true God, and all will be right in the world again.

Lord, hasten the day when You take control of our messed up world. Restore Your creation to its natural beauty, and set the hearts of mankind on You. In Jesus' name, amen.

March 20

Now this is what the Lord Almighty says: "Give careful thought to your ways."

—Haggai 1:5

According to the New Oxford American Dictionary, the definition of *ways* is "the customary modes of behavior or practices of a group." So ways are traditions, customs. When groups with different customs interact, their ways do have the tendency to mingle.

Adopting the ways of those around them is usually what got the Israelites in trouble. That is probably why verse 7 repeats the Lord's words. "Give careful thought to your ways."

However, when I read God's words to Israel, I find myself thinking about something I have heard in every church I have ever belonged to: "This is the way we have always done it." New ideas are often shot down because things have never been done that way before.

Even we today need to remember God's words. Maybe our traditions are not so great after all. I'm not saying that we cannot keep traditions. But let's give thought to why we do things, rather than blindly following the ways of those who came before us.

Lord, teach me to examine my ways, and help me to be open to new ideas while still maintaining the integrity of my faith. In Jesus' name I pray. Amen.

March 21

For the wages of sin is death, but the gift of God
is eternal life in Christ Jesus our Lord.
—Romans 6:23

Can you think of a time when you did something wrong but were not punished as severely as you thought you would be? Maybe it was when you were a child and your parents went easy on you when you accidentally broke a window. Maybe it was in school when you inadvertently left an assignment at home. Maybe it was on the job when you goofed up the paperwork for one of your boss's biggest clients.

Whatever the situation, think about how you felt when the punishment you received did not, in your opinion, fit your crime. Did you feel relieved? Did you feel lucky? Did you feel blessed?

For our sins against God, we deserve death. That is the punishment that fits our crimes. But God is willing to give us a way out of that punishment. God chooses to give us the gift of mercy, to overlook our sins because Christ went ahead and took the punishment for us. And that's definitely a reason to feel blessed!

Thank You, O God, for Your gift of eternal life through Your Son Jesus. Keep me ever mindful of Christ's sacrifice, and let me remember this blessing every day of my life. I pray this in Jesus' holy name. Amen.

March 22

Be silent before the Sovereign Lord, for the day of the Lord is near. The Lord has prepared a sacrifice; He has consecrated those He has invited.

—Zephaniah 1:7

To me, this verse is the perfect verse for Lent. The Lenten hymns tend to be more somber, more thoughtful, more reserved. "Be silent before the Sovereign Lord...." Lent is a quieter season.

The Lenten hymns, liturgy, and Scripture readings tend to call our attention to the sacrifice God prepared and then carried out on Good Friday. The Lamb of God was born to be sacrificed, and the time of Christ's sacrifice is at hand. The Lord has sentenced His Son to a gruesome and brutal death. Out of respect and awe, we must be silent.

We should also be silent with gratitude. The death Christ faced was the death we deserved. By that sacrifice, the Lord has indeed consecrated us. God calls us each by name and invites us to return to Him. And Christ has made us worthy to enter the Lord's presence.

Be silent. Be respectful. Be filled with awe. Be grateful. And above all, accept the Lord's invitation.

Lord, no words can express my humble gratitude for the sacrifice of Your Son. I come before You in silent reverence and accept Your invitation to be washed in the blood of the Lamb. Amen.

March 23

So with you: Now is your time of grief, but I will
see you again and you will rejoice, and no one
will take away your joy.

—John 16:22

Jesus said this to His disciples the night He was betrayed.
They were soon going to see Him arrested and killed, and
they would grieve. But Jesus would rise again, return to His
disciples, and replace their grief with joy.

I think it's important to note that Jesus does not tell His
disciples not to grieve. Jesus does not forbid grief. Rather, He
gives His disciples hope. And Jesus gives us that same hope.

Whenever we lose a loved one, we grieve at the time of the
loss. But we only grieve because our loved one is no longer with
us. We have the hope that one day we will see all of our loved
ones again. We will be reunited with our family and friends.
We will rejoice.

So we grieve now. But amid the grief, we look with hope to
the day when all our pain and sorrow will be replaced with joy.

Jesus, You gave Your disciples hope amid their impending grief.
When we are grieving, remind us of that same hope—the hope
that someday we will all be together again. Amen.

March 24

The third time He said to him, "Simon son of John, do you love Me?" Peter was hurt because Jesus asked him the third time, "Do you love Me?" He said, "Lord, You know all things; You know that I love You." Jesus said, "Feed My sheep."

—John 21:17

Peter was right—Jesus did know that Peter loved Him. So, why then did Jesus ask Peter three times? Did Jesus need to hear it? Maybe, but not likely. After all, Jesus, knowing all things, would have no doubts to be put to rest. I'd be willing to venture that it was more that Jesus knew Peter needed to say it.

Periodically we all need to hear someone say that they love us because our simply knowing isn't always enough. We all have those doubts pop up every so often. However, we also need to periodically say "I love you" to others. When we do, we reaffirm our feelings, even to ourselves. The tone of voice we use to say those three little words can prove or disprove to everyone, including ourselves, that they are really meant.

Of course God knows that we love Him. But do we know that we love Him? Let's find out. Let's say it out loud!

Dear Jesus, You know everything. You know how I feel about You. Help me to prove it to myself in the way I speak this aloud. I love You! In Your name, amen.

March 25

Now faith is confidence in what we hope for and assurance about what we do not see.

—Hebrews 11:1

I once heard a story about a terminally ill man who asked his Christian doctor what happened after death. The doctor couldn't say for sure, which resulted in the man questioning if he did need to fear death. The doctor walked over to a door and let a dog into the room. The doctor explained that this dog, his dog, had never been in that room before but was excited to come in because the dog knew his master was there.

Although that story is undoubtedly fiction, it does prove a point about faith. Death is not the only time we face something we do not see. Throughout life, we face many transitions, and we cannot see how the life change is going to work out. Faith gives us the assurance that we will be just fine once we get through the transitions.

The scariest thing to face is the unknown. However, we can face the unknown with confidence because we have the hope of God being in control. We have faith.

Lord God, as I face the unknowns in my life, remind me of Your everlasting presence. When my faith falters, renew within me the confidence and assurance that only comes from trusting in You. Amen.

March 26

Then the Lord reached out His hand and touched
my mouth and said to me, "I have put My words
in your mouth."

—Jeremiah 1:9

Jeremiah was young and inexperienced. He didn't feel he
could be a prophet for the Lord. But God put His words in
Jeremiah's mouth, and Jeremiah went out into the world as
God's prophet.

Kathy had never written a song before in her life. Sure, she
was a musician, but she played songs. She didn't write them. Yet,
while in the Leadership Program for Rural Musicians put on by
her church's synod, Kathy felt compelled to write a song. Not
only did she go ahead and write it, but she also shared it with
her fellow program members.

Being open to God's word does not mean simply listening to
what God has to say. It means going where God sends us and
speaking what God wants us to say.

The lyrics of the simple song that Kathy wrote are as much
a testament to being open to God's word as Kathy's actions of
writing the song. Today, and every day, let's use those lyrics as
our prayer.

"God of mercy, where I am needed send me, where I am needed
send me. God of mercy, where I am needed send me." Amen.

March 27

Rejoice always, pray continually, give thanks in all circumstances; for this is God's will for you in Christ Jesus.

—1 Thessalonians 5:16-18

Rejoice. Pray. Give thanks. These are not simply good pieces of advice. These are not suggestions for a happy life. This is how God wants us to live.

We all face struggles in our lives. These struggles can cause us to lie awake at night, worrying about how we are going to make it through another day. When that happens to me, I do what I do best—look to songs for comfort.

One song I am particularly fond of is "Count Your Blessings (Instead of Sheep)" from the musical *White Christmas*. My favorite line in that song is, "When my bankroll is getting small, I think of when I had none at all."

No matter how difficult things get, we always have a reason to rejoice and to give thanks. Many of us are good at praying when we want something from God, but we don't always pray when things are going well. If we pray continually, we will pray in good times and bad.

God, teach me how to always rejoice and give thanks to You, regardless of how difficult things get for me. And help me to continually pray, regardless of how good things get for me. Amen.

March 28

In the same way, the Spirit helps us in our weakness. We do not know what we ought to pray for, but the Spirit Himself intercedes for us through wordless groans.

—Romans 8:26

Praying can be difficult. We may know what we want, but will our requests sound acceptable before God?

For awhile, I worked in a livestock feed store that, among other things, sold feeds manufactured on site. There were usually three to four guys working back in production. One day, the production manager came rushing up to the front to call 911. I heard him tell the dispatch that one of his employees had fallen a relatively large distance onto a concrete floor. That day there were only two other guys besides the production manager working back there. I was friends with one of those two guys. I found myself praying earnestly that it was not my friend who had fallen.

I felt terrible when I realized that I essentially prayed that the other guy was the one who had fallen. I felt even worse when I learned that the other guy was indeed the one who fell. But I know that the Spirit takes my prayers before the Father, not with the words I have said but with feelings that are in my heart.

Father, thank You for sending Your Spirit to help me pray when I can't find the right words to express myself. Amen.

March 29

For physical training is of some value, but godliness has value for all things, holding promise for both the present life and the life to come.

—1 Timothy 4:8

Some people are obsessed with physical fitness. It took a herniated disc for me to start caring about my health, but even now, I do not obsess. I will still partake of sweets on occasion, but there are some people who feel they must run five miles if they eat even one piece of candy.

Paul is by no means telling young Timothy in this verse that physical training is a bad idea. Physical fitness does result in the ability to lead a more fulfilling life. However, we should never focus so much on our physical health, or anything else for that matter, that we neglect our spiritual health. Even the healthiest person will eventually die. Then what? If we have faith in Christ, we have the promise of another life to come.

It is okay for us to be passionate about things, be it our physical fitness, our hobbies, charities, etc. But we need to take care that our passion does not turn into obsession. With Christ in the center of our lives, He will lead us to the proper balance.

Jesus, I want You at the center of my life. Do not let my passions turn into obsessions that pull me away from my heavenly home with You. Amen.

March 30

The purposes of a person's heart are deep waters,
but one who has insight draws them out.
—Proverbs 20:5

My favorite book is Harper Lee's *To Kill a Mockingbird*. In that book, Atticus Finch tells his daughter that, to truly understand someone, she needs to look at things from the other person's perspective. While through most of the book, he tells his daughter to climb inside the other person's shoes, the first time he teaches her this lesson, he tells her climb inside the other person's skin.

I really like the thought of climbing inside the other person's skin. I find that to be a much more meaningful way to look at things from another's perspective. It's one thing to stand in someone else's shoes. But by climbing into their skin, you are forced to look at things through their eyes.

We may not always understand why someone reacts to us the way they do. However, if we take the time to crawl inside their skin, we can see that they may be facing challenges we did not know about. And when we attempt to understand the other person, conflicts can be resolved quickly or even avoided entirely.

God, when I do not understand someone, help me to climb inside their skin and look at things through their eyes. In Jesus' name, amen.

March 31

The Lord Himself goes before you and will be
with you; He will never leave nor forsake you.
Do not be afraid; do not be discouraged.
—Deuteronomy 31:8

Although this verse was spoken to the Israelites before they
took control of the promised land, these words are just as true
for us today. We all face times of depression, frustration, and
fear. Those times can leave us feeling completely alone.

When difficult times come, we can take heart in the fact
that the Lord is always with us. He walks in front of us to guide
us, but He also walks beside for support. No matter what life
throws at us, God is there to help us cope.

There's a saying that the downtrodden rarely look up. But
whenever we do feel afraid, discouraged, or otherwise down,
that is precisely the time to look up. When we look down, all we
can see is where we currently are. When we look up, we see our
Lord with us and leading us. That's not to say we'll instantly
feel better, but at least we will be open to receive God's comfort
and support.

Lord, when I am down, raise my eyes and heart heavenward.
Let me feel Your presence and see You guiding me. Amen.

April 1

Do not conform to the pattern of this world, but be transformed by the renewing of your mind. Then you will be able to test and approve what God's will is—His good, pleasing and perfect will.

—Romans 12:2

We teach our children to resist peer pressure. A common response to a child's comment that everyone else is doing something is that infamous, "If everyone else jumped off a bridge, would you jump too?" We want our children to learn that the right thing to do is not always the popular thing to do.

Yet somehow, we lose sight of that lesson ourselves. We let society dictate everything for us, from what we wear and what we eat to how much of an education we get. We have designer clothes and fad diets. And we all have to go to college and get a 4-year degree, even if that's too much education for the profession we really want.

We need to resist our own peer pressure—the pressure society places on us. When we allow God to transform us, we are open to see and embrace His will for us.

Help me, O God, to resist conformity, and transform me into the person You want me to be. Show me Your will, and allow me to fully embrace it. Amen.

April 2

Here I am! I stand at the door and knock. If anyone hears My voice and opens the door, I will come in and eat with that person, and they with Me.

—Revelation 3:20

In one of the Sunday school classrooms in my home church, there was a picture of Jesus knocking on a door with no doorknob. When I first saw that picture, I was too young to understand the symbolism in it. Mom explained to me how the door, like a person's heart, could only be opened from the inside.

That picture was undoubtedly inspired by today's Bible verse. Jesus wants to be accepted, to be invited in, to provide life-giving nourishment for the soul. But we can't just holler a "come in" to Him because He cannot open the door from the outside.

I also find it interesting that Jesus says, "If anyone hears My voice and opens the door…." Have you ever opened the door, maybe to leave or maybe to let a dog outside, and discovered a visitor who had not yet knocked or rung the doorbell? We can't do that with Jesus. There is no accidentally discovering Jesus at the door to our heart. That's because Jesus has been knocking all along. We can only suddenly hear His knock and answer the door. And why shouldn't we?

Jesus, open my ears to hear Your voice as You knock on the door to my heart. I want to invite You inside. Amen.

April 3

Commit to the Lord whatever you do, and He will establish your plans.

—Proverbs 16:3

There are people who believe the only profession a person can be "called" to is ministry. It has been my experience, however, that God calls people into many professions. Yes, God calls pastors. But God also calls doctors, teachers, counselors, therapists, and every other profession a person could have. Regardless of our vocation, if we are committed to doing God's will, then we are indeed doing God's work.

It has also been my experience that God calls us to more than merely our jobs. Think about your interests, your hobbies, your passions. God can call you into those as well.

Whatever we do, whether we are paid for it or not, we need to commit our work to the Lord. God will take our deeds and our plans, even those plans that are years down the road of becoming reality for us, and will use us to further His kingdom on earth. It may be scary for us, as God may use activities or interests that we do not realize He can use. But we belong to the Lord, and He will not let us fail at what He calls us to do.

Lord, I commit myself—my job, my interests, my hobbies, my passions, my entire being—to You. Use me as You see fit. Amen.

April 4

A friend loves at all times, and a brother is born for a time of adversity.

—Proverbs 17:17

There is a saying that you know who your true friends are when you need help moving. While it might have originally been said as a joke, there is a lot of truth to that statement. You know who is truly your friend by looking at who's around when you need help, regardless of what help you need.

It is very easy to be a friend to someone when things are going well for them. As long as life is going a person's way, being that person's friend is all fun and games. That person may feel like they have all the friends in the world.

But what happens when life is no longer a bed of roses? We all experience those low times. We may be struggling financially. We may be coping with a loss. We may be suffering from depression. Those are the times when we need to lean on our friends, but some "friends" don't want to be around in the tough times.

This verse not only shows us how to identify our friends. It also shows us how to be a friend to others. Be there for your friends in their times of trial. Love your friends, especially when they feel unloveable.

Jesus, You are a friend who will never leave me in my hard times. Help me to be a true friend to others. Amen.

April 5

> And the Lord said to me, "I have seen this people, and they are a stiff-necked people indeed! Let Me alone, so that I may destroy them and blot out their name from under heaven. And I will make you into a nation stronger and more numerous than they."
>
> —Deuteronomy 9:13-14

Being stubborn is rarely a good thing. And stubbornness can so easily result in damaging effects on relationships. This passage in Deuteronomy is a prime example of that.

The Israelites were being stubborn, and God was ready to wipe them off the face of the earth. They were proud. They were arrogant. But worst of all, they were stubborn.

It's stubbornness that keeps two people from making up after a fight. It can also be stubbornness that led to the fight in the first place. Stubbornness prevents someone from seeing what is right and focuses their attention on what they want.

Never confuse stubbornness with determination. Determination will keep you working toward a positive goal. Stubbornness will be what hurts you and those around you.

Lord, break my stubbornness. Let me be determined, rather than stubborn. I do not want to hurt my relationship with You or others. Amen.

April 6

And without faith it is impossible to please God, because anyone who comes to Him must believe that He exists and that He rewards those who earnestly seek Him.

—Hebrews 11:6

At first glance, this seems to be a statement of the obvious. Of course we cannot have a relationship with God if we do not know that God exists, any more than we can have a relationship with a parent, sibling, or any other family member we have never met. But there is so much more to this statement if we take a closer look at it.

Some people will argue that even atheists believe in God. They just simply refuse to acknowledge God's power or authority. I don't know if that's true or not because I've never heard an atheist say anything other than flat-out denial of God's existence.

The point is, faith is not simply believing that God exists. It is also the belief that God wants us to come to Him, to have a relationship with Him. Which would we rather have from family and friends—acknowledgement of our existence or an actual relationship? Naturally, it is pleasing to God to have us seek Him to have a relationship with Him. He wants us to not only know about Him, but to love Him. And that is accomplished through faith.

God, I want to know You. I want to have a relationship with You. I need Your help to accomplish this. Amen.

April 7

In everything I did, I showed you that by this kind of hard work we must help the weak, remembering the words the Lord Jesus Himself said: "It is more blessed to give than to receive."
—Acts 20:35

Christmas has always been my favorite holiday. I can remember as a child getting down on my hands and knees by the Christmas tree to find the presents with my name on the tag. I would look at each of my presents—their size, shape, weight, etc.—and try to figure out what they were. Sometimes I would shake them. The only reason I never tried to open one end was because I didn't think I could get away with it.

I still enjoy the gifting aspect of Christmas, but I totally ignore the presents for me under the tree until it's time to open them. Now, the pleasure comes in my year-long search to find the perfect present for the other person and then seeing their reaction as they open the present. In fact, I enjoy giving presents so much that I will give "just because" gifts to people throughout the year.

Whether for holidays, a birthday, or for someone in need, the biggest delight in gifting always is experienced by the generous giver.

Jesus, You said it is more blessed to give than to receive. Help me be a generous giver. Amen.

April 8

Better is one day in Your courts than a thousand elsewhere; I would rather be a doorkeeper in the house of my God than dwell in the tents of the wicked.

—Psalm 84:10

We all have a "happy place"—a place that is guaranteed to boost our mood, no matter how down we feel. We seek out that place when we need comfort or relief from stress. We may even go to our "happy place" when we are already happy, just because we like being in that place.

The psalmist seems to be describing his own "happy place." For him, the best place to be is in God's presence. The psalmist would rather be just outside God's house than to be living among people who have no fear of or respect for God.

I don't know about you, but my "happy place" has nothing to do with church. When I'm at church, in the house of my God, I am more focused on the responsibilities I have there, like Sunday school music and putting together the bulletin. Wouldn't it be awesome if we all could think of no better place to be than in the house of the Lord? That can happen if we first and foremost focus on God.

Dear God, make Your house my "happy place." Teach me to focus on You, so that I can see that being in Your presence truly is the best place to be. Amen.

April 9

"For I know the plans I have for you," declares the Lord, "plans to prosper you and not to harm you, plans to give you hope and a future."
—Jeremiah 29:11

After a winter of limited jogging, I got it in my head to run a 5K breast cancer benefit race. With the decision made, I had only six and a half weeks to train to run a half-mile farther than I had ever run before. I also gave myself a fairly ambitious time goal for that benefit race.

Two weeks into my training, I experienced a nasty setback. My new activity level put too much pressure on an ankle that I had sprained the previous summer. Despite my bracing the ankle, it swelled up and began throbbing. The pain and swelling made me question my ability to run a 5K race at all. I wondered if I should just give up.

My boss, who was also my unofficial coach for this training, gave me a pep talk not unlike the talk God gave Jeremiah. My boss reminded me that I could run this race. All I had to do was stick to the training plan he had for me. My ankle would heal, and I would be fine. Just stick to the plan.

Lord God, I know You have plans for me. Help me abide by Your plans, as You know how to keep me from harm. I will prosper under Your guidance. Amen.

April 10

So then, just as you received Christ Jesus as Lord, continue to live your lives in Him, rooted and built up in Him, strengthened in the faith as you were taught, and overflowing with thankfulness.

—Colossians 2:6–7

How many of us know people who were raised in a church family but who abandoned their faith as adults? Unfortunately, it does happen. A lot. Sometimes these young Christians disappear from the church after they are confirmed. Other times it happens when they go off to college. And still other times it happens when they are ready to embark on a new life as an adult.

With this being such a problem in the church, how can we keep our young people coming? I'm not sure there is a simple answer to this question. All I know is that Paul has great words of wisdom. We also can encourage our youth to stay rooted in Christ. Wherever their lives take them, Christ goes with them.

This time of year, many young people are preparing for graduations—from high school and from college. Let's take a few moments to pray for these young Christians that they are indeed strengthened in the faith as they were taught.

Christ, You walk with each one of us throughout our life. As graduations approach for so many, keep Your young followers living their lives in You. Amen.

April 11

Come to Me, all you who are weary and
burdened, and I will give you rest.
—Matthew 11:28

We all have crosses to bear. We all have things that weigh
us down, burdens we carry with us through our daily activities.
Sometimes these crosses are burdens from the past that we
simply have not let go. Sometimes these crosses are current
struggles.

Regardless of what the burden is, it is exhausting to carry
that weight around. The crosses we bear take their toll on us
physically, not just mentally or emotionally. They can leave us
physically tired, as though we have been carrying a 50-pound
barbell across our shoulders.

Thankfully, we do have someone to whom we can turn.
Jesus does not chastise us for carrying these burdens. After all,
not every cross we bear is one that we have chosen. But whether
we are essentially punishing ourselves for past mistakes or we
are dealing with a curveball life has just thrown at us, Jesus
will give us the rest we need. We may have to pick up our cross
again, but when we turn to the Lord in prayer, we can at least
put the weight down for a little while and rest.

Jesus, I am weak and heavy-laden. I now come to You. Please
give me the rest I need to persevere with this cross I bear. Amen.

April 12

I have told you these things, so that in Me you may have peace. In this world you will have trouble. But take heart! I have overcome the world.

—John 16:33

In this verse, Jesus plain and simply tells His disciples that they will have trouble. He did not say that we "might" have trouble or that we "could possibly" have trouble. Nope. We *will* have trouble!

But not only do we have the promise of hard times, we also have the promise of peace and ultimate victory. No matter how big our problems are, Jesus is bigger. There is nothing that Jesus cannot overcome.

While we face the troubles of this world, we also have the peace that only Jesus can give. In Jesus, we have the peace that allows us to carry on in our daily lives, amidst the trouble we are facing. We have the peace that keeps us calm when the storm is raging all around us.

So yes, we will have trouble. There's no question about that. The only question is how will we respond to the trouble? My suggestion is to listen to Christ and to take heart! In the end, Jesus always wins!

Lord Jesus, thank You for the promise of Your peace. May Your peace surround and fill me so that I do not lose heart in You. After all, You have already overcome the world. Amen.

April 13

Therefore do not worry about tomorrow, for tomorrow will worry about itself. Each day has enough trouble of its own.

—Matthew 6:34

Worrying can be addicting. I personally struggle with "what if" worries. What if I don't have enough clients for the week? What if my weekly paycheck isn't big enough to cover all my bills? What if the rust on my car's hood eats clear through, forcing me to replace the entire hood?

Unfortunately, worry does absolutely no good. All it does is raise our blood pressure and cause us to lose sleep. And most of the things we worry about never actually happen at all. Worrying is a lot like a little hamster running on its exercise wheel. That hamster is working really hard but is getting nowhere.

I'm sure that is what Jesus had in mind when He told His followers to not worry about tomorrow. We all have enough to handle just getting through the current day. We certainly don't need to "borrow trouble" by worrying about something that hasn't even happened yet.

Teach me, dear Lord, to not spend my time worrying. Help me instead to focus on the present time and to deal with "tomorrow" when it becomes "today." In Jesus' name I pray. Amen.

April 14

Do you not know? Have you not heard? The Lord is the everlasting God, the Creator of the ends of the earth. He will not grow tired or weary, and His understanding no one can fathom.

—Isaiah 40:28

This verse has it all. It starts with the desire to spread the word about God. It continues with a statement of faith. Then it finishes with a word of comfort and an expression of awe.

Personally, I am most partial to word of comfort. "He will not grow tired or weary." I know someone who has driven friends away because of his negative attitude and self-pity. His friends got tired of his attitude and were worn out trying to pull him out of his pity parties.

While I may not drive friends away like this other person did, I know that I am also susceptible to negative attitudes and self-pity. Sometimes my friends see these in me, and sometimes only God knows. The comforting part for me is that even though God always knows my negativity and always hears my complaints, He will never grow tired of listening to me or weary of dealing with me.

God will never grow tired or weary. Yes, that means God is always awake to look out for us. But it also means we will never drive God away from us.

Thank You, God, for never growing tired or weary of me, no matter how exhausting I may be. Amen.

April 15

> He said to them, "Then give back to Caesar what
> is Caesar's, and to God what is God's."
> —Luke 20:25

The chief priests were going to use taxes against Jesus. If Jesus said it was wrong to pay taxes to Caesar, then the Roman government would come after Him. If Jesus said it was right to pay taxes to Caesar, the Jewish people would turn against Him.

Nobody likes paying taxes, but Jesus' answer to the question of paying taxes reminds us that nothing we have is truly ours. We like to think the money we have is our own and that our government has no right to it. Really, though, everything we have comes from God.

The paychecks we feel we earn are actually the result of the jobs God led us to find. More often than not, the jobs we have are the result of the gifts and talents that God gave us in the first place. Our homes, possessions, even our family and friends are all gifts from God.

So before any of us complains about the taxes we have to pay, let's stop to think for a moment. Have we given back to God what is God's? If not, now is the time to start.

God, everything I have is a gift from You. Help me to give back to You everything that is Yours, including my very life. Amen.

April 16

The beginning of wisdom is this: Get wisdom.
Though it cost all you have, get understanding.
—Proverbs 4:7

My mom was a middle school teacher. Her job was difficult. She had spent a lot of time and money on her own education for a job that didn't pay well. She dealt with students who wanted the grades without the work and with parents who believed their child could do no wrong.

I learned a lot from Mom. She taught me science in her classroom. But I also gained an understanding from her that has served me well in my adulthood.

From Mom, I learned that a job should never be about money. She was a teacher because she loved what she did. Consequently, I work in a chiropractic clinic, even though I could make more money in a spa, because that is where I am happiest.

I also learned from Mom that what is popular is not always right and what is right is not always popular. She angered students and parents alike by doing the right thing for her classroom. I have also come to hold to what is right, even if it's not what everyone else thinks.

That understanding, taught by my mom, was the beginning to the wisdom I continue to get.

Thank You, Lord, for those who have taught me understanding and wisdom. Amen.

April 17

The Lord is my shepherd, I lack nothing.
—Psalm 23:1

Since most people have little to no experience with sheep, it can be really hard for them to understand the depth of this verse, or the verses that follow, for that matter. We raised sheep when I was growing up. That was an experience I wouldn't trade for the world!

Sheep do not know how to take care of themselves. Through the years of domestication, sheep have lost the instinct that their wild relatives have. Sheep cannot protect themselves. They cannot find their way if they get lost. They do not know where to go without someone else to lead them. Sheep are pretty helpless.

What sheep are to humans is not unlike what humans are to God. We may like to think we can take care of ourselves, but when it comes right down to it, we are helpless. Sheep need their human shepherd to provide food, water, safety, and direction. How many times do we pray for these very things? We pray for food for the hungry. We pray for water for areas of drought. We pray for safety from all sorts of dangers. We pray for direction for our lives. And God provides all of that for us, His flock.

Lord, my shepherd, thank You for providing me with everything I need. In You, I do lack nothing. Amen.

April 18

[Love] always protects, always trusts, always
hopes, always perseveres.

—1 Corinthians 13:7

This is part of a passage commonly read at weddings.
However, there are many different types of loves, and this
statement holds true for all of them. Whether the love is
between spouses, friends, or parents and their children, these
characteristics of love are always there.

Love causes a parent's desire to shield their child from any
kind of pain, physical or emotional. Love causes a person to stand
up for a friend being insulted. Love will even cause a complete
stranger to defend someone being bullied. Love protects.

In today's society, people tend to believe the worst about
other people. Rumors about something negative, whether they
are true or not, spread like wildfire. Rumors about good things
are rarely shared. That's because this world lacks love. Love
always trusts, always hopes. Love looks for the good in people.
The cool thing is, love always finds the good in people.

Loving God, teach me to love as You love. Teach me how to
protect those around me. But more importantly, teach me how
to always look for and find the good in the people around me.
This world needs more of Your love, and I want to help spread
Your love to the world. Amen.

April 19

If we are faithless, He remains faithful, for He cannot disown Himself.

—2 Timothy 2:13

There's a saying that you can't change the spots on a leopard. It means that a person will always have certain characteristics that cannot be changed. Those traits are part of who that person is. To go against those traits is to essentially disown oneself.

The same thing is true of God. There are certain things that are characteristic of God that will never change. One of those traits is God's faithfulness. No matter what happens, God is always faithful.

There's something very encouraging, very comforting, in that thought. Let me say it again. No matter what happens, God is always faithful. Nothing will ever change God's faithfulness because that faithfulness is part of what makes God who He is.

And who God is does not depend on who we are. That is why we can be unfaithful (or faithless, as this translation says) and God will still be faithful to us. So when we go astray, God still waits for us. And when we return, God is welcoming us back with open arms.

Lord God, thank You for being faithful to me, even when I am unfaithful to You. When I wander from You, remind me that Your faithfulness never depends on what I do and grant me the courage to return to You. Amen.

April 20

A bruised reed He will not break, and a smoldering wick He will not snuff out. In faithfulness He will bring forth justice; He will not falter or be discouraged till He establishes justice on earth. In His teaching the islands will put their hope.

—Isaiah 42:3–4

Having grown up in the rural Midwest, I have seen a lot of brush piles burned. I have watched my dad many times as he stood guard over a large fire, the hose ready in case it started to get out of hand. I have also watched Dad use the hose when the fire has almost burned out. He would douse the few remaining glowing embers and put an end to the fire that had obviously run its course.

There are times when we may feel like that glowing ember. We don't feel like we have anything left. Those are the times when we need to turn back to Jesus. Jesus won't douse our fire, even if we're down to just one glowing ember.

All that it takes to get a fire started again is a some fuel and some oxygen. Rather than extinguishing our flame, Jesus will throw more wood on and gently fan our flame. Jesus can and will bring our fire back to life.

Jesus, when I am feeling spent, like I have nothing left, come tend to my flame. Add fuel to my fire so that I may burn all the brighter for You. In Your holy name I pray. Amen.

April 21

The Lord is close to the brokenhearted and saves
those who are crushed in spirit.
—Psalm 34:18

One of my friends had shared a picture with this verse on
Facebook. The day she shared it happened to be a day when
I was struggling with grief. It had been almost two months
since this particular loved one had died. Yet for some unknown
reason, I couldn't stop thinking about her.

Grief is like that though. I've lost enough loved ones in my
life that I have experienced more grief than I'd like to at this
age. One thing that I have noticed is that people in general are
more sympathetic immediately following the death than they are
months later. They also tend to be more sympathetic toward a
person who has not experienced many deaths.

This verse reminds me, though, that just because others
around me may not understand or be supportive of my grief
months and years down the road does not mean that I am alone
in that grief. God is always there. When we are struggling with
griefs we don't even understand, God is with us to comfort us
and to lift our spirits again.

Lord, thank You for being close to me, especially when I am
brokenhearted. Thank You for the comfort that can only come
when You put Your arms around me. Amen.

April 22

> For everything that was written in the past was
> written to teach us, so that through the endurance
> taught in the Scriptures and the encouragement
> they provide we might have hope.
> —Romans 15:4

In my desk drawer at work, I have a New Testament Bible. I love that little Bible, and I have read it several times. However, that is an incomplete Bible. Thankfully, that is not the only Bible I own.

The New Testament is what we Christians base our faith on. We accept Christ as our Savior and strive to follow His teachings. Some Christian denominations are so focused on the New Testament that they believe that's all a person needs to read.

But the Old Testament is still important. When He taught in synagogues, Jesus read from the Scriptures, which is what we now refer to as the Old Testament. And in his letter to the Christians in Rome, the apostle Paul also stated the importance of the Scriptures.

Our Christian faith may be based on the New Testament. However, like Paul said to the Romans, everything that was written in the past was written to teach us. The Old Testament still has much to offer us.

Lord God, You have provided a wonderful teaching tool in the form of Your holy Word. Help me to not focus solely on one part, but guide me to spend ample time in both Old and New Testaments. Amen.

April 23

"[N]o weapon forged against you will prevail, and you will refute every tongue that accuses you. This is the heritage of the servants of the Lord, and this is their vindication from Me," declares the Lord.

—Isaiah 54:17

One of my favorite songs is "The Lord is My Defense," sung by the group Dakota Road. The verses name all kinds of different situations that a person can be in while acknowledging that the Lord is always our defense. For example, one line says, "When somebody slanders me, the Lord is my defense."

As long as we are in this world, we will have to deal with other people. Some of the people we meet will be good people, but others will not. There will always be people in this world who will start vicious rumors about an innocent person. There will also always be people who will blindly believe any negative rumor they hear about a person.

But the Lord is our defense. He has promised vindication to all who follow Him. People may slander us. They may do worse things to us than simply speak lies of us. Yet they will not prevail. In the Lord, we have an impenetrable defense.

Lord, You are my defense. No harm can come to me as long as I am in Your shelter. Thank You for Your promise of vindication. Amen.

April 24

And everyone who calls on the name of the Lord
will be saved.

—Acts 2:21

It seems to be human nature to want to be a part of something exclusive, to belong where not everyone is allowed. Fraternity and sorority houses are very popular on most, if not all, college campuses. Why? Because not everyone can join.

Throughout the years, people have tried to make God's grace an exclusive club. That was in the very beginning of Christianity. Jews were considered to be God's "chosen people." Therefore, they believed that salvation through Christ was only for those of Hebrew descent.

We all enjoy being included in special groups, but how do you feel when you are the one being excluded? Were you ever refused membership to a Greek house on campus? Did you ever try out for honor band or honor choir only to not be selected? Rejection is painful!

Thankfully for those of us who are not of Hebrew descent, God's grace is not an exclusive club. Salvation is available to anyone and everyone who turns to the Lord. No auditions or tryouts necessary. And the only initiation rite is baptism.

Thank You, Lord, for making Your grace available to everyone, including me. Amen.

April 25

You are the salt of the earth. But if the salt loses
its saltiness, how can it be made salty again? It is
no longer good for anything, except to be thrown
out and trampled underfoot.

—Matthew 5:13

If you know much about chemistry, you will know that salt's flavor is the result of the bond between sodium and chlorine. When those two elements come together, they make sodium chloride, which is the fancy, scientific name for table salt.

Similarly, it is the bond between Christ and us that makes us Christians. Without that bond, we cannot be saved or bring Christ's message of salvation to the world. This bond is crucial!

Also, the human body needs salt for things like fluid balance and muscle and nerve function. Without salt, our bodies cannot be healthy. In the same way, this world needs Christians. More specifically, the world needs the message of Christ that Christians bring.

As long as we have that bond with Christ, we serve our purpose. If we break that bond, we are of no use to Christ anymore. Don't let your bond break.

Jesus, through my bond with You, I become the salt of the earth. Strengthen the bond between us so that I may continue to bring Your life-giving message to the world. Amen.

April 26

In their hearts humans plan their course, but the
Lord establishes their steps.

—Proverbs 16:9

Throughout my middle school and high school years, my
plan was to become a veterinarian. In the summer between my
junior and senior years of college, I decided that I was more
interested in animal behavior than I was in animal medicine. So
I earned my Bachelor of Science degree in animal science with
the plan to study animal behavior in graduate school.

As I write this, I am sitting at my desk in the chiropractic
clinic where I work as a massage therapist. This is a far cry from
the veterinarian I was so determined to be during my teenage
years! But I am very happy where I am now, and I am certain
that I am doing what God wanted me to do all along.

Even though I started out with different plans, it doesn't
mean that I was ever actually going against God. I know I have
touched many lives on the road that has led me to where I am
today. By guiding my steps, God aligned my plan with His plan
and used me for other parts of His plan along the way.

God, thank You for guiding me, for establishing my steps
through life. Your plan always comes together, and it humbles
me to know that You will use me to carry out Your plan. Amen.

April 27

Then Peter came to Jesus and asked, "Lord, how many times shall I forgive my brother or sister who sins against me? Up to seven times?" Jesus answered, "I tell you, not seven times, but seventy-seven times."

—Matthew 18:21–22

I must admit, forgiveness is something I struggle with. I have a terrible time letting go of wrongs I feel were committed against me. I internalize those feelings of anger and frustration. Then I brood over them until my blood pressure skyrockets.

The same is true whether the wrong was committed by another human being or by one of my pets. And the sad thing is, the "offending party" may not even have realized they did something wrong. Still, I am bound and determined to punish them, even though the sin may only be in my head.

I can understand Peter's question all too well. How many times do I have to put up with something? Jesus expands on His response to Peter with the Parable of the Unforgiving Servant. God continues to forgive us, so we should forgive one another. Besides, when we hold on to sins of the past, we aren't punishing anyone except ourselves.

Lord, please teach me to forgive others the same way You so graciously continue to forgive me. In Jesus' name I pray. Amen.

April 28

Then you will know the truth, and the truth will
set you free.

—John 8:32

This verse is frequently taken out of context. What Jesus is
really saying in this verse is that, by following His teachings, we
will know the truth about Jesus. That truth is that Jesus is the
Messiah, and we are set free from the burden of sin.

When taken out of context, people quote this verse to say
that one should always tell the truth. That is sound advice, as
lying will only entangle you in a web of deceit. But let's consider
all aspects of honesty.

How many times do we lie to ourselves? We tell ourselves
we don't need help with something when, in reality, we do. We
tell ourselves that we cannot do something when we know we
actually can but just do not want to. Then there's the way I tend
to be most dishonest with myself—lying to ourselves about how
we truly feel about someone or something.

In all of these cases, we can free ourselves from burdens
we bear. No more dealing with disasters that could have been
avoided. No more sabotaging ourselves. And no more suppressed
or denied emotions. We shall be free!

Help me, dear Lord, to face the truths I want to deny, especially
the truths about myself. Set me free. Amen.

April 29

[T]he Lord will watch over your coming and going both now and forevermore.

—Psalm 121:8

If you spend very much time browsing your friends' posts on Facebook, you will see that people are really busy these days. My own Facebook newsfeed is full of pictures that my friends have posted from one of their many activities. And most of those Facebook posts were made from the person's cell phone.

Step away from Facebook and look at the world around us. People always seem to be going somewhere. They're going to work. They're going home. They're running errands. They're transporting kids to activities. They're heading off to a social engagement. They're returning from a business trip.

With all the hustle and bustle our lives have today, isn't it reassuring that the Lord is always watching over us? No matter where we are going or what we are doing, we are always under the watchful eye of our God. God is looking after us today. God is looking after us tomorrow. God is even looking after us forty years down the road because God will watch over us for all eternity!

God, I thank You for always watching over me. I seem to come and go a lot, and it is very reassuring for me to know that I am never out of Your sight. Amen.

April 30

Pride goes before destruction, a haughty spirit before a fall.

—Proverbs 16:18

We've all been there—trapped in an argument with someone who just cannot admit that they are wrong. Many times, arguments occur because both parties have done something wrong and neither side is willing to admit their error. That means it is entirely likely that we ourselves have been the person unwilling to admit error.

It's pride, plain and simple, that causes the problem. We are too proud to say "I was wrong" or even the more light-hearted "my bad."

But think of the damage done when people cling to their pride. When pride takes control in arguments, saving face becomes more important than saving relationships. What's worse is it only takes one person's pride to damage the relationship. Too often in arguments, only one person apologizes. The other person remains proud and refuses to admit their part in the conflict.

But is it really worth it? Is saving face truly better than saving the relationship? Personally, I don't think so.

Lord, please keep my pride from destroying my relationships. Teach me to admit when I'm wrong and to apologize. Amen.

May 1

See! The winter is past; the rains are over and gone. Flowers appear on the earth; the season of singing has come, the cooing of doves is heard in our land.

—Song of Solomon 2:11–12

Spring is my favorite season! Having always lived in the upper Midwest, winter is such a long, dreary season. Everything is either brown or white, depending on whether or not there is snow on the ground. Days are short. Once Christmas is over, the rest of winter is depressing.

For several years now, I have seen the first robin well before the winter releases its cold grip on the land. Still, it's nice to see some color return to the area. But then, the grass turns green. Trees blossom and bud out. My tulips sprout and bloom. My barn cats start having their litters of kittens.

All the blooming flowers and chirping birds make me want to break out in joyful song! The earth is alive again! This May Day, let's celebrate nature's rebirth! And while we're at it, let's celebrate our own rebirth in Christ.

Lord of all creation, I thank You for spring. Thank You for the beauty of the earth that comes when nature is reborn in You. And thank You for the beauty in me that comes from my rebirth in Your Son, Jesus, in whose name I pray. Amen.

May 2

Then Naomi said to her two daughters-in-law, "Go back, each of you, to your mother's home. May the Lord show you kindness, as you have shown kindness to your dead husbands and to me."

—Ruth 1:8

In so many words, Naomi was saying "thank you" to her daughters-in-law. She was expressing gratitude for what these two young women had done for her. Naomi may have even been thanking these women for being who they were.

"Thank you" are two very simple words, yet many people seem to have difficulty saying them. Many times gratitude is only expressed at obvious times, like upon receiving a gift. Yet there are so many other times when we could say "thank you" to someone.

I am fortunate to work for a boss who thanks me on a daily basis. It seems like every day, he finds something to express gratitude for. There are times when he has thanked me simply for being me. As a result, I probably thank him more than I thank anyone else. I know how great it feels to be appreciated, so I want to reciprocate and make sure my boss knows how grateful I am to him, even for his just being who he is.

God, teach me to express gratitude. Help me to thank You for all that You do for me and to thank others for all that they do. Give me a grateful heart. Amen.

May 3

And do not forget to do good and to share with
others, for with such sacrifices God is pleased.
—Hebrews 13:16

"What's in it for me?" "What do I get out of it?" "I'll help you,
but you're going to owe me."

While those things may not be openly said, more often
than not, the sentiments are there when someone agrees to help
someone else. People seem to only want friends who can benefit
them. We as a society have embraced the "it's not what you know,
it's who you know" philosophy and look to make connections
that will help us at some point down the road.

But that is not what we as Christians are supposed to do.
We are supposed to befriend people who have nothing to offer
us in return. Note how the apostle Paul referred to good deeds
and sharing. He called them "sacrifices."

To sacrifice means to give up something of value. Doing
good is not supposed to be a trade, where something of value
is given up in return for something else of equal value. We
should willingly give of ourselves—our time, our talents, our
treasures—to help those around us and expect nothing in return.

God, help me to give of myself to help others and expect nothing
in return. I want to please You with my sacrifices. Amen.

May 4

Therefore I do not run like someone running aimlessly; I do not fight like a boxer beating the air. No, I strike a blow to my body and make it my slave so that after I have preached to others, I myself will not be disqualified for the prize.
—1 Corinthians 9:26–27

The chiropractic clinic where I work contains a functional training center. It gives me a place to do my own workouts and an opportunity to see other people working out. Sometimes people who are working out need encouragement.

Whenever I find myself in a position to encourage another in their workout, I am thankful that I work out myself. I understand the struggle between mind and body. So, I can help the person master his or her body.

The philosophy of practicing what you preach and the struggle between mind and body are not limited to personal training. They also apply to ethics and morals. Whenever our body and our spirit want two different things, we face the struggle. And others face the struggle. We can only help others through their struggles when we practice what we preach and conquer our own body.

Lord, please give me the strength to win my own struggles between body and spirit so that I may in turn help others conquer their bodies. Amen.

May 5

For the Spirit God gave us does not make us timid, but gives us power, love and self-discipline.
—2 Timothy 1:7

There's a Kenny Rogers song, called "Coward of the County," that talks about how people thought Tommy was a coward because he would never fight. That song describes only too well how society views people who will refrain from getting physical over their beliefs. But the words Tommy's father tells him in the song are very true: "Now it don't mean you're weak if you turn the other cheek."

Actually, quite the opposite is true. In a fit of anger, anyone can throw a punch. But it takes strength to hold back that fist.

Christ taught us to turn the other cheek. However, that does not make us cowards. We are not weak; we are not timid. When we choose to walk away, we do so because of the power, love, and self-discipline we have been given through the Holy Spirit.

That's not to say that there aren't some things worth fighting for. But as Christians, we should use the Spirit to discern what battles we should fight, and we should use that same Spirit to help us walk away.

Show me, dear Lord, when I should stand my ground and when I should walk away. And by the power of Your Spirit, help me turn the other cheek. Amen.

May 6

Dear friends, do not believe every spirit, but test the spirits to see whether they are from God, because many false prophets have gone out into the world.

—1 John 4:1

Things are not always as they appear to be. Magicians make their living off the power of illusion. They seem to do things that are impossible. Even if they do not share their secrets, we know that they did not really saw their assistant in half or escape from a box that had only one locked opening.

Magicians are not the only ones making their living by deceiving others. I once had a person tell me that, as a Christian, I should automatically trust everyone. In the back of my mind, I was daring him to say that to his daughter if he ever had one.

However, there is no rule that says every Christian must automatically trust everyone. In fact, one could argue that today's verse recommends the exact opposite. We should not blindly trust those around us. Rather, we need to "test the spirits." That is to say, we need to take a close look at the people we meet. And we should only trust those who fear and trust in the Lord.

God, by Your Holy Spirit, help me to distinguish between those who follow You and those whom I should not trust. Amen.

May 7

I have fought the good fight, I have finished the
race, I have kept the faith.

—2 Timothy 4:7

This day marks the anniversary of when I went from simply
being a runner to actually being a race runner. After I had
adopted a new, healthier lifestyle, I began using running as
a way of handling stress, coping with problems, or otherwise
clearing my head. And then, on May 7, 2016, I ran my first race.
It was a 5K (which is 3.1 miles) breast cancer benefit race.

Going through life is a lot like running a race. In a race, the
crowd of runners around you can cause you to take a faster pace
than what you are used to. How many times in life are we swept
up by the pace of things happening around us?

When I take too fast of a pace in a race, eventually I cannot
keep going at that speed and must walk. But that's okay, just as
it is okay to slow our lives down. We do not need the approval
of anyone around us.

And in the end, we will approach the finish line. If we keep
our faith, we will finish the race. And we will be surrounded by
all the saints, cheering us on to our heavenly goal.

Lord, when the pace of life gets to be too much for me, remind
me to slow down for awhile. Give me the strength to persevere
and finish the race. Amen.

May 8

"I am the Alpha and the Omega," says the Lord
God, "who is, and who was, and who is to come,
the Almighty."

—Revelation 1:8

Have you ever stopped to look at the relationships you've had
over the years? How many of us had childhood friendships that
we thought would last forever only to drift apart in adulthood?
How many of us have had relationships with siblings fall apart
for one reason or another?

Such thoughts can be depressing, especially for someone
like me who does not keep in touch with any childhood friends
and with very few college friends. It seems like once a chapter
in my life ends, so do the relationships that were formed during
that time.

Revelation 1:8 reminds us that no matter what relationships
form and end, God is always there. In a lifetime of changes, God
remains constant. Regardless of where we have been, where we
are, or where we are going, God will be with us.

But not only will God always be with us, He will always
remain in control. He's not like some retired politician whose
only claim to fame lies in the past. No, God is always the
Almighty. We can always depend on the Lord.

Almighty God, thank You for always being present in my life.
Your consistency is my comfort. Amen.

May 9

My dear brothers and sisters, take note of this:
Everyone should be quick to listen, slow to speak
and slow to become angry.

—James 1:19

As a child, I remember hearing that God gave us two ears and one mouth so that we would listen twice as much as we talked. Like so many things we are taught in childhood, this lesson is something that we really need to remember as adults. After all, adults can be just as talkative as children!

However, it's not so much that we shouldn't speak. It's that we need to spend more time listening that we do speaking. Not only is listening a sign that we are truly interested in those around us, but listening is also a sign of wisdom.

Think about it for a minute. Have you ever noticed how the people who seem to be the most knowledgable about a given topic are the ones who say the least? They wait until they are asked before voicing their opinion or sharing a piece of their vast knowledge. And maybe the reason these people have become so knowledgable, so wise, is because they spent more time listening. Maybe that's how they learned in the first place.

Lord, teach me to listen so that I may learn from what others have to say. Amen.

May 10

Make sure that nobody pays back wrong for wrong, but always strive to do what is good for each other and for everyone else.

—1 Thessalonians 5:15

In the Old Testament, the Israelites were given a law that, when damage or harm was inflicted upon them, they could literally inflict that same damage or harm upon the person who had wronged them. But when Jesus came, He changed that with the command to "turn the other cheek."

The problem is that we humans are not content with balancing the scale, so to speak. We want to always tip the scale in our favor. So, when someone wrongs us, we want to wrong them worse. For example, someone pokes us in the eye, and we rip their eye out.

We want to "get even," but seeking revenge never evens anything. In fact, we may end up hurting even more people because we get "tunnel vision." We only see what our revenge does for us. Many times, though, our revenge spills over onto innocent people.

I believe that is why Jesus tells us to turn the other cheek. Leave the vengeance to God. With God, the punishment will fit the crime, and no innocent people will be involved.

God, let me leave the punishments to You. Help me to let things go and to not seek my own revenge. Amen.

May 11

When I said, "My foot is slipping," Your unfailing
love, Lord, supported me.

—Psalm 94:18

When I read this verse, I think about a scene from the movie
Clash of the Titans, the version that was released in 1981. In that
movie, there is a scene where Perseus and some soldiers are
climbing a mountain. As they scale that mountain in single file,
the camera zooms in on a soldier's foot as it slips off the rock.
Immediately the soldier below catches and supports the slipped
foot of his comrade.

One might argue that the soldier who caught the slipped foot
was protecting himself as he could have been knocked from the
mountain had the guy above him fallen. While that may have
been one reason, they were also comrades in arms. In battle they
had to trust each other. And scaling this mountain was a battle
in its own right. They were in the climb together.

We cannot pull God down if we fall. But the Lord is in our
climb with us. That means when our foot slips, He will catch
and support us, not because He needs to protect Himself but
because He loves us and wants to protect us.

Thank You, Lord, for Your love that protects me and supports
me every step of the way and on every mountain I must climb.
Amen.

May 12

How great You are, Sovereign Lord! There is no one like You, and there is no God but You, as we have heard with our own ears.

—2 Samuel 7:22

One of the most important lessons we can learn in life is that we are not God. Only God is God. No matter how much we want to control every aspect of our lives, we simply do not have that kind of power.

Once we accept that we do not have the power to control everything, we open ourselves up to a calming peace. When we let God have the control that really only God has anyway, we are free from worry about what is happening in the world around us. We are free from the stress of trying to control the uncontrollable.

When we reach that peace and freedom, we then can notice all the wonderful things around us that God is doing. We can truly see the sunrise that only God can make. We can stop and smell the roses that only God can cause to bloom. We can hear the birds singing the songs that only God can give them to sing.

Lord, You alone are God! And Your works are marvelous in my sight! Help me to surrender all control to You, so that I am free to see and enjoy the beauty of Your creation. In Jesus' name I pray. Amen.

May 13

Let the peace of Christ rule in your hearts, since as members of one body you were called to peace. And be thankful.

—Colossians 3:15

The 13th of any month can be very stressful for some people, especially when it falls on a Friday. Oh, the terrible things that can happen on Friday the 13th! Break out the lucky four-leaf clovers!

Superstitions can be fun, but mostly they are debilitating. And they are not Christian responses to the world around us. Some people are so terrified about Friday the 13th that they refuse to leave their homes. Some people are so certain that black cats are bad luck that they will harm any cat with black fur.

But if we truly believe that we are part of the body of Christ, we realize that God is more powerful than any date falling on a particular day of the week, than any animal of any color, than any type of plant. And when we accept that our superstitions are pointless, we once again experience God's peace, a peace for which we should always be thankful.

Christ, teach me to treat superstitions as fun only but not to put any real faith in them. Keep my faith in You alone, so that I may experience the peace You so graciously give. Amen.

May 14

For we are God's handiwork, created in Christ
Jesus to do good works, which God prepared in
advance for us to do.

—Ephesians 2:10

We all have work to do in the world and in our churches.
This is the time of year when Sunday schools are ending for
the summer and congregation members start looking ahead to
vacation Bible school. All over the country, maybe even around
the world, there is gratitude being expressed to those who have
helped teach the youth of the congregations, and there is a plea
for volunteers to assist with summer Bible education.

I have become a regular part of the Sunday school teaching
staff at my church. Unfortunately, due to my work schedule, it
is very rare that I am able to help with vacation Bible school. I
simply cannot take odd times off from work. I have too many
clients depending on me.

When your church asks for volunteers, are the same people
always stepping up? The next time your church needs volunteers
and you're met with the resistance of people who claim to have
already "put in their time," remind them that we are all God's
handiwork. That means we are all created to do God's work.

God, guide me to do the work You have created me to do, both
at my job and in my church. Amen.

May 15

For I am convinced that neither death nor life, neither angels nor demons, neither the present nor the future, nor any powers, neither height nor depth, nor anything else in all creation, will be able to separate us from the love of God that is in Christ Jesus our Lord.

—Romans 8:38–39

As I write this, my church is without a pastor. While I have experienced this several times over the years, this time I have found myself taking on way more responsibilities than what I was used to. Sometimes it gets a little overwhelming.

One supply pastor we've had come in a few times has become great support for me. I look forward to every time he comes to lead worship. Today he was again back to lead our worship, and after the service, he gave me a large coin that has Romans 8:39 on it. At the top it said "No Matter What."

I don't know if he gave that to me because he knew that the extra responsibilities were getting to me or for another reason. But as long as the pants I am wearing have a pocket, that coin will be with me. It's a wonderful reminder that no matter what happens, I am never separated from the God who loves me.

Thank You, God, for Your love, which is so big and strong that nothing can ever separate me from it. Thank You, also, for those who remind me of Your love. Amen.

May 16

But godliness with contentment is great gain.
—1 Timothy 6:6

When we talk about contentment, most people think about money or possessions. And while it is good to be content with those things, there are other things we should also be content with. Contentment does not only mean we are not greedy. It means we are not envious at all.

I have naturally curly hair. It used to really irritate me to see the different hair styles people with straight, or even wavy, hair could have. I could never do anything like that because my hair would always do its own thing. No amount of hairspray could make my hair curl in a way it did not want to.

The best thing that ever happened to me was when I accepted what I had to do with my curls. Now, instead of fighting to make my hair do what I want it to do, I pick it in the morning, allowing it to curl however it chooses. And I will get some of the cutest curls!

I may not be able to have the fancy hairstyles others have, but I have curls that some people would kill for. And now that I have learned to accept my curls, I am no longer envious of fancy hairstyles. I am content with my curls. I am happy with my curls.

Lord, teach me to be content with what I have, be they possessions or physical characteristics. Amen.

May 17

You shall not misuse the name of the Lord your
God, for the Lord will not hold anyone guiltless
who misuses His name.

—Exodus 20:7

You may recognize this as one of the Ten Commandments.
When I was a teenager learning the Ten Commandments
in confirmation class, I never really stopped to think about
reasons behind the various commandments. This particular
commandment is one I simply memorized and moved on.

However, I started thinking about this commandment again
when I saw a meme on Facebook that said, "If you want to swear,
use your own name. —God." Several people had commented on
it, substituting their own name where generally people use the
Lord's name in vain. That really stuck with me.

Do you ever use the Lord's name in vain? How would you
feel if someone swore using your name? I'd be willing to bet that
most of us would not like that so much. And the Lord's name
is much more powerful than our own names! The Lord's name
saves, so let's do our part to keep the Lord's name sacred.

Lord God, Your name is holy. Forgive me when I misuse Your
name. May I only speak Your name with the love and respect it
commands. Amen.

May 18

The fruit of that righteousness will be peace; its
effect will be quietness and confidence forever.
—Isaiah 32:17

I loved growing up on an acreage on a gravel road. After
school, there was nothing I enjoyed more than taking a walk
through our hayfield. School days were frequently full of
constant activity, especially once I started middle school and
moved from one classroom to another. Then there was all the
noise! School bells ringing. Classmates talking, sometimes
shouting.

Living on a gravel road meant that there was not a whole
lot of traffic on our road. So, although I could see the road
from anywhere in our hayfield, I felt like I could get away from
civilization. There was peace, and there was quiet.

Isaiah writes about how righteousness results in peace,
quietness, and confidence. We cannot achieve righteousness
on our own. We need Christ for that. Therefore, ultimately,
Christ is the one who provides the promised peace, quiet, and
confidence.

This peace is a promise mentioned several times throughout
the Bible, but it's a promise worth noting. Even those of us who
thrive on hectic schedules still have a desire for peace. And
Christ will always provide that.

Christ, thank You for the promise of peace, quietness, and
confidence that comes from my faith in You. Amen.

May 19

Shout for joy to the Lord, all the earth, burst into jubilant song with music.

—Psalm 98:4

It was December, and I was in the basement of the office where I work, doing laundry. As is my habit, I started singing while I folded the sheets for the massage tables. Since it was December, the songs I broke into were, naturally, Christmas carols.

Our office manager was upstairs at the front desk. She did not have the radio turned on, so she could hear a woman's voice singing Christmas songs. It took her awhile to figure out she was hearing me.

Doing laundry is not the only time I'll break into song. I have found that I will sing almost anywhere. I will even sing during allergy season, when my sinus congestion makes me sound more like a bullfrog than a human. However, I don't sing to impress other people. I sing because I'm happy. I sing because I'm joyful.

No, folding sheets does not bring me happiness or joy. I find it to be an obnoxious chore. But obnoxious chores are a part of life, and life is something worth being happy and joyful about! So whether I'm folding laundry, hand washing dishes, or cleaning my cat's litter box, just being alive is all the reason I need to sing for joy.

Lord, teach me to sing for joy at simply being given one more day here on earth. Amen.

May 20

Indeed, there is no one on earth who is righteous,
no one who does what is right and never sins.
—Ecclesiastes 7:20

Recently, a local group of atheists started advertising on billboards around the town in which I work. One of their signs talked about how it is possible to be good without God. When I read that billboard, I simply thought, "They have missed the point." I do not need God to be good. I need God because I am *not* good.

Sure, I do good deeds. I will hold doors open for people. I will mow grassy areas that are not my responsibility. I will let vehicles make turns or change lanes in front of me in the midst of heavy traffic.

The thing is, though, that I will also let doors fall closed on people coming behind me. I will ignore my neighbor's jungle of a yard and only mow my own yard. I will turn a blind eye to the driver needing to make a lane change during rush hour.

The local atheists are correct in their thought that good deeds come easily to good-natured people. However, every human has the ability to be selfish. No, we do not need God to be good. We need God because there are too many times when we are not good.

God, forgive me when I am selfish. Thank You for redeeming me and freeing me from sin. Amen.

May 21

A gentle answer turns away wrath, but a harsh word stirs up anger.

—Proverbs 15:1

Most people know that heat makes sore muscles feel better. Thus, it's not uncommon for someone who has been injured to apply heat to the sore area. Then they are puzzled when the heat fails to ease their pain but rather makes the pain worse.

In one of my classes in massage school, we were taught that you can never go wrong applying ice to an injury. Heat, however, should only be applied to areas where there is no inflammation. You see, where the body is inflamed, there is already excessive heat. Applying more heat to such an area is like adding fuel to a fire.

Anger could be described as emotional inflammation. In fact, we often describe someone who is mad as being "hot." When a person is mad and yells at us, our instinct may be to yell right back at them. That is like putting a heating pad on an inflamed injury. We have just added heat to heat, and we make the situation worse.

A gentle response, though, is like putting ice on an injury. It cools and soothes. Most importantly, it heals.

Lord, teach me to respond to anger with gentleness. Let me put ice on the emotional injury to ease the other person's pain and promote their healing. Amen.

May 22

Therefore each of you must put off falsehood and speak truthfully to your neighbor, for we are all members of one body.

—Ephesians 4:25

"It's just a little white lie. It won't hurt anybody." Though commonly spoken, these words just are not true.

A few short months after I began working at my current job, I jumped off a step in the basement. I forgot about the low ceilings, got too much height in my jump, and hit the side of my head on a light. Nothing broke, but the impact made a lot of noise. My boss heard it and came to check on me. But I hid out of his sight, secretly icing my head, and assured him I was fine. I even told him it was my hand that had hit the light.

About a month later, I finally confessed to him what had actually hit the light that day. He jokingly told me that he felt betrayed. I know he was just kidding, but I can't help but wonder if he did question his ability to trust me. Sure, I had said a little white lie to keep him from worrying about me. But a lie is still a lie, and no matter what the dilemma is, a lie is never the answer. More damage can be done to a relationship after being caught in a lie than the truth ever would have caused.

God, may I be truthful in all that I say. Do not let me speak falsehoods that may cause irreparable damage to the relationships I have with others. Amen.

May 23

[F]or all have sinned and fall short of the glory of God, and all are justified freely by His grace through the redemption that came by Christ Jesus.

—Romans 3:23–24

Nobody is perfect. I don't know about you, but I have known some people who somehow appear to be perfect. One particular person I once knew never spoke badly about anybody. Another person I know will go out of his way to help others. It seems like some people can do no wrong.

Such people can be intimidating to be around. But they are still humans, and that means they are not perfect. We only know what they say and how they act around us. We have no idea what thoughts and feelings they may have. Jesus taught that even our innermost thoughts can cause us to sin.

But don't let that knowledge drop these seemingly perfect people from any pedestal you choose to place them on. After all, they are still great role models for us. They show us how to treat other people. Just remember that you do not have to be intimidated by them. Spend time with them, and learn from them. You are justified by the same grace that they are.

Lord, thank You for saving me by Your grace. And thank You for giving me role models who may not show how much they need Your grace too. Amen.

May 24

For God so loved the world that He gave His one
and only Son, that whoever believes in Him shall
not perish but have eternal life.

—John 3:16

This may very possibly be the first Bible verse I ever
memorized, just not the translation I learned. Actually, though,
I like the wording of this translation. "…His one and only Son."

I do not have children, except my four-legged "fur babies."
And even there, I have more than one. I love them all dearly
and could never consider giving up any of them, especially not
into a situation that would mean certain death for them. I would
rather die myself!

God did what I could never do myself. God sent His one and
only Son to certain death. I can't even do that with one of the
many dogs and cats I have!

But God also did what I would do. You see, Jesus is God.
Jesus said Himself that He and the Father are one. That means
God would rather die Himself than to see any one of us perish.

That is some powerful love! And that is why this Bible verse
also sums up Christianity. We have a God that loves us and
would rather die than see death come to us. All we have to do is
believe that Jesus did take our place in death.

Jesus, I do indeed believe in You. Amen.

May 25

And let us consider how we may spur one another on toward love and good deeds, not giving up meeting together, as some are in the habit of doing, but encouraging one another—and all the more as you see the Day approaching.

—Hebrews 10:24–25

This is one of many different verses found in the Bible that encourage us to continue meeting together. It is true that we can worship anywhere we are. And as this passage shows, the idea of worshiping alone is nothing new.

But there is a reason we are supposed to meet together. That reason is support, plain and simple. There are times that we need a little extra encouragement. There are also times when other people may come among us and seek encouragement from us.

Also, when we break away from the community of believers, it is much easier for us to be led astray. There is safety in numbers. We encourage each other to continue to believe, and we help each other from having our faith twisted into lies.

We really do need each other. We need to belong in a community of believers. We need to spur others on, just as we ourselves need to be spurred on.

God, when I begin to think that I do not need to belong to a community of believers, gently remind me that I need the encouragement of others. Amen.

May 26

Whatever you do, work at it with all your heart,
as working for the Lord, not for human masters.
—Colossians 3:23

It has gotten to the point that I spend very little time on Facebook on Sunday afternoons. It seems like every other post I read says something about dreading Monday, wanting more weekend, or not wanting to return to work.

I happen to love Mondays. The reason I love Mondays is because I return to work after having two days off. I won't ever say, "I have to go to work," except to my dog, who doesn't fully comprehend what I'm saying. Otherwise, I will say, "I get to go to work."

For me, work is not really work. My job is my calling. The person who signs my paychecks may be human, but I do truly believe that my boss is the Lord. God called me into my profession, so when I serve others in my place of employment, I am serving the Lord.

Think about it for a minute. Every year has at least 52 Mondays. Some years have more, depending on what day of the week the year starts. Wouldn't it be nice to not automatically dread 52 days? Even if you don't love your job, give it your all. You are still serving God.

Lord, teach me how to approach my job as though You were signing my paychecks. Remind me that, even at my work, I am serving You. Amen.

May 27

Obey them not only to win their favor when their eye is on you, but as slaves of Christ, doing the will of God from your heart.

—Ephesians 6:6

If you read the context in which this verse is found, you will learn that this was being directed to slaves. However, even free people should heed the advice of this verse, of this entire passage. What kind of person are you when nobody is looking?

Are you polite toward other drivers when you have passengers but are rude when you are driving alone? Do you work hard when your boss or supervisor is around but then waste time when you aren't being watched? At church, are you welcoming of strangers when the pastor is nearby but ignore guests when the pastor is distracted?

God is always watching us. He knows our true nature, and it is God's opinion of us that truly counts. We may be alone in our car, but the Lord is riding shotgun. Our supervisor may be in another room, but God is still at our desk with us. The pastor may talking to someone else, but the Lord is observing us. By remembering that we never are completely alone, we will be the people God wants us to be.

God, let me be the person in private that I am when others are watching, since I am never out of Your sight. Amen.

May 28

For if you forgive other people when they sin against you, your heavenly Father will also forgive you. But if you do not forgive others their sins, your Father will not forgive your sins.
—Matthew 6:14–15

Forgiveness is a very big part of Jesus' teachings. He even used a parable to stress the importance of forgiving others. Remember the Parable of the Unforgiving Servant?

I can think of many reasons why Jesus would want to teach about forgiveness. One reason is demonstrated by the Parable of the Unforgiving Servant and is also described in today's passage. Why should God extend to us a courtesy that we are not willing to extend to one another?

By expecting God to forgive us when we refuse to forgive others, we are essentially saying that we believe ourselves to be more important than our neighbor. For whatever reason, we see ourselves to be worthy of something that nobody else deserves.

However, it is not our place to decide who deserves forgiveness and who does not. It is simply our place to forgive others. Let's leave the judging to God. After all, we all are in need of forgiveness.

Lord, when I struggle to forgive others, remind me that I need forgiveness myself. Amen.

May 29

This day I call the heavens and the earth as witnesses against you that I have set before you life and death, blessings and curses. Now choose life, so that you and your children may live.

—Deuteronomy 30:19

Have you ever watched a friend or family member do something that you know they shouldn't do? Maybe it's getting into a bad relationship. Maybe it's accepting a challenge or dare that could have dangerous consequences. Have you ever just wanted to tell that loved one what decision you think they should make?

If you are at all familiar with the Old Testament, you will know that the Israelites did not always heed these words from Moses. All the Israelites had to do was obey God's law, spoken to them by Moses. Moses even concludes by summarizing what he has given them—life and death—and encourages them to choose obedience to God. Yet, how many times did the Israelites end up in exile because they chose the way of death?

Fortunately, God gives us all the way back to Him. We may keep choosing death, but Christ died that death for us. So, all we have to do for life now is to choose Christ. When we choose Christ, we choose life.

Christ, I choose You. I choose life in You. Thank You for dying the death I deserve, and keep me from straying away from You. Amen.

May 30

Blessed is the nation whose God is the Lord, the people He chose for His inheritance.

—Psalm 33:12

While Memorial Day is observed on the last Monday of May, the actual date of Memorial Day is May 30. This day started out as the day to decorate the graves of those killed in the Civil War. Then it transformed into the day to remember all those who were killed in action, or have died since their military service.

Every Memorial Day, I wear my grandpa's dog tags. If you have never seen military dog tags, you may not know that a person's religion is represented on their tags. Despite the separation of church and state, the military decided that a person's religious affiliation was just as important as their blood type, also found on dog tags.

There is a saying that goes, "There are no atheists in foxholes." I do not doubt that. When staring death in the face, how could a person not feel the need for God? And maybe our nation would be better off today if we all spent a little time in a foxhole, staring at our dog tags that have the life-saving information of blood type and religious affiliation!

Lord, I thank You for the service of those who put their faith in You, even though they may have died on a battlefield. Amen.

May 31

The birds of the sky nest by the waters; they sing among the branches.

—Psalm 104:12

One day, I was sitting alone at my dining room table with my dogs lying quietly on the floor at my feet. I was eating breakfast and thinking about all that I would need to get accomplished outside before the forecasted storm came. The storm was already close, as I could see dark skies out the windows on one side of my house. Occasionally I could even hear the faint rumble of thunder.

As I sat there in quiet planning, I became aware of another sound. Birds were singing. At that moment, my mind shifted from my mental "to-do" list to the lesson that could be learned from those beautiful songbirds.

Animals have their own way of knowing when storms are approaching, and they must brace themselves for whatever fury the weather brings. But there is no sense in worrying about what's coming or bracing for trouble prematurely. At the proper time, it's okay to batten down the hatches. But in the meantime, just keep singing!

God, teach me when it is time to be concerned and when I should carry on like usual. Let me learn from the birds of the fields and continue to sing, even when there are storms brewing in the distance. Amen.

June 1

All you need to say is simply "Yes" or "No";
anything beyond this comes from the evil one.
—Matthew 5:37

"With God as my witness, I will be in class tomorrow."
These words were spoken to me by a college classmate of mine
who was notorious for missing our microeconomics class. Then
she would ask me for my notes when she saw me in another one
of our classes. I don't know which annoyed me more at that
point, the fact that I'd been attending that class for the both of
us or that she felt it necessary to swear an oath with God as a
witness.

She, like so many other people who use the phrase, "with
God as my witness," probably did not mean anything bad by it.
But Jesus said that swearing an oath is not necessary. All we
should say is "yes" or "no."

I happen to take my word very seriously. If I say I'm going
to do something, then I will do it. I swear no oath. I do not call
upon God—or anyone else, for that matter—to be my witness.
And people who know me know that I am true to my word.

Hold to your word. Then a simple "yes" or "no" is all that
you will need.

God, help me to always be true to my word, so that my "yes"
and "no" answers may stand without the need for me to swear
any oaths. Amen.

June 2

The man said, "The woman You put here with me—she gave me some fruit from the tree, and I ate it." Then the Lord God said to the woman, "What is this you have done?" The woman said, "The serpent deceived me, and I ate."

—Genesis 3:12–13

The original sin may have been eating the forbidden fruit, but Adam and Eve didn't stop there. In this part of the story, they both blame someone else for their mistake. "It was the woman's fault!" "It was the serpent's fault!"

Failure to take responsibility for one's mistakes is just as prevalent today. When I was rear-ended, the driver of the vehicle bailed; I never saw her. The owner of the vehicle tried to blame a water truck that had been obstructing one lane of traffic on a four-lane street. Seriously, people, just admit you weren't paying attention to traffic! I'd been stopped at a traffic light for awhile!

I'm not saying that it's easy to admit one's mistakes, but it is still something we need to do. Like Adam, we might follow the lead of others when we know that path is wrong. Like Eve, we may allow ourselves to be deceived because we don't know how to be content. We need to own our mistakes and ask for forgiveness.

Lord, when I sin against You or against my fellow man, grant me the courage to own up to my mistakes and ask for forgiveness, rather than passing the blame. Amen.

June 3

For by the grace given me I say to every one of you: Do not think of yourself more highly than you ought, but rather think of yourself with sober judgment in accordance with the faith God has distributed to each of you.

—Romans 12:3

There was an organist at a small country church who not only had a lot of talent, but she knew she was talented. She flaunted her talent every chance she had. She would even showboat by playing hymn arrangements that were not really singable.

As talented as this country church organist was, her talent was nothing compared to another organist in a big congregation in a nearby city. The city church organist, however, would blush whenever someone complimented her playing. This city church organist also made sure that the pastors never chose hymns that she knew the congregation would not be able to sing.

The country church organist thought very highly of herself. The city church organist, on the other hand, was humble. Both had God-given talents, but only one seemed to acknowledge that her talent was a gift.

We all have talents. But we would be wise to remember that our talents are gifts from God. Therefore, we should never let our talents go to our head.

Thank You, God, for the talents You have gifted me with. Please keep me humble when I share my talents. Amen.

June 4

Do everything without grumbling or arguing.
—Philippians 2:14

I remember as a kid resenting it any time my parents asked me to do something. Whether it was cleaning my room, feeding the chickens, or setting the table, I would grumble about it. Although I always obeyed, I did so reluctantly.

I wish I could say that I'm different as an adult, but I'm not. When my parents ask me to do something, I still obey reluctantly. I am just a grown-up version of that kid who did not want to be inconvenienced in any way or interrupted from current plans in progress.

How about you? When a friend, family member, coworker, or boss asks you to do something, do you willingly go about the task? Or do you only do what you've been asked after a certain amount of grumbling? Or do you argue your way out of doing it at all?

To be perfectly honest, I don't like admitting my childish behavior. But now that I have admitted it, I have a new freedom. I have the freedom to choose a different response, a better response to my parents' requests. That same freedom is yours too, if you are willing to face the truth and to change your response.

Lord, teach me to respond to requests without grumbling or resentment. Remind me that when I serve others, I am also serving You. Amen.

June 5

For the grace of God has appeared that offers salvation to all people.

—Titus 2:11

In 2016, several states started addressing a very controversial issue—transgender restrooms. There were people who believed that a person should be able to use the public restroom that agreed with the gender they "felt," even if it was not their physical gender. Other people insisted that perverts would start pretending to identify with the opposite gender just to get into those restrooms. It was a battle that only seemed to be quieted when social media found a different obsession.

But the whole restroom issue brought out some very ugly remarks about prejudice and religious judgment. There were a few comments along the way that echoed the sentiment of today's Bible verse. Regardless of race, sexual orientation, or any other label we might put on a person, that person is offered the same salvation we are.

God's grace knows no limits. So whenever a controversy arises, let's be respectful in our debates. Every single one of us has the same offer of grace. Salvation is not only available to those who agree with us. It is offered to all people.

Forgive me, God, when I try to limit Your grace. Remind me that Your salvation is for everyone. Amen.

June 6

The way of fools seems right to them, but the wise listen to advice.

—Proverbs 12:15

My boss once made the observation that I do not like asking for help. That observation was made while I was dealing with a herniated disc flare-up, which I had caused by doing the same thing that had caused me to herniate that disc two years prior. In both cases, I was bound and determined to handle this problem myself, even though it meant doing things that I knew I should not do.

Asking for help is difficult. Whether we are in need of help doing something physical or handling some other problem, many of us would like to think we can take care of ourselves. We would like to think that we know what we are doing.

I have a disc in my low back to remind me that I do not always know what I am doing. There is not a single one of us who can know everything there is to know. We need to seek out the wisdom of others. Sometimes we need that extra muscle strength. Other times we need that different perspective. We need to ask for help.

Lord, teach me to ask for help. Guide me to seek the wisdom and advice of the people You have put in my life for that reason. Amen.

June 7

And now you will be silent and not able to speak
until the day this happens, because you did not
believe my words, which will come true at their
appointed time.

—Luke 1:20

Zechariah did not believe the angel Gabriel's words that
Elizabeth would conceive a child in her old age. As a result,
Zechariah was literally rendered speechless. Some people
speculate that he was also rendered deaf during that time. That
seems like a harsh punishment for a little disbelief!

When I am giving massages, I frequently close my eyes. In
doing so, my sense of touch becomes more sensitive, and I find
the my clients' problem areas faster. I also become more aware
of the relaxing atmosphere I have created through the music I
play and the essential oil I burn. Thus I become more relaxed,
enabling me to focus on my client rather than on my stresses.

Zechariah was distracted by worldly limitations. That is
why he did not believe that he and his wife would actually still
be able to have a child. God took away Zechariah's ability to
speak, maybe even to hear, so that Zechariah would be able to
focus better on God. It wasn't so much a punishment for disbelief
as it was a tool to nurture his faith.

God, remove my distractions so that I may focus on You and
nurture my own faith. Amen.

June 8

When they saw the courage of Peter and John and realized that they were unschooled, ordinary men, they were astonished and they took note that these men had been with Jesus.

—Acts 4:13

This verse is out of the story of Peter and John standing before the Sanhedrin after healing a man in Jesus' name. In those days, schooling was not available to everyone. That is why "ordinary" men were "unschooled."

Today's society seems to put a lot of emphasis on four-year colleges. I will not use this verse to argue against college. Nor will I use it to condone dropping out of high school. Rather, I want to call attention to one important phrase: "these men had been with Jesus."

We can all do amazing things, with or without formal education. All we need is to associate ourselves with Jesus. Jesus can take our knowledge, or lack thereof, and cause us to work wonders in our world.

Being with Jesus will also give us the same courage the chief priests saw in Peter and John. We, like the apostles, will be able to stand against those who would seek to bring us down. All this comes from simply being with Jesus!

Jesus, grant me the ability to do amazing things and the courage to stand against opposition all in Your holy name. May I always be with You. Amen.

June 9

Children are a heritage from the Lord, offspring
a reward from Him.

—Psalm 127:3

There are special days set aside every year for all sorts of things. We all know that the third Sunday in June is always Father's Day. But did you know that the second Sunday in June is Children's Day?

For several years now, I have been given the privilege of teaching Sunday school music. That undertaking has presented me with several challenges. There is nothing like trying to corral twenty or more kids, none of which are older than fifth grade, all on a sugar high from the snacks served after worship! And there is nothing as frustrating as hearing kids complain that there won't be any food left because the church started serving a potluck dinner prior to the conclusion of Sunday school.

But one year, when the last day of Sunday school fell on Mother's Day and the Sunday school and youth group led the worship service, I sang the song "Thank God for Kids" as part of the prelude. Even with every challenge and frustration I have experienced, I wouldn't trade my Sunday school kids for anything! They are truly a gift from God and a blessing to everyone they meet!

God, I thank You for kids, whether they are my own flesh and blood or not. Amen.

June 10

Set a guard over my mouth, Lord; keep watch
over the door of my lips.

—Psalm 141:3

My mom has a sign hanging near the front door that says,
"Lord, keep Your arm around my shoulders and Your hand over
my mouth." In essence, the psalmist is asking God for that same
thing. Those are two different ways of praying the same prayer.

How often do you say something that you later regret? You
might not regret it for several days, or you might regret it the
moment you speak it. Unfortunately, once a word slips past our
lips, we cannot take it back.

As children, many of us probably learned the rhyme, "Sticks
and stones may break my bones, but words will never hurt me."
Unfortunately, many of us also learn as children just how untrue
that rhyme really is. Words can hurt.

Words can hurt the person who speaks them as much as they
do the person who hears them. Words can destroy relationships
in a matter of moments. So, every day, let's make the words of
the psalmist be our own prayer. Let's ask God daily to guard
our mouths against the words it would be best to leave unsaid.

Lord, please do set a guard over my mouth. Let me always
remember that words can be painful and that, once spoken, can
never be taken back. Amen.

June 11

And this is my prayer: that your love may abound more and more in knowledge and depth of insight, so that you may be able to discern what is best and may be pure and blameless for the day of Christ.

—Philippians 1:9-10

At first glance, these verses seem a bit confusing. What does love have to do with knowledge and insight? Love is a matter of the heart, but knowledge and insight are matters of the mind.

Yet, I am reminded of a sermon I once heard. The pastor was talking about how we might do better if we were to follow our heart, rather than letting our conscious be our guide. It's one thing to understand something in your mind. It's a totally different thing to understand something in your heart.

So, if we follow our heart, we might actually find ourselves in deeper knowledge and insight. We will certainly be better at discerning what is best because through love, we are able to put the needs of others ahead of our own. We will be able to see what is best for everyone, not just what is best for ourselves.

And we need to not just know what is best, we need to feel it. Don't try to wrap your head around this concept. Wrap your heart around it. Follow your heart.

Lord God, teach me how to follow my heart. Let love guide me to deeper knowledge and insight. Amen.

June 12

And now these three remain: faith, hope and love. But the greatest of these is love.

—1 Corinthians 13:13

On this day in 2016, there was yet another terrorist attack. This one came in the form of a single gunman targeting a gay nightclub. The results were not surprising. Government officials called for gun control, and the public hatred for the Islamic community (of which the gunman was a radical) skyrocketed.

Every time I hear about another act of terrorism, I think back to September 11, 2001. Alan Jackson released a song that summarized the emotions of that day, called "Where Were You (When the World Stopped Turning)." In the chorus, this very Bible verse is paraphrased: "Faith, hope, and love are some good things He gave us, and the greatest is love."

The greatest is indeed love. That is why there was an outpouring of financial and blood donations to help the victims of the June 12 shooting. That is why there is always an outpouring of help after any terrible act of terrorism, regardless of the nature of the act or the religious beliefs of the attacker. Terrorists will never win as long as we continue to respond to their acts of terror with our own acts of love. Love is greater than hatred.

God, may my response to terrorism always be one of love. Amen.

June 13

Teach us to number our days, that we may gain
a heart of wisdom.

—Psalm 90:12

Once when I was jokingly calling myself old around someone sixteen years older than I am, this person responded by pointing out that he had a few years on me. I resisted the urge to point out that while he may have lived on this earth more than one and a half decades longer than I have, our maturity levels do not reflect it. My maturity reflects my confidence. Thus I do not feel the need to joke about absolutely everything. I can have serious conversations with people. This guy has all the insecurities of a teenage boy and, as a result, the maturity of a teenage boy.

I don't think the psalmist is necessarily talking about age in this verse. I don't think he's insisting that age automatically creates wisdom. To me, it sounds more like the psalmist is asking to learn how to make each day count, rather than how to count each day.

Want to be truly wise beyond your years? Instead of counting the days you've been on this earth, try counting the days you've helped make this world a better place. That is how we should all number our days.

Lord, teach me how to make my days count, instead of counting my days. Help me to leave this world a better place than it was when I entered it. Amen.

June 14

But for those who fear You, You have raised a
banner to be unfurled against the bow.
—Psalm 60:4

Today is Flag Day, the day officially set up to commemorate
the adoption of the United States national flag in 1777. Our
nation's flag has been a sign of hope for many people. The
words of our national anthem were penned as Francis Scott
Key observed a battle in the War of 1812. As long as the "star-
spangled banner" was flying over the fort being attacked, the
United States could still be victorious.

I grew up reciting the Pledge of Allegiance every day in
elementary school. One of my favorite lines in the pledge is a
reason the pledge has been dropped from most schools now—
"one nation under God." Our nation was founded by God-fearing
men. Our nation was led through many wars by God-fearing
men (and women).

The current condition of our nation may lead us to wonder
where all the God-fearing people are now. As a country, we no
longer seem to have our focus on God.

But our flag can still offer us hope today. Our "star-spangled
banner" has not fallen yet, so there's still time for us as a nation
to return to God. There is still hope for us God-fearing people.

God, return this and every nation to You. Guide us so that our
banner may still be unfurled. Amen.

June 15

But a Samaritan, as he traveled, came where the man was; and when he saw him, he took pity on him.

—Luke 10:33

I have heard the Parable of the Good Samaritan countless times in my life. But only recently did this verse of the story really start to stand out with me. I began to think about what it means to truly see someone.

In the parable, a priest and a Levite also encounter the same man that the Samaritan did. The priest and the Levite also see the man. At least, they see his body.

Only the Samaritan truly saw the man who had fallen victim to the robbers. Where the priest and the Levite only saw a broken and bleeding body, the Samaritan saw a human being. The Samaritan saw beyond the surface, beyond the body's skin to the man's soul below.

When was the last time you truly saw someone? When was the last time you noticed someone in raggedy clothing and wondered what their story was? When was the last time you looked at a successful businessperson and wondered what struggles they had overcome in their life? When was the last time you took a step back from a disagreement so you could put yourself in the other person's shoes?

Lord, teach me how to truly see people, as the Good Samaritan did, as You do. Amen.

June 16

Do not be deceived: God cannot be mocked. A man reaps what he sows.

—Galatians 6:7

"God cannot be mocked." One dictionary definition of the word *mock* is to make something seem laughably unreal or impossible.

There are many people who would try to make God unreal or impossible. Yet at least some of those same people spout off warnings about karma biting body parts. They are also quick to remind people of the saying "what goes around comes around."

Those warnings about karma are saying the same thing as the last sentence in this verse from Galatians. The only thing karma leaves out is that God will be the one to bring about a person's harvest. To talk about karma in the abstract is to attempt to mock God. However, when the fateful "karma" comes back to bite, everyone will see that God is not laughably unreal or impossible. Everyone will see that, in fact, it has been God setting things right from the start. And those who have put their faith in God will reap their spiritual reward. Talk about your ultimate karma!

God, when others try to mock You by denying Your existence while crediting other forces for Your work, help me to remain steadfast and faithful to You. Do not let me be deceived. Amen.

June 17

Very truly I tell you, when you were younger you dressed yourself and went where you wanted; but when you are old you will stretch out your hands, and someone else will dress you and lead you where you do not want to go.

—John 21:18

There is a church I drive by occasionally that has a tagline on its sign. That tagline says, "Where faith is fun."

In today's verse, Jesus is telling Peter what is going to happen to him because of his faith. Church history says that Peter was crucified upside down because he refused to be crucified the same way as his Lord. Either way, crucifixion is an excruciating way to die. So I'd wager that Peter did not believe his faith was fun.

What we all need to remember is that faith is not meant to be fun. Church is not meant to be an hour of entertainment. To expect fun and games is to completely miss the point of faith.

Faith is putting God first and foremost in our life. That may have us doing things that are uncomfortable for us. We might even face some danger because of it. But as long as we put God first, we will have the blessed reward of eternal life.

Jesus, You warned Peter that faith in You was not going to be fun. When we start trying to make our faith fun and easy, draw our focus back to You. Amen.

June 18

Do not take revenge, my dear friends, but leave room for God's wrath, for it is written: "It is Mine to avenge, I will repay," says the Lord.
—Romans 12:19

Revenge is an interesting concept. Just stop and think for a moment about how revenge works. I do something to you, perhaps unintentionally. You are upset by it, so you do something to inflict pain on me. However, you want to make sure I don't forget my lesson, so you want to make my pain worse than yours was. Then I, having learned a different lesson than what you wanted to teach me, decide to show you who you are messing with. So I purposely inflict worse pain on you than what you had done to me. And then the cycle continues.

There is no end to revenge. More often than not, the initial crime was accidental. But even if it was intentional, each person feels it necessary to "one-up" the other person. Both parties end up hurt, and justice was never served.

That's why we need to leave the revenge up to God. God knows where to draw the line. He will balance the scale, as opposed to our desire to tip the scale in our favor. Let God do the avenging.

God, stop me from taking revenge on those who wrong me. Instead, help me let You serve justice. Amen.

June 19

Then the Lord said to Cain, "Where is your brother Abel?" "I don't know," he replied. "Am I my brother's keeper?"

—Genesis 4:9

"Am I my brother's keeper?" That question has been asked in many forms throughout the generations. Brother, sister, parent, coworker, boss, friend. Many people have been "missing," and yet very few others seem to care.

In Cain's case, he knew exactly where his brother was. But still, he did not care that he had just killed Abel out of jealousy. More to the point, Cain did not care about Abel. Period.

I am by no means saying that we must always keep track of everyone in our life. If I were making us all responsible for knowing everyone else's location, I'd make my boss wear a cowbell around his neck!

But there are better things to ask than if we are somebody's keeper. Instead, we can volunteer to help find the person who isn't where they should be, or we can offer to relay a message should we see the "missing" person. We can show that we care, even if the person isn't truly lost.

Lord, teach me how to care about those around me and to be more helpful if someone around me cannot be found. Amen.

June 20

The Lord is not slow in keeping His promise, as some understand slowness. Instead He is patient with you, not wanting anyone to perish, but everyone to come to repentance.

—2 Peter 3:9

We all have a different understanding of what it means to be slow. For example, have you ever pushed the speed limit only to get stuck behind someone who is driving five miles per hour below the posted limit? Do you describe that person as being slow?

Now reverse roles and put yourself in the car traveling at the lesser speed. You've left home plenty early, giving yourself all the time you need to get to your destination. You also know that your vehicle will use less gasoline at slower speeds, so you choose a speed that will help improve your car's gas mileage. When you suddenly have someone riding your bumper, do you describe yourself as slow?

We only seem to use the word "slow" to describe someone who is not moving at the speed we ourselves want to go. Consequently, we may even go so far as to call God slow when He isn't responding to us on our time. But we would be wise to remember that God is not slow. Rather, God works on His time, and we need to accept that.

God, help me to wait while You fulfill Your promises on Your time. Amen.

June 21

No temptation has overtaken you except what is common to mankind. And God is faithful; He will not let you be tempted beyond what you can bear. But when you are tempted, He will also provide a way out so that you can endure it.

—1 Corinthians 10:13

During my own effort at weight loss, I found myself being tempted by cheap, generic sandwich cookies. I didn't even really care for those cookies, but one evening I was really being tempted by them. I reached out via text messaging to a couple friends of mine. Each friend responded in a way that helped me through that temptation. I resisted the cookies.

No matter what temptation we face, it's never a temptation that is unique to just us. Others have faced the same temptations. And those people who have experienced the same temptations may be the way out God provides for us. After all, they've been in our shoes, so they'll know how to resist the temptation.

So the next time you face a temptation, whether it's as little as eating something you shouldn't or as big as breaking the law, ask for God's help and wait for Him to provide you the way out.

God, grant me the strength to endure the temptations I face. And thank You for always providing me a way out of those temptations. Amen.

June 22

There is no fear in love. But perfect love drives
out fear, because fear has to do with punishment.
The one who fears is not made perfect in love.

—1 John 4:18

I once read that a horse trained out of fear was no good
because there would always be something the horse feared more
than humans. But when a horse trusts its trainer, it will turn to
its trainer to learn what it should do when it is afraid.

People are more like horses than I think most would be
willing to admit. But take a moment to consider the various
relationships in your life. Compare the relationships based on
fear and punishment to those based on trust and love. Can we
not also find something to fear more than the people trying to
instill us with fear? When we are afraid, do we not turn to the
people we love, people we know we can trust?

We also need to take that same frame of mind to our
relationship with God. The Lord does not want us to fear coming
to Him. He sent Jesus to take our punishment for us. We are
not only free from our sins, but we are also free from the fear
of punishment. So when we are afraid, we can seek guidance
from the Lord.

Lord, thank You for sending Jesus to take my punishment. Let
me seek You when I am afraid and to trust You for guidance.
Amen.

June 23

Let us not become weary in doing good, for at the proper time we will reap a harvest if we do not give up.

—Galatians 6:9

There's a story about a man who would walk miles of shoreline after the tide had gone out, throwing starfish back into the water. A passerby asked the man why he would waste his time doing that, as the beach was covered with starfish that had been stranded by the receding tide. The passerby told the man what he was doing would not make a difference. The man simply threw another starfish back into the ocean and said, "It made a difference to that one."

In today's society, we can feel like we are fighting a never-ending battle against the evils of the world. We may even become discouraged and want to give up. But when we question if the good we are doing is making any difference, we need to remember the story of the man and the starfish. The good we do makes a difference to those for whom we do it.

So let's keep at it. And, as this verse in Galatians reminds us, there will come a time when we can see the fruits of our labors. We will see just how much our good deeds did indeed matter.

Lord, do not let me grow weary of doing good in this evil world. When I get discouraged, remind me that the good I do does make a difference to those around me. Amen.

June 24

Whoever loves discipline loves knowledge, but whoever hates correction is stupid.

—Proverbs 12:1

I don't know of anyone who likes being corrected. However, there is a big difference between disliking correction and hating correction. That difference is how we respond to it. When we dislike correction, we can still acknowledge the fact that we were wrong. Hating correction is to deny any error.

We need to accept discipline and correction because if we do not, we end up looking foolish. A stretch of highway I drive a lot had the "stop ahead" near a four-way stop repainted. Someone ended up having to be corrected, as the marking was painted "stop ahaed." To leave that alone would have made the state workers look stupid.

While correction is difficult, it brings knowledge. I'd like to think that the workers who had been painting the highway learned to double-check the order of the stencil letters before painting the pavement. So the next time you get disciplined, think of it as a learning experience and embrace it.

Lord, help me to accept correction graciously as a learning experience and to remember that it is better for me to be corrected than to remain in error. Amen.

June 25

Peter replied, "Even if all fall away on account of You, I never will." "Truly I tell you," Jesus answered, "this very night, before the rooster crows, you will disown Me three times." But Peter declared, "Even if I have to die with You, I will never disown You." And all the other disciples said the same.

—Matthew 26:33–35

Spoiler alert! Peter did, in fact, deny knowing Jesus three times, just as Jesus foretold. So much for Peter's "never" statements.

However, before we start criticizing Peter for disowning Jesus, let's take a good, hard look at ourselves. Do we ever disown Christ? Are we really that different from Peter and the other disciples?

How many of us sing songs of worship and praise in church on Sunday but refuse to even mention Christ's name during the other six days of the week? How many of us, like Peter, fear what will happen to us if we let others know we are Christians?

The good news is that, also like Peter, we are forgiven for the times we fail to keep our word. As long as we keep coming back to Him, seeking repentance and showing our willingness to try again, Christ will keep forgiving us.

Christ, I am truly sorry for every time I have disowned You. Please forgive me and let me try again to be Your disciple. Amen.

June 26

And should I not have concern for the great city of Nineveh, in which there are more than a hundred and twenty thousand people who cannot tell their right hand from their left—and also many animals?

—Jonah 4:11

Jonah has got to be one of the strangest prophets of the Bible. First, he ran away from God's call and ended up in the belly of a whale. Then, after obeying the call, he got upset that the people of Nineveh did repent and that God spared the city. While pouting about God's grace, Jonah threw a fit about a tree that died as quickly as it appeared. He just didn't seem to understand the way God works.

Unfortunately, if you think about it, we all have a little Jonah in us. We can all get upset when God shows the same grace to others that He bestows upon us. Think about it for a minute—how do you feel about the possibility that Adolf Hitler, a man most of the world would describe as evil, may be in heaven? That is how Jonah felt about Nineveh.

We all need to remember that grace is God's alone to bestow. After all, God created all people. Thus, there should be no surprise that God cares for all people.

God, teach me to accept that Your grace is available to everyone, and not just the people I want to receive it. Amen.

June 27

If your hand causes you to stumble, cut it off. It is better for you to enter life maimed than with two hands to go into hell, where the fire never goes out.
—Mark 9:43

Maybe it's just because of my nature, but I like to look at this verse in a less literal sense. What other things could Jesus have meant when He talked about removing things that cause us to stumble? The first thing that comes to my mind is the company I keep.

I'm sure we all know people who are fun to be around but who convince us to do things we shouldn't do. Perhaps you have a coworker who engages in gossip at the water cooler. Perhaps you have a family member who fuels a family conflict. Perhaps you have a friend who plays malicious, tasteless pranks on people.

Peer pressure is as real for us adults as it is for our children. It can be very easy to follow the lead of others, and before we know it, we are engaging in the same acts that we know are wrong.

No matter how difficult or painful it can be, we should remember Jesus' words and cut these people loose if they lead us astray. We'll be better off in heaven without them than in hell with them.

Lord, give me the eyes to see who or what is causing me to stumble and the strength to remove that stumbling block from my life. Amen.

June 28

So the poor have hope, and injustice shuts its mouth.

—Job 5:16

This short verse is full of encouragement, which might seem strange coming from this book of the Bible. Job lives through all sorts of disasters and almost comes across as whiny later in the story. Yet maybe that's what makes this verse of hope so powerful.

Job's story starts out with him having everything. As the story progresses, Job loses his riches, his family, even his own health. He loses everything. The story ends with Job once again having everything. The moral of the story is summed up by this verse that actually comes fairly early on. Call it foreshadowing—a hint about what is going to happen later.

Even in times of great distress, we are reminded that God will make everything right in the end. No matter what happens to us, we have the hope that God will come through for us. All of the injustices we experience in our own lives or witness in the world around us will be corrected.

Remember this verse, the moral of Job's story. Let it foreshadow our own story as well. Everything is going to be all right.

God, help me to hold fast to the hope that, in You, all injustices will eventually be made right. Amen.

June 29

We love because He first loved us.

—1 John 4:19

During the summers when I was in college, I worked for someone who owned a harness racing stable. My duties ranged from cleaning stalls to jogging the racehorses to helping halter-train the foals. My first summer working there, I took a special interest in a three-year-old filly.

This young racehorse started getting special treatment from me. I'd put a little extra bedding in her stall. I'd pick clover around the barn to give her as a treat. I'd spend a little extra time grooming her.

Eventually, this filly would whinny at me to call me to her stall. When turned out in the paddock, she would play "hard to catch" with her owner but would walk right up to me. Our unique relationship ultimately resulted in her becoming my horse upon her retirement from racing.

This horse came to love me, but only because I had shown love to her first. And the same thing is true for us humans. We have come to love because God first showed His love for us. We have a unique relationship with God that results in our belonging to Him forever!

God, I love You! Thank You for first loving me and for showing me how to love. May I always reflect Your love as proof of the relationship I have with You. Amen.

June 30

But seek first His kingdom and His righteousness,
and all these things will be given to you as well.
—Matthew 6:33

One Sunday at worship, the children's message was about keeping God as a priority. The youth leader had a jar and several marbles, all of the same size except for one large marble. The smaller marbles represented the various worries and responsibilities we faced. The large marble represented God.

When the youth leader began putting marbles in the jar, he began with all the little marbles. When he put the large marble in last, he could not put the lid on the jar. The marbles did not appear to fit. But when he poured all the marbles out and began by putting the large marble in first, he could get all the smaller marbles in the jar and put the lid on it. All of the marbles did indeed fit.

Even though this was a children's message, it was a good lesson for us adults too. If we do not put God first, we will find there is no room for Him in our lives. We may also find a lack of room for other things as well. But when we put God first, everything in our lives will come together. Everything will fit. We just need the right start.

God, help me keep the right priority and put You first and foremost in my life. Then I know everything else will fall into place. Amen.

July 1

And God said, "Let there be light," and there was light.

—Genesis 1:3

According to this story in Genesis, light is the very first thing God created. That speaks volumes about the importance of light. Light is life.

You may recall from some of your general science classes in school that plants use light to create their own food. You may also know that our own bodies will make vitamin D when we are exposed to sunlight. Plants and animals alike need light.

Light also provides us with safety and security. That is why we will put lights on timers while we are on vacation. Many children will have a nightlight in their bedroom to protect them from their own imaginations. Some adults will even use nightlights to provide just enough light in dark places to make light switches easier to find.

Is it any wonder that Christ referred to Himself as the "light of the world"? Light is the perfect metaphor to describe how much we need our Savior. Christ also gives us life, safety, and security. We need light, and we need Christ.

Lord, thank You for creating light. Thank You for all the blessings You provide through light. And thank You for Your Son, the light of the world. Amen.

July 2

Because of the Lord's great love we are not consumed, for His compassions never fail. They are new every morning; great is Your faithfulness.

—Lamentations 3:22-23

I am a morning person. Over the years, many people have teased me or have been annoyed by my morning perkiness. I have the most energy in the morning, making that my most productive time of the day.

One of the things I love about morning is seeing the world wake up again. Sunrise brings with it brilliant colors that paint the eastern sky. Birds that have spent the night in the safety of their nests resume their songs. Animals that slumbered through the night return to their playful antics.

With morning comes a fresh start. My mistakes of the previous day are left in the past. A new day gives me a new chance to do the things I should do, to be the person I should be. Through God's compassionate grace and mercy, which come anew each morning, I get to try again. And every morning begins with the hope that on this day spread out before me, I will get it right.

Lord, Your faithfulness is indeed great. Thank You for Your compassions, new every morning. Help me to acknowledge each day as another chance to be the person You want me to be. Amen.

July 3

I praise You because I am fearfully and wonderfully made; Your works are wonderful, I know that full well.

—Psalm 139:14

Have you ever been asked to name one thing about yourself that you would change? What was your answer? Was it something about your physical appearance? Was it something about your personality? Did you have trouble deciding on just one thing you'd change? Or did you decide that you're fine with yourself just the way you are?

There was a time when I would have wanted to change some things about my personality. But that was before I took a personality test, learned my personality "type," and began to better understand myself. I now see that the things I used to think were weaknesses may actually be my greatest strengths.

Each one of us is made to God's specifications, and we need to embrace our many unique traits. Whether it's something physical, like curly hair or really long legs, or something about our personality, like being emotional or talkative, it was a trait designed for us by our Maker. And God knows what He's doing.

Maker of all things, You designed me the way You wanted me to be. Show me how to use the traits You have given me for the purpose for which You created me. Help me to see that my weaknesses can be my strengths. Amen.

July 4

But our citizenship is in heaven.
—Philippians 3:20a

Today, all across the United States, people are celebrating the birthday of a nation. For many, this is a day off from work. Thus it is a day full of parades, backyard barbecues, get-togethers with family and friends, and, come nightfall, fireworks. Okay, in states where fireworks are legal, some people won't wait for sundown!

There is nothing wrong with celebrating Independence Day. We just need to remember one very important thing. We are merely pilgrims here on earth. And, unlike the Pilgrims who landed on Plymouth Rock, we are not to make ourselves at home here. Our home is above. Our citizenship is in our Father's heavenly kingdom.

We should still be good "guests" during our time here. We need to take care of our nation's resources and its inhabitants. Let's leave this world a better place than when we arrived, keeping it available for the pilgrims who will make their journeys behind us.

Father, it is in Your heavenly kingdom where we find our true citizenship. As we journey through this life, bless the land we temporarily call our home, and teach us how to be good stewards of this nation's resources. Amen.

July 5

There is no one holy like the Lord; there is no one besides You; there is no Rock like our God.

—1 Samuel 2:2

As part of a compliment, my boss once told me that I was "one of a kind." I felt it was necessary to lighten the mood, so I jokingly told him, "It's a good thing, too, because this world couldn't handle two of me!"

Our God is also one of a kind. No one else can do what God does. No one can even come close!

Only God was able to bring everything into existence by simply speaking a word. Only God can carry out a plan to redeem a fallen humanity. Only God can provide us with what we need when we need it.

God not only provides for our physical needs of food, water, clothing, and shelter. He also provides for our emotional needs in the form of the friends He brings into our lives. He provides for our spiritual needs by giving us pastors, teachers, and role models for our faith.

And, of course, God provided for our eternal souls by sending Jesus to die for us. Through Jesus' death and resurrection, God—the only truly Holy One—gives us a share of His holiness. He gives us enough that we can live with Him forever.

Holy God, You are my rock and my salvation. Thank You for providing for me as only You can. Amen.

July 6

Have I not commanded you? Be strong and courageous. Do not be afraid; do not be discouraged, for the Lord your God will be with you wherever you go.

—Joshua 1:9

It is very difficult to take that first step outside one's comfort zone. That is, after all, the reason why it's called a "comfort zone." We feel comfortable there. We feel safe there.

The downside to staying in our comfort zone, however, is that we do not grow there. We can only grow when we face challenges and take chances. Challenges are uncomfortable, and chances can definitely be risky. But without them, nothing in our lives will change.

Some people may question their need to grow. They may feel that they want their lives to remain exactly the same. And yet those are probably the people who need the most growth.

The Bible is full of people who took that step outside their comfort zones: Abraham, Noah, Moses, Isaiah, Ruth, Mary, the twelve disciples, Paul. The list could go on. The Lord was always with them, just as He will be with us as well. So go ahead. Take that step out of your comfort zone.

Lord, grant me the courage to step outside my comfort zone so that I may do Your will. Remind me that You will always accompany me. Amen.

July 7

I will not fear though tens of thousands assail me on every side.

—Psalm 3:6

At first, one would probably interpret "tens of thousands" to refer to an army. But as I reflect on this verse, I find myself thinking about the many things that can assail each of us in our daily lives. We have so many worries and concerns that it can feel like we have tens of thousands of stresses assailing us.

We have demands in our workplace. Even a massage therapist like me has stress from the job. We have demands in our home, especially if we have children and spouses. But even "fur babies" can cause stress. We have demands from our church. Stress is everywhere!

Yet, like the psalmist, we need not be afraid. God will always deliver us, even when we feel like we're drowning in our stresses. No matter what the worry or concern is, God is by our side.

Though tens of thousands of anything assail us, God is with us. These things may attack us on every side, but that doesn't matter because God is able to cover us on all sides. And when we start to feel run down, God will sustain us.

God, when I am afraid, worried, or stressed, remind me of Your constant presence and sustain me by Your grace. Amen.

July 8

For everything God created is good, and nothing is to be rejected if it is received with thanksgiving.

—1 Timothy 4:4

The context of this verse explains why it is not necessary to abstain from eating certain foods. However, like so many other Bible verses, this verse can be interpreted many different ways. This is especially true when one switches from one Bible translation to another.

For example, the King James version says, "For every creature of God is good...." The animal lover in me really appreciates the words of that translation. Every creature is indeed good!

Regardless of the translation used, pulling this verse out of context turns it into a good stewardship reminder for us. We know from reading the first chapter of Genesis that God saw all of His creation as good. And who are we to argue with God? We should also acknowledge that every aspect of God's creation is good.

Not only should we see the goodness of creation, but we should also be thankful for it. With that thanksgiving comes our duty to properly care for it. God has entrusted us with His good creation.

Teach me, dear God, to give Your good and wondrous creation the care it deserves. Let me feel truly thankful for every rock and tree and creature Your hand has made. Amen.

July 9

Abraham answered, "God Himself will provide the lamb for the burnt offering, my son." And the two of them went on together.

—Genesis 22:8

This is an interesting verse to think about. Sacrifices were the price that humans had to pay to God to make up for their sins. God demanded the blood sacrifice, and yet God provided the blood for the sacrifice. That's like you owing me money, and then I give you the money to pay me back. The debt is settled because of a gift.

What humans had done for centuries with blood sacrifices was really to borrow from others to make small payments toward a debt that could never be paid off. The blood of animals would never entirely atone for our sins. The only way we could get out of debt with God was with our own human blood.

So, God found a way to settle the debt. He gave us His Son's blood. And blood that holy was enough to pay off the debt of every human that has ever and will ever walk the face of this planet.

What a gift!

Lord, thank You for the gift of Your Son. Thank You for providing the Lamb for the sacrifice that paid off my debt to You, as well as the debt of all mankind. Amen.

July 10

If we confess our sins, He is faithful and just and will forgive us our sins and purify us from all unrighteousness.

—1 John 1:9

I first heard these words as part of the "brief order for confession and forgiveness" at the start of Sunday morning worship. It took me a long time to learn that these words originate in the Bible, not the hymnal! But they are good words to remember.

It's a simple truth. We goof. We screw up. We sin. That's just the way we are. We can't help it. Try as we may to do right, we will fail. It's our nature as humans.

But there's another simple truth. God purifies. God restores. God forgives. There is nothing that must be done to earn His forgiveness or His favor. No matter how many times we fail, God sets us right. That's God's nature.

However, there is one catch. God can do anything, but He chooses to give us free will. Consequently, God will not fix us until we admit to Him that we are broken. He will not interfere with our mistakes, but He will help us as soon as we turn to Him and ask for His help and forgiveness. All we must do is confess.

Faithful and just Lord, I confess to You all of my sins, even the sins that are unknown to me. Please forgive me and restore me in Your image once again. Amen.

July 11

But I tell you, love your enemies and pray for
those who persecute you.

—Matthew 5:44

You're kidding, right? Why should I love anyone who
obviously hates me? Why should I extend any courtesy to
someone who will not extend that same courtesy to me? Jesus,
do You have any idea of what You are asking of me?

Actually He does. The first of Jesus' last seven words from
the cross demonstrated exactly what Jesus meant by these words
recorded in Matthew. "Father, forgive them!" Jesus Himself
loved those who were the ultimate enemy. He prayed for those
who were literally killing Him.

Jesus' prayer from the cross did not change anything at that
moment. They still crucified Him. Jesus still died. But Jesus
was free from any hard feelings or ill will toward those Roman
soldiers.

When we love our enemies, we also may not see immediate
changes. In fact, we may never see any change in those people.
However, when we turn their actions over to God, we are free
from the negative impact our enemies have on us. We will be
able to see the change in ourselves.

Jesus, You taught us to love our enemies. Guide us to follow
Your example to pray for our persecutors. Amen.

July 12

Dear children, let us not love with words or speech but with actions and in truth.

—1 John 3:18

I'm sure we can all think of circumstances where someone's actions contradicted their words. When a coworker has done something that disrespected you, are you going to believe her if she says she cares about you? If your friend gossips about you behind your back, are you going to believe him if he says you can trust him?

In this letter, John is not saying that we should not express our love to one another in words. I'm sure he knew as well as anyone how wonderful it can be to hear someone say they love us. What John is saying, however, is that we need to make sure our actions agree with our words.

Remember that "just because" is a perfectly acceptable reason to give your spouse flowers or a gift. When your friend tears up, don't worry about finding the right words to say. Skip straight to the hug. There are many ways to express love without saying a word. Actions done in love can be just as powerful, sometimes more so, than the spoken word.

Heavenly Father, You have shown Your love for us through Your actions. Help us, in turn, to show our love for our neighbors through our actions toward them. Amen.

July 13

The Lord gives strength to His people; the Lord blesses His people with peace.

—Psalm 29:11

Have you ever needed to make a very difficult decision? While you were trying to decide what to do, how did you feel? Did you feel any better once the decision was made?

Many times when faced with a difficult decision, a person will feel like there is a war raging inside. Each option is fighting to become the solution. Such turmoil can leave a person feeling confused, tired, and maybe even weak.

Weighing the options and deciding on a course of action can be very difficult to handle alone. So a lot of people will ask for the advice of their close friends or family. But the truly wise people will seek the counsel of God.

The Lord knows exactly what path is right for us. He can tell us what option we should choose. All we must do is ask and then open ourselves up to His answer. Then, when we have followed the advice of our God, we will experience the peace our soul longs for and will find the strength to follow through with the decision that has been made.

Lord, when I face a dilemma, call me back to You, so that I may seek Your counsel and receive Your peace. Amen.

July 14

If you declare with your mouth, "Jesus is Lord," and believe in your heart that God raised Him from the dead, you will be saved. For it is with your heart that you believe and are justified, and it is with your mouth that you profess your faith and are saved.

—Romans 10:9–10

I was in middle school when Tim LaHaye and Jerry B. Jenkins published their first book in the Left Behind series. When I read that book, I was caught off guard by one of the characters left behind after the Rapture. The character who surprised me so much was a pastor.

The authors did a wonderful job of explaining how this pastor missed the Rapture. Basically this character professed with his mouth a faith that he did not believe in his heart. There is a difference between saying something and truly believing it.

While the Left Behind series is fiction, the authors do encourage us to consider our faith. We call ourselves Christians. Many of us regularly profess our faith in church by reciting one creed or another. But when was the last time you thought about the words of those creeds? Do you truly believe in your heart what you are declaring with your mouth?

Lord, grant me the courage to profess my beliefs with my mouth and the faith to truly believe in my heart what I am professing. Amen.

July 15

Ah, Sovereign Lord, You have made the heavens and the earth by Your great power and outstretched arm. Nothing is too hard for You.
—Jeremiah 32:17

I love being out in nature! I am fascinated by the variety of plants and animals in this world. And when I gaze up at the night sky, I am amazed by the countless stars that shine so brilliantly.

Sometimes I turn to nature when I need to focus my thoughts on something specific. Other times I turn to nature when I wish to quiet my mind and clear my head of all thoughts. Regardless of what state of mind I am in, I turn to nature so that I can turn to God.

We all have a place where we feel closest to God. For me, it is definitely far away from the hustle and bustle of civilization. Every flower, every tree leaf, every animal, and every star in the sky reminds me of God's great power. I'm left feeling small, but in a good way.

If God can not only create the entire universe but can also tend to everything on a daily basis, how difficult is it for Him to tend to me as well? God has everything under control, including my life. As today's verse says, nothing is too hard for God.

God, Your power is amazing and humbling! There is not a speck of creation that is outside Your care, and I am truly grateful for the attention You give to me. Amen.

July 16

Don't grumble against one another, brothers and sisters, or you will be judged. The Judge is standing at the door!

—James 5:9

Do you ever stop to think about how many times you hear a person complaining about someone else? Or do you ever consider how many times you complain about other people? It seems that we humans are notorious for grumbling against each other.

Many of us know all too well how unfair the criticisms of others can be. We've heard the complaints that have been made against us by people who do not understand what we are going through at the time. Even the most professional of people cannot always push their personal problems aside forever.

We may not know the struggles and burdens of those around us. Therefore, we are not qualified to complain about them. Grumbling about someone is to pass judgment on that person, because we think we know how or what they should be doing.

Only God knows everyone's whole story. That is why we need to leave the judgment to God. Let God decide what is right and what is wrong. God knows best.

God, teach me to not grumble or complain against another person. Remind me that only You know what others are going through. Therefore, only You can judge fairly. Amen.

July 17

For the Lord gives wisdom; from His mouth
come knowledge and understanding.
—Proverbs 2:6

My very first devotion project was a Lenten discipline.
Rather than giving something up, I wrote a devotion every day
during that Lent. Something happened during that project that
I had not expected.

While writing one devotion, a thought occurred to me that
I had never thought of before, even though the verse on which I
was writing was in a very familiar passage. I found myself with
insight that had only come to me through reading and reflecting
on the Bible. I had not learned it from any human teachers.

God has many ways of speaking to us. It's not always as
direct as the way He spoke to me while I was writing that
devotion. In fact, God usually does speak to us through human
mouths. He gives us teachers, pastors, and mentors to speak
His word to us.

Yet, regardless of how God speaks to us, the result is always
the same. He imparts wisdom to those who will listen. If we are
open to receive it, God gives us understanding that we cannot
reach on our own. Thanks be to God!

Lord, open my ears to hear You speak to me. Guide me to Your
wisdom and understanding as only You can. Amen.

July 18

He replied, "I have been very zealous for the Lord God Almighty. The Israelites have rejected Your covenant, torn down Your altars, and put Your prophets to death with the sword. I am the only one left, and now they are trying to kill me too."

—1 Kings 19:10

Elijah was in a tough spot. He had been bringing God's words to the Israelites only to be met with resistance. The Israelites were so resistant, in fact, that they killed anyone who told them what they did not want to hear.

Wouldn't it be nice to say we live in a civilized society where disagreements were handled in a calm, rational manner? Unfortunately, that is not true. We might not physically kill someone who says what we don't want to hear, but we can try to kill their spirit.

One pastor I knew hadn't even been at his church for a year and a half when certain congregation members started trying to kill his spirit. But, despite the blows he was taking for his sermons, this pastor did not back down. He needed to pull back to regroup periodically, but so did Elijah. The main thing is to keep saying what needs to be said, no matter what kind of reception the words are met with.

Lord God, remind me that when my zeal for You is met with harsh resistance, I am in good company and give me the strength to press on. Amen.

July 19

This is how we know what love is: Jesus Christ laid down His life for us. And we ought to lay down our lives for our brothers and sisters.

—1 John 3:16

Christ's sacrifice on the cross was the ultimate expression of love. There's no question about that. But before we all start going out and looking for people to die for, let's take a broader look at what it means to lay down our lives.

In the Disney movie *Frozen*, love is defined as putting someone else's needs ahead of your own. That is what Jesus did. Because the result of our sin is death, the only way Jesus could fully put our needs ahead of His was to die for us. However, we can "lay down our lives" without actually dying.

How do you respond if someone asks you for help moving? If you respond by finding any excuse possible to avoid helping, you are putting your needs first and not showing love. However, if you put your own plans or desires on the back burner, you are essentially laying down your life for this friend. By putting your life on hold, you are putting your friend's needs first, so you are demonstrating Christian love. No actual death is required, only true selflessness.

Jesus, teach me to love as You do, by putting the needs of others ahead of my own. Amen.

July 20

For this is what the Lord says: "I will extend peace to her like a river, and the wealth of nations like a flooding stream; you will nurse and be carried on her arm and dandled on her knees."
—Isaiah 66:12

There is a relatively large river that flows through the city where I work. And one of my favorite retreats in that city is a section of bike trail that comes very close to the river. In fact, at one spot on this section, there is a bench that faces the river.

Sure, I know all about the dangerous undercurrents and other violent hazards that lurk under the surface of a river. I know to be careful swimming in rivers. But I still find it peaceful to watch the surface current gently gliding along.

God promised in Isaiah that He would extend peace like a river. God's peace is truly like a river. On the surface, there is gentle motion. However, below the surface are stronger currents that can either sweep a person away or hold them steady while cutting new paths. The difference between riding the current or getting pulled under is respect. Fearful respect of God's current is all that it takes to reap the benefits of the peaceful river.

Lord, give me a healthy respect of Your power so that I may truly appreciate Your peace. Amen.

July 21

So he got up and went to his father. But while he was still a long way off, his father saw him and was filled with compassion for him; he ran to his son, threw his arms around him and kissed him.

—Luke 15:20

When I was in college, I helped with a few junior high lock-ins. As part of the icebreaker time for one lock-in, we had to share with our partner what our favorite Christian symbol is and why. I had never thought about it before that moment, but it didn't take me long to come up with my answer. My favorite symbol is the cross because it reminds me of someone inviting me in for a hug.

I have one friend who is very good about hugging me when he sees I need one. And he never says a word to me before giving me the hug. Rather, he comes toward me with his arms outstretched, inviting me into his compassionate embrace.

Today's verse comes from the Parable of the Prodigal Son. Jesus was symbolizing how our Father will lovingly embrace us whenever we return to Him. No words are needed. Jesus' outstretched arms on the cross are an open invitation for us to rush in for the hug we all so desperately need.

Father, thank You for the open invitation for me to come to Your loving embrace. Amen.

July 22

Do not set foot on the path of the wicked or walk in the way of evildoers.

—Proverbs 4:14

In the TV mini-series *Lonesome Dove*, one character ends up being hanged because he fell in with the wrong crowd. Set in the time of the Old West, this law-abiding character needs to get through the territory and knows the dangers of traveling alone. He joins a gang, just for safety in numbers. The gang turns out to be a band of murderous horse thieves. When they get caught, they all get hanged. Unfortunately, even though he didn't participate in any killings, this law-abiding character is also hanged, just because he had become part of the gang.

One could make arguments about that being a work of fiction and set in a previous time. However, we do face the same struggles in this day and age, in our reality. We may have the best of intentions, but we fall in with the wrong crowd.

Therefore, we need to be diligent when choosing companions for our life journey. We can easily be led astray, just by surrounding ourselves with the wrong people. And if we ever question the company we find ourselves in, we need to pray for guidance.

Lord, protect me from the wicked. Surround me with people who want to avoid evil as I do. Amen.

July 23

But you, keep your head in all situations, endure hardship, do the work of an evangelist, discharge all the duties of your ministry.

—2 Timothy 4:5

It has been proven that, by remaining calm, a person can escape a car submerged in water. The person must wait, however, until the inside of the car is completely filled with water. Only once the water pressure inside the car matches the water pressure outside the car will the door be able to be opened. In the meantime, the vehicle occupant must remain calm. Any panic will raise the person's breathing rate, causing them to use up oxygen too quickly.

Granted, most of us will never find ourselves trapped inside a submerged vehicle. However, the lesson is good for every aspect of our lives. Whenever we are in a sticky situation, remaining calm will help us to find the solution. Sometimes, we simply have to bide our time while the situation works itself out.

Paul's advice to Timothy is important for us to remember also. "Keep your head." Remain calm. Stay focused.

God, when I find myself in over my head, help me to remain calm and focused on You. Teach me to trust that You will show me the solution when the time is right. Amen.

July 24

The pride of your heart has deceived you, you
who live in the clefts of the rocks and make your
home on the heights, you who say to yourselves,
"Who can bring me down to the ground?"
—Obadiah 1:3

The worst thing that can happen to a person is that they start thinking too highly of themselves. Just look at athletes. For a specific example, look at Arnold Palmer in the 1966 US Open. Arnold Palmer had a strong lead, only to lose that lead and ultimately lose the title.

A little self-confidence is a good thing. We should believe in ourselves. However, as the self-confidence grows, our faith needs to be growing also. We are not invincible. If we fail to acknowledge God's hand in our success, God may feel the need to knock us down a peg or two.

God's word of warning spoken by Obadiah to Edom is also God's word of warning to us. Go ahead and build your self-confidence. But make sure that you are also building your faith so that you have the correct balance of confidence in yourself and confidence in God.

God, grant that I may never gain so much self-confidence that I forget that You alone give me the strength and skills I need to succeed. Amen.

July 25

Your righteousness is like the highest mountains,
Your justice like the great deep. You, Lord,
preserve both people and animals.

—Psalm 36:6

For a few years now, this date has been a difficult one for me. It was on this date in 2013 that I came home from work to find my beloved Arabian mare dead in the pasture. And every year, bittersweet memories of that horse come flooding back to me on this day.

Some people will argue about whether or not animals go to heaven. I am not going to participate in such a debate here. However, I do find this Bible verse to be very comforting when I find myself grieving over the death of any of my animals.

The comfort comes from my knowing that the Lord shares my love of animals. The story of Noah and the flood testifies to that. The ark held more than just Noah and his family. It also held two of every kind of animal.

The psalmist also recognized God's care for animals. The Lord loves all of creation. In fact, He cares for animals so much that He appointed humans to care for them. And when we love our pets, we are reflecting the love that the Lord has for them.

Thank You, Lord, for the animals You have given me to care for. May I always show them the love that You have for them. Amen.

July 26

Do not judge, and you will not be judged. Do not condemn, and you will not be condemned. Forgive, and you will be forgiven.

—Luke 6:37

Abraham Lincoln is credited with saying, "Whether you look for the good or look for the bad, you are going to find it." Those words are very true, regardless of whether you are looking at a situation or at another person.

Jesus' words recorded here in Luke are also true whether we are looking at a situation or at another person. Generally, we think about how we should not judge or condemn other people. However, it's not just people we form premature opinions on.

How many times have we looked at a task before us and thought, "This isn't going to go well"? Then we are not surprised when that task doesn't go well. Our very own attitude can sabotage our work.

So, whether we are looking at another person or at a situation, let's remember to look for the good. We will find whatever it is we are looking for. We might as well look for the good. That way, we will indeed find the good!

Lord, teach me to always look for the good in every person and every situation I encounter, today and every day. Amen.

July 27

However, as it is written: "What no eye has seen, what no ear has heard, and what no human mind has conceived"—the things God has prepared for those who love Him.

—1 Corinthians 2:9

The human mind can conceive quite a lot. Countless authors have dazzled us with the stories they have written. Countless screenwriters have penned movie scripts that leave audiences amazed and entertained. Countless artists have created paintings, sculptures, or other masterpieces that may confuse as well as inspire the viewer.

With all that the human mind can conceive, it can be difficult to believe that there is more that we have not conceived. In fact, it can be mind-blowing to even attempt to consider that there are things our minds actually are not capable of conceiving.

There have been many speculations about what heaven will be like. But this verse makes such speculations pointless. Paul is telling the church in Corinth—and us today—that we cannot even begin to imagine the things God has prepared for us. Our minds are just incapable of conceiving or comprehending the bliss that will be ours for eternity. How mind-blowing and exciting!

God, I eagerly await the things You have prepared for all who love You, things I know I cannot imagine. Amen.

July 28

But Jesus often withdrew to lonely places and prayed.

—Luke 5:16

Here is a Bible verse for every introvert out there! It is proof that there is nothing wrong with going off alone for quiet time. Even Jesus did so frequently.

Being an introvert myself, I understand the need to withdraw to recharge. Some occasions my time is spent in active prayer. Other occasions I quiet my heart and mind to be open to whatever God wants to speak to me.

Even extroverts will occasionally feel the need to withdraw, or so I've been told by a highly extroverted friend. We all experience times when we need to quietly reconnect with God. Maybe we need to talk to God about something weighing heavily on us. Or maybe we need guidance, so we come to God only to listen.

The point is that we should never feel bad about the need to withdraw. It does not mean that we have suddenly become antisocial. It is not a sign that we are slowly turning into hermits. There is nothing negative coming from our withdrawal. We are simply acknowledging a lost connection with God that we are seeking to reestablish.

Lord, please encourage me to withdraw when I feel the need, so that I might strengthen my connection with You. Amen.

July 29

[F]or wisdom is more precious than rubies, and
nothing you can desire can compare with her.
—Proverbs 8:11

"Knowledge is knowing that a tomato is a fruit. Wisdom
is knowing not to put it in a fruit salad." Every time I see that
saying, I think about how true that is. I also think about how
many things are obvious to some people yet other people have
no comprehension of those same things.

For example, why is it that whenever there is an altercation
involving a police officer, suddenly all police officers are
stereotyped as evil racists? Knowledge is knowing that there
are bad apples in every profession. Wisdom is knowing to not
classify everyone by the few bad apples.

The wise know to look at more facts than just what they
first see. As a result, the wise end up seeing things that are very
obvious to them yet escape other people.

Seek wisdom. Not only will it keep you from putting tomatoes
in a fruit salad, but it will also keep you from becoming blinded
by bigotry. Wisdom brings understanding. Understanding
brings harmony. Wisdom is truly precious.

Lord, grant me the wisdom to see beyond the convenient facts
to the whole truth. Amen.

July 30

Lazy hands make for poverty, but diligent hands bring wealth.

—Proverbs 10:4

There's one on every team. There is that member who fails to do their fair share of the work, making more work for everyone else. There is that one member who cannot be bothered or just wants to reap the benefits without putting forth the effort.

If you have ever been on a team and have dealt with the lazy member, you know the frustration that it involves. But be assured that even if no one else notices, your Father in heaven does. In the end, God will reward those who work hard—those who pull their own weight and those who do the work of others.

If you have never experienced the burden of a team member who isn't contributing fairly, then you either have the perfect team or you are the one failing to hold up your end. So take a good look at your work. Are you doing all that you can? Are you even doing all that you should? Remember that God will reward those who work hard, not the ones who ride on their team members' coattails.

Heavenly Father, give me patience with the people who add to my workload and grant me the sight to see when I am causing someone else to have extra work. Amen.

July 31

Therefore this is what the Lord says: "If you repent, I will restore you that you may serve Me; if you utter worthy, not worthless, words, you will be My spokesman. Let this people turn to you, but you must not turn to them."

—Jeremiah 15:19

Have you ever found yourself going the wrong direction and needing to turn around? Depending on where you are, turning around is not always easy. If you miss your exit on an interstate, for example, you may have to go several miles before you reach the next exit where you can turn around.

Sometimes it can even be difficult to turn around when walking. Nothing screams, "Hey, look at me!" like a very sudden u-turn in a hallway or corridor. I, for one, like to make an exaggerated about-face to poke fun at myself for going the wrong way.

Fortunately, with God, u-turns are much easier. There is no need to continue going the wrong direction because we don't have to wait for a specific place to turn around. And God will not ridicule us for abrupt turns. In fact, He celebrates that we have noticed the error of our ways and have made the necessary changes. When we acknowledge our mistakes and repent, God restores us and sets us in the right direction again.

God, thank You for restoring me every time I repent and for making u-turns in life a simple process. Amen.

August 1

Peter said to Jesus, "Lord, it is good for us to be here. If You wish, I will put up three shelters— one for You, one for Moses and one for Elijah."
—Matthew 17:4

Jesus was shining like the sun and was talking with Moses and Elijah. We could speculate why Peter wanted to build the shelters or if he even realized what he was saying. But I want to look at the very first thing Peter said. "Lord, it is good for us to be here."

Peter, James, and John were getting to see a side of Jesus that nobody else, not even the other disciples, had seen. It was a learning experience like none other! It was indeed good for those three disciples to be there to witness this event. It was also good for them to just be there in close communion with their Lord.

Likewise, it is good for us to also spend some time in close communion with our Lord. One of the ways we have such experiences is through worship services. There the gospel is opened up to us, and we can learn things about God that we never knew before.

Churches all over experience decreased church attendance during the summer. Yet, those who faithfully come to worship have those additional times of close communion with God. It is good for us to be at church.

Lord, please let me never forget that it is good for me to spend time in close communion with You. Amen.

August 2

"So do not fear, for I am with you; do not be dismayed, for I am your God. I will strengthen you and help you; I will uphold you with My righteous right hand."

—Isaiah 41:10

Inspired by my dogs, I did an online search for Bible verses related to living in the moment. Dogs naturally live that way. Even when my dogs watch me empty the last of their food into their dishes, they do not worry about where their next meal is coming from. All they are concerned with is getting the food currently in their dishes.

We humans tend to worry about more than just food. This verse, which turned up in the online search I did, not only acknowledges the fact that we have many concerns, but also reminds us how we should respond to our various concerns. Whether we are worried about trying to make ends meet when our expenses are bigger than our income or we have concerns about how to care for an ailing loved one, we need not be afraid.

God knows our needs, and He will take care of us. Just as my dogs trust me to meet their needs, so we should trust God to meet our needs. We need to take a lesson from our dogs and live in the moment.

Teach me, dear God, to trust in You to take care of me. I want to live in the moment that You have given me, rather than living in fear. Amen.

August 3

He replied, "Whether He is a sinner or not, I don't know. One thing I do know. I was blind but now I see!"

—John 9:25

There are many types of blindness, especially physical blindness. People can be colorblind, where they are unable to distinguish between certain colors. There is single-eye blindness, where a person cannot see out of one eye. There is also legal blindness, where a person has enough difficulty seeing without the aid of glasses or contact lenses that they are not allowed to drive without their eyesight corrected.

Then there is the blindness experienced by the man speaking in today's verse. He had been completely blind. Back in those days, total blindness meant total helplessness. Even in today's society, complete blindness can make life very complicated.

However, there is another type of blindness, one that is not physical. It's the blindness experienced by the Pharisees who kept questioning the man in this story. It's not that they *can* not see, but that they *will* not see. And that's the worst kind of blindness because that is not easily corrected. Only God can fix that blindness and only if the person allows it.

Lord, open my eyes. Correct my spiritual blindness so that I may see Your great works in the world and the people around me. Amen.

August 4

Let my teaching fall like rain and my words descend like dew, like showers on new grass, like abundant rain on tender plants.

—Deuteronomy 32:2

Young plants need rain. That's why we water trees when we plant them. Grass and gardens also get watered a lot. Plants cannot grow without water, so we tend to be very meticulous with our young plants.

We ourselves are young plants in God's garden. But the water we need to grow comes from God's teaching. We cannot grow in our faith without God's Word.

There are many ways for plants to get water. The easiest way to water our plants is through rain. However, sometimes the rain just doesn't come often enough. That's why we have sprinkler systems, soaker hoses, and field irrigation systems.

We can get our "water" through Sunday worship services, but sometimes that is not enough to quench our soul's thirst. So never underestimate the importance of daily devotions and small group Bible studies. There is always more than one way to get the teaching we need to grow.

Lord God, Your teaching is the water that allows my faith to grow. Guide me to the many sources of Your Word. Amen.

August 5

A cheerful heart is good medicine, but a crushed
spirit dries up the bones.

—Proverbs 17:22

You can learn a lot of good life lessons from Disney movies.
For example, one lesson I learned from *Mary Poppins* is that even
the most horrible of tasks can be a delight to do if approached
with the correct attitude. That's what young Jane and Michael
learned when Mary Poppins made them clean their nursery.

We all have tasks we do not want to do. For me, one such
task is dusting. I despise dusting! Dusting means I must move all
of my various decorations, which can be very time-consuming. I
also must be mindful of what I am using to dust. Is the chemical
strictly for wood? Can I use it on my plastic model horses? Is it
just for electronics? It's a chore I don't do very often because I
dislike doing it so much.

However, our terrible tasks are easier to do if we don't think
about how terrible they are. Rather, we should approach them
with a cheerful heart. Then, like Mary Poppins taught, it will
be like that "spoonful of sugar [to make] the medicine go down"!

Lord, give me a cheerful heart to willingly do the unpleasant
tasks that lie ahead of me. May I have an attitude that turns
misery into fun. Amen.

August 6

Do you think I came to bring peace on earth?
No, I tell you, but division.

—Luke 12:51

Jesus really did bring division to earth just with His very presence. There are divisions even among Christians. But, I don't think Jesus meant to create the divisions that occur between Baptists, Lutherans, Catholics, Methodists, Episcopalians, etc. Those divisions are ones we have created ourselves.

Instead, Jesus brings a special kind of division. Consider sweet corn for a moment. Before you indulge in your garden treat, you must first remove the husk and the silk. That is part of the corn plant, but it is of no use to you. Actually, the husk and silk keep you from enjoying the sweet corn as you were meant to.

We also have "husk and silk" in our lives. Those may be things or people. Jesus wants to separate us from everything that prevents us from having the relationship with God that we were meant to have. So Jesus must strip away the things that distract us. And if there is a person who is interfering with our relationship with God, Jesus will divide us from that person as well. Jesus' divisions may hurt us at the moment, but they are ultimately for our own good.

Jesus, open me up to Your divine divisions and help me see that You are doing what is best for me. Amen.

August 7

But you are a chosen people, a royal priesthood,
a holy nation, God's special possession, that you
may declare the praises of Him who called you
out of darkness into His wonderful light.

—1 Peter 2:9

If you had to evacuate your house in a hurry and only had time to grab three things, what would they be? A photo album? A family heirloom? A favorite blanket?

My three things to save would be my alto clarinet, my guitar, and my baritone ukulele. Those are my three special possessions. They are not mere musical instruments to me. The sentimental value they have to me results in my willingness to risk life and limb to make sure they are not left behind to be destroyed.

We are God's special possession. God would not leave us to be destroyed. Instead, He sacrificed His only Son to make sure that we would be saved. We are not mere humans to our Lord. We are His chosen people.

Each one of us has special value to God that made us worth saving, worth Jesus' sacrifice. But, unlike the "things" we would label as our special possessions, we can do much more than trigger memories. We can declare our Lord's praises. We can, and we should!

God, thank You for making me Your special possession. May I always sing Your praises, as You have called me to. Amen.

August 8

But from everlasting to everlasting the Lord's love is with those who fear Him, and His righteousness with their children's children— with those who keep His covenant and remember to obey His precepts.

—Psalm 103:17–18

Many things fail to pass from one generation to the next. For example, I had a great-aunt who rendered her own lard long after she'd moved off the farm. I haven't the foggiest idea how one even does that!

But God's love is something that does indeed get passed on down the generations. God loves those who fear and obey Him. Parents are the first "faith instructors" their children have. And by their example, their children learn God's way and then teach their own children.

My parents were very faithful about taking my sister and me to church. My sister is very faithful about taking her own boys to church. One Sunday, my older nephew was disappointed that he wasn't going to be able to go to church because his younger brother had gotten sick. I just know that he will be faithful in taking his children to church also.

Lord, thank You for the faith that is passed from one generation to the next and for Your love, which will flow to all generations. Amen.

August 9

He has saved us and called us to a holy life—not because of anything we have done but because of His own purpose and grace. This grace was given us in Christ Jesus before the beginning of time.

—2 Timothy 1:9

A very common struggle people have is to figure out their purpose in life. Some people hope to find their purpose in their job. Others seek to find their purpose in the relationships they have.

Really, though, if we want to learn our purpose in life, we need to stop looking around. We need to look up. Our life's purpose is not determined by how we earn money or who we associate ourselves with. Our purpose comes from God.

God has had a purpose for each of us long before we were born, long before our ancestors were born. Through Christ we have been brought close to God, so we are able to find our purpose in Him.

As part of an exercise my boss had us employees do once, I thought about my purpose. I have it posted at my desk, where I can see it every day I come to the office. It is truly a God-driven purpose, though, as I acknowledge that I am called to be the light of the world.

God, show me what Your purpose for my life is and grant me the strength to live according to that purpose. Amen.

August 10

I am the true vine, and My Father is the gardener.
—John 15:1

The Gospel of John is my favorite Gospel. The writer of John also includes some wonderful imagery that Jesus used to explain things. Being the visual person that I am, I learn a lot with imagery.

Now, I did not grow up around vineyards, but I do know a thing or two about vines just from the plants that were around on my parents' acreage. One such vine was the morning glory. The vines were all over our pasture fences. The flowers blossomed beautifully while on the vine but withered almost immediately upon being picked.

A person really must know what they are doing if they are going to use morning glories for any decorations. They must understand the plant and what it needs in order for the blossoms to flourish.

God is our gardener. He knows exactly what we need in order to thrive and flourish. But, as Jesus says a few verses later, one thing that we need is connection to the main vine—to Jesus. Under God's gentle care, we also blossom with a beauty that can only come from our attachment to the True Vine.

Divine Gardener, care for me as only You can. Bring my budding flower to full bloom so that I may show Your glory to the world. Amen.

August 11

"For the eyes of the Lord are on the righteous and His ears are attentive to their prayer, but the face of the Lord is against those who do evil." Who is going to harm you if you are eager to do good?

—1 Peter 3:12-13

I must begin by pointing out what Peter is *not* saying in this passage. Peter is not saying that we should totally disregard our safety when we are on a mission to help others. There are people in the world who take advantage of those who just want to help.

Notice the Scripture that Peter quoted. He points out that the Lord is attentive to the righteous and is against evildoers. That means that the Lord does not approve of those who seek to harm the world's helpers.

We still need to exercise caution when we render aid to someone. We still need to be aware of those who would want to harm us. But God is on our side. No matter what happens to us, the Lord has His eye on us. He will hear us when we cry to Him. And should anyone seek to harm us while we are on a mission of good, the Lord will look out for us and will avenge us.

Lord, You call me to do good in the world, even though there are those who would seek to harm me. Protect me from those evildoers and teach me to trust in You for any evil that is done against me. Amen.

August 12

The Lord said, "If as one people speaking the same language they have begun to do this, then nothing they plan to do will be impossible for them. Come, let us go down and confuse their language so they will not understand each other."
—Genesis 11:6-7

At first glance, one might think that God introduced different languages because He wanted to punish the people or somehow restrict them. But I have since come to question if this was a punishment at all. By introducing new languages, God scattered the people, and maybe that was for the best.

Maybe the Lord scattered the people not because they were doing great things together but because they could do greater things once divided. Consider the great things that have come from competitions between nations. For example, Russia and the United States had a competition regarding space travel. We put humans on the moon because of this competition. That's much greater than building a tower.

Sometimes it's good to work together. Sometimes it's better to work apart from each other. Don't fear being scattered. Greater things lie ahead.

Lord, show me when it is time to separate from the crowd to achieve the greater things You have set before me. Amen.

August 13

Impress them on your children. Talk about them
when you sit at home and when you walk along
the road, when you lie down and when you
get up.

—Deuteronomy 6:7

Moses is telling the people how they should receive God's
commandments. They are so important that God's people should
be constantly talking about them. Is it really necessary for us
to constantly talk about God's commandments? Well, if you're
anything like me, you remember things better the more often
you say them aloud.

There was one time when I walked from my car all the way
inside constantly repeating out loud the size of my car's tires.
I was about to start tire shopping, so I needed to know what
size to look for. And I had nothing on which I could write that
information. As a result of that verbal repetition, it took a week
or more of not thinking about tires for me to finally forget my
car's tire size.

We don't want to forget God's commandments. Ever. Thus,
we should always keep them in our hearts and minds and on
our lips. Let's talk about God's commandments so that we keep
His commandments.

God, imprint Your commandments on my heart. May I keep
talking about them so that I never forget them. Amen.

August 14

"Am I only a God nearby," declares the Lord,
"and not a God far away?"

—Jeremiah 23:23

This is the time of year that many teenagers are preparing to head off to college. Some of those students are attending a school that is not in their hometown. That means they will be away from the watchful eye of their parents. That thought can be as terrifying, if not more so, for the parents.

But God is not found in just one area. When I headed off to college for the first time, I was more than 160 miles away from my parents and my home congregation. Now I live more than 250 miles away from where I grew up. Miles cannot separate us from God. We are never away from His watchful eye. Perhaps a more comforting thought is that we are never away from God's loving embrace.

So whether you are sending a child off for a new adventure or are starting out on an adventure of your own, remember that God Himself declared that He is both nearby and far away. God will go with those who are traveling. God will also remain with those who stay behind.

Thank You, dear God, for being near to me regardless of where I am. It is a great comfort knowing that my loved ones and I are always in Your sight. Amen.

August 15

He is before all things, and in Him all things hold together.

—Colossians 1:17

Have you ever felt like your world was falling apart around you? That tends to be a fairly common description people have for their lives when they hit a rough patch. They might be facing health issues. They may be coping with grief. They might be facing the uncertainty of unemployment. They might be going through the heartache of divorce.

When things feel like they are falling apart around us, our tendency is to try to hold them together. But that is something that we simply cannot do. It's like trying to hold an ice sculpture together as it melts. There is nothing we can do to stop it.

However, that's not to say that if we let go, things will completely fall to pieces. When we step back, God can step in, and God is perfectly capable of holding the entire world together. When God does let things come apart, it's only because He needs the pieces to build a bigger and better masterpiece. We just need to trust God's judgment.

God, I commend my life and my world into Your hands. Hold things together according to Your will. And when You need the pieces for a better plan, help me to let go and to trust You. Amen.

August 16

Shout for joy to God, all the earth! Sing the glory of His name; make His praise glorious.
—Psalm 66:1-2

One evening as I was driving home, I had a contemporary gospel CD playing in my car. I'll sing along with most of the songs on this album, but this particular evening, as I was singing along with "Shout to the Lord," I really started thinking about the lyrics. While I continued to sing along, I reflected on the words that were coming out of my mouth.

The verse talks about the wondrous things that God has done. In the Lord, we have a Savior, a refuge, a protector, a comforter. And then the chorus breaks into praise for those reasons.

There are many reactions a person can have when they finally reach a safe place. One reaction is to celebrate the arrival and all that it means. And that's what "Shout to the Lord" reminded me of on that drive. We should shout for joy and celebrate all that the Lord has done.

When we do shout out to the Lord, our voices join in with all of creation. All of the earth finds refuge and strength in the Lord. Thus, all of the earth praises God.

Lord, let me not hold back my shouts of joy for all that You have done. May my voice blend in with the rest of creation, lifting up Your praise. Amen.

August 17

Therefore go and make disciples of all nations, baptizing them in the name of the Father and of the Son and of the Holy Spirit.

—Matthew 28:19

One of my college roommates, a Christian, once commented to me that she couldn't understand how God could be both Father and Son. I had never really thought about it until then, but that it a difficult concept to grasp. Then you throw the Holy Spirit in there, and you've got a concept that will even baffle biblical scholars.

I cannot explain the Holy Trinity any better than a scholar can, but after that conversation with that college roommate, I decided that I needed to find an analogy to simplify things a little. What I finally came up with does not explain how the Holy Trinity works, but rather the roles I see each play in my life. Thus was born my "apple analogy."

God the Father creates life, represented by the apple's core—where the seeds are. God the Son satisfies our hunger and gives us new life, represented by the "meat" of the apple. God the Holy Spirit gives us the gifts that makes us each unique, represented by the apple peel. It's definitely not the perfect analogy, but it helps me.

Holy Trinity, You are a mystery, but I still thank and praise You for all that You do in my life. Amen.

August 18

Humble yourselves, therefore, under God's mighty hand, that He may lift you up in due time.

—1 Peter 5:6

In this verse, Peter reminds his readers about something that Jesus Himself had said. Recall how Jesus talked about where to sit at a dinner banquet. It is better to sit down at the farthest end of the table and have the host move us up to a seat of honor than to seat ourselves in a place of honor and have the host ask us to move because someone more important had arrived. Peter echoes this lesson.

Think for a moment about humility. If we are already humble, we are better able to cope when things work against us. However, when we are cocky and arrogant, we are humiliated when something goes wrong.

In fact, if we think too highly of ourselves, we may even go so far as to blame someone else our mistakes. For example, I knew a seasoned 4-Her who broke a "cardinal rule" of 4-H dog showmanship and stepped between her dog and the judge. When she lost the show, she blamed the judge for being soft-spoken. That experienced 4-Her had a harsh lesson in humility as she ended up losing to a younger, less experienced 4-Her. Humble yourself, or God will humble you.

Lord, keep me humble so that, when the time is right, You alone may raise me to glory in You. Amen.

August 19

Jesus answered him, "Truly I tell you, today you
will be with Me in paradise."

—Luke 23:43

I was heartbroken when I was forced to make the decision
to have my 14-year-old Schipperke euthanized. When I settled
on a date, I resolved to make his last day one to be remembered.
He was going to leave this world feeling loved.

I took that day off from work, so that I could spend the
entire day with him. We stopped at our groomer, so she could
say goodbye to him. We had a picnic lunch at the dog park,
where I shared my food with him. I didn't know any other way
to make his last meal more special than letting him have "people
food." For a better part of the day, it was just this old dog and
me, sharing our company and our love until the time came for
his last vet appointment late that afternoon.

Jesus and the criminal were dying on the cross when
Jesus made this assurance. A public execution may not seem
like "paradise." But, when it comes right down to it, paradise
is really a place where we feel loved and at peace. Therefore,
spending time with loved ones and with Jesus is indeed paradise,
regardless of our actual location.

Thank You, Jesus, for letting me be in paradise with You, no
matter where I am. Amen.

August 20

What I mean is this: One of you says, "I follow Paul"; another, "I follow Apollos"; another, "I follow Cephas"; still another, "I follow Christ."

—1 Corinthians 1:12

A friend of mine got me started attending a midweek prayer service. The first two times I went, this friend was also there. I sat with him both times because this was an Episcopal church and I am a Lutheran. I could follow my friend's lead with the traditions that I was unfamiliar with.

The third time I went was the first of many weeks that this friend was unable to attend due to his work schedule. I was very apprehensive about attending this prayer service without this friend. Somehow I felt that I would only be welcomed if I was associated with someone who was a regular at that service.

However, that first time I was "on my own" at that service, both the priest and one of the other members were very encouraging about my attending without having someone's lead to follow. Essentially, they echoed what the apostle Paul was saying in today's verse. Lutheran, Episcopal, Methodist, Baptist, Catholic—it doesn't matter. We all belong to Christ.

Lord Christ, I am Yours. Please do not let me become so focused on my religious denomination that I fail to remember that we all belong to You. Amen.

August 21

Before a downfall the heart is haughty, but humility comes before honor.

—Proverbs 18:12

When I was fourteen years old and just learning how to drive, I had the tendency to get a little cocky. Many times I would become overconfident in my driving ability. Mom never liked riding with me when I got like that and for good reason. When I had that false confidence, I would weave or would terribly fluctuate in speed. My thinking more of my driving skill than what was proper always caused me to drive below my actual skill level, humiliating me in front of my mother.

To be haughty is to be arrogant. That superiority complex will always be our downfall. It might not come as quickly as did my downfalls after my cockiness concerning my driving ability. But the time will come when our arrogance catches up with us. The fall will be hard, and it will be humiliating.

But when it does come, we should embrace the humility that results from our downfall. As this verse says, humility comes before honor. We need to learn our lessons in humility, so that we may experience honor later.

God, when my heart is haughty, teach me humility. Help me to learn my lesson so that I may receive the honor that only comes to those who are truly humble. Amen.

August 22

A perverse person stirs up conflict, and a gossip separates close friends.

—Proverbs 16:28

I am fortunate to work in a small office. Including my boss, there are five of us who work together. As a result, there is not much, if any, gossiping in my workplace.

However, I know that many of my massage clients are not so lucky. Clients often use their massage time to vent about the stresses that have caused the tight muscles I am massaging. Too often their stresses come from having that one coworker who thrives on conflict and relishes in spreading gossip throughout the workplace.

There is no easy solution to handling such people, and, unfortunately, this Bible verse does not offer much help. However, I would not say that this verse offers no help because it actually does. Even if the person thriving on conflict does not realize the misery they are causing, the rest of us can take heart in the fact that the Bible even refers to such individuals as "perverse." Then we can pray for the perversion and stop ourselves from joining in the gossiping.

Lord, grant me the strength to cope with those around me who thrive on conflict. Keep me from participating in gossip, so that I may not add to any discord. Amen.

August 23

Do not let your hearts be troubled. You believe
in God; believe also in Me.

—John 14:1

We live in troubling times. It doesn't help that social media
spreads bad news like a wildfire. And the publicity each disaster
receives can inspire copycats.

Some people, when faced with bad news, will react in fear.
For example, if they know someone who is in the same city
where a shooting occurred, they will fear that their loved one
was shot and will obsessively worry until they finally hear from
that loved one, regardless of how big the city is or where the
shooting took place. And some people will become anxious at
the sight of protestors, out of fear that their protesting will turn
into rioting.

However, Jesus calls us to a different response to bad news.
He calls us away from worry and toward faith. Rather than
giving into our fears, we need to turn back to God and trust that
He will take care of us as He always has. Remember that Jesus
calms storms. He calmed a storm on the sea, and He can calm
the storms in our life. All we have to is believe in Him.

Jesus, the storms of this world rage all around me. I confess that
sometimes I become afraid. When that happens, please calm my
fears and help me to trust in You. Amen.

August 24

But Jonah ran away from the Lord and headed for Tarshish. He went down to Joppa, where he found a ship bound for that port. After paying the fare, he went aboard and sailed for Tarshish to flee from the Lord.

—Jonah 1:3

Have you ever found yourself being called to something you just do not want to face? Maybe it was a place you had to go, a person you had to interact with, or a situation you did not want to be in.

I have a few massage clients whom I dread seeing on my schedule. I just do not want to enter my massage room after those people have gotten on my table. However, there is nothing I can do because they have never done anything inappropriate. Whenever one of those difficult clients gets a massage, I always have a choice. I can either run away from the appointment, even though I have no good reason to, or I can face my calling and give the best massage I am capable of.

We all have our "Ninevas"—the place or situation God calls us to, even though we do not want to go. Jonah ran away from his calling. We, too, can run away from our calling. Or rather, we can try to run away. God will find us. It's in our best interest to obey God's calling right from the start.

God, teach me to obey Your calling, even when I would rather run away. Amen.

August 25

Gracious words are a honeycomb, sweet to the
soul and healing to the bones.

—Proverbs 16:24

"Sticks and stones may break my bones, but words will
never hurt me." That saying was very popular in my elementary
school, used to teach us kids how to not let mean words get to us.
However, even then, we knew how hurtful cruel words could be.

When we look at the power of words, we usually tend to
look at how destructive they can be. However, today's verse
reminds us that there is another side to the power of words.
Cruel words do indeed hurt and destroy. However, kind words
heal and renew.

Do you realize that there are some people who go to work
day after day and never receive any compliments from their
boss? Have you ever stopped to think that there are people who,
due to the nature of their job, never hear a kind word spoken to
them all day? Can you imagine never hearing a gracious word
spoken to you?

Before you speak, remember the power words have. Do not
just refrain from speaking harshly, but make a point of speaking
kindly. Your words may be the only gracious words that person
will hear all day.

Lord, grant that I may speak the gracious words that bring
healing and comfort to the souls I encounter. Amen.

August 26

But the Lord is faithful, and He will strengthen
you and protect you from the evil one.
—2 Thessalonians 3:3

For many years, I had always assumed that "the evil one"
in this verse referred to Satan. But when I found myself in a
verbally abusive professional relationship, suddenly "the evil
one" no longer meant the devil to me. No matter what I said or
did around this person, I was always wrong. Even what this
person probably deemed as teasing was harsh, abrasive, and left
me feeling both small and angry.

Verbal abuse does not leave the same visible marks that
physical abuse does, but the damage is just as real. Whenever
I learned that this person had arrived to see me, I would feel
my blood pressure skyrocket and my stomach knot up. After
this person would leave, I would need time to cry out my anger,
frustration, and hurt. I was left so stressed that my chest would
even tighten.

However, the Lord gave me protection from this "evil one."
This protection came in the form of friends who gave me ways
to cope with the verbal assaults and who offered suggestions on
how to handle my abuser. I still occasionally had to face "the evil
one," but I had protection from the damage done.

Lord, thank You for protecting me from all the evil ones in my
life. Amen.

August 27

All Scripture is God-breathed and is useful for
teaching, rebuking, correcting and training in
righteousness, so that the servant of God may
be thoroughly equipped for every good work.
                                        —2 Timothy 3:16–17

Truth be told, the first time I ever started writing devotions,
I was apprehensive about sharing them with anyone. I've heard
too many people take the Bible out of context to make it back
their opinion, whether it really did or not. And since I would
take a verse or two at a time—which is also taking verses out of
context—I was afraid I would be twisting the words of the Bible
myself. However, there is a difference between using Bible verses
to back opinions and using Bible verses to write devotions. The
purpose of voicing opinions is self-righteousness. The purpose
of devotions is to promote spiritual growth.

More often that not, devotions and other spiritual writings
are as much "God-breathed" as the Bible itself is. In fact, I grow
as much as, if not more than, the person who reads my devotions.
Like my readers, I am a fellow servant of God, trying to become
equipped for every good work.

God, speak to me through Your Holy Scriptures that I may only
use Your Word to nurture spiritual growth, my own as well as
those around me. Amen.

August 28

Hear my voice when I call, Lord; be merciful to me and answer me.

—Psalm 27:7

One woman I know once told me that when she gets mad at her husband, she will not leave the room. Instead, she will remain in the same room as her husband but will simply stop speaking to him. She told me that he is really bothered by being so blatantly ignored.

However, if you stop to think about it, how many of us like being ignored when we speak? Ignoring can happen any time, not just during an argument. Have you ever been involved in a conversation where one person has been telling a story but never finishes because they realize nobody is listening?

It's even more frustrating to be ignored when you are calling for help. Best case scenario, you are left unable to do something that needs to be done. Worst case scenario, you are left in harm's way and are unable to save yourself.

The psalmist apparently needed God's help but was feeling ignored. Fortunately, for both the psalmist and for us, God is indeed merciful. He will answer us. He will not leave us hanging for long.

Lord, thank You for hearing and answering me. Teach me how to listen to others as You listen to me. Amen.

August 29

Then the Lord called Samuel. Samuel answered, "Here I am." And he read to Eli and said, "Here I am; you called me."

—1 Samuel 3:4-5

I have a close friend who has, on several occasions, expressed amazement at those of us who are intuitive. He even once made the comment that since I am highly intuitive, I am probably more open and receptive to God's speaking than is this friend. In fact, my friend even likened himself to Samuel, running to whoever is handy at the time when it is really God speaking to him.

Because I am intuitive, I do not know what it's like to not have this intuition. So I really cannot say whether I am more in tune to God's voice than those who, like this close friend, are not intuitive at all. What I do know, however, is that a lack of intuition will not stop God from speaking to us.

Yes, Samuel ran to Eli three times, mistaking the voice of God for Eli's voice. But God waited while Eli guided Samuel to tune in to the voice of God. Likewise, God will wait while our own mentors guide us to recognize and listen when God is speaking to us.

God, I may not always recognize You when You speak to me. Please be patient with me and give me people who can tune me in to Your voice. Amen.

August 30

The Lord watches over you—the Lord is your
shade at your right hand.

—Psalm 121:5

I was in high school before my parents put window air
conditioner units in our house. So for most of my childhood, I
had to find other ways to keep cool in those hot, humid southern
Iowa summers. One of the most common things I did to cool off
was to seek out some shade. In fact, a favorite place of mine was
a grove of trees out in the horse lot that my sister and I called
"Shady Glen."

Sometimes it still amazes me just how much cooler it can
be in the shade. The direct rays of the sun can be unbearable,
regardless of where you live. Shade is so beneficial that first aid
for someone suffering from heat exhaustion involves moving
that person into shade.

God is indeed as refreshing as shade on a hot summer's day.
When we grow weary from our life's struggles, God is ready and
waiting to give us the shade we need for our rest and recovery.
And if life's toils have pushed us beyond weariness to outright
exhaustion, the Lord is watching us and will bring us to the
spiritual shade we cannot reach on our own.

Thank You, Lord God, for constantly watching over me and for
providing the spiritual shade for my soul. Amen.

August 31

I have come to bring fire on the earth, and how
I wish it were already kindled!

—Luke 12:49

Fire fascinates me. It is so destructive, and yet such destruction is often necessary in nature. I once learned that there is a type of tree that will only release its seeds when exposed to the intense heat of a forest fire.

The fire burns off diseased plants and dead overgrowth that will choke out otherwise healthy vegetation, but some of that vegetation—such as trees—can be at risk of also being destroyed. So this particular tree releases seeds to grow in the aftermath of the fire. And when these seeds take root and grow saplings, they are thriving free of the dead brush that would choke them. A new forest is born.

Jesus came to kindle a fire of His own. His fire, which is still burning today, cleans our world and our lives of the overgrowth that would hinder our growth and the diseased aspects that harm us. Jesus was anxious to get that fire going. He wanted to see us thrive. All we need to do is welcome this fire into our lives and let it burn off all that is choking our souls.

Jesus, please come and kindle Your fire in my life. Rid me of the unnecessary and even dangerous elements that hinder my growth in You. Amen.

September 1

For the time will come when people will not put up with sound doctrine. Instead, to suit their own desires, they will gather around them a great number of teachers to say what their itching ears want to hear.

—2 Timothy 4:3

I have two horses, Bear and Red. It can be very interesting watching them out in the pasture. They will walk practically single-file, with Bear in front. However, Red is the one deciding where they go. She will tell Bear what direction he is to turn by moving to one side or the other. And if Red wants Bear to move faster, she crowds him, pushing him from behind.

We humans will do the same things. We will choose leaders but then will tell our leaders where to take us. In a democracy, that's fine. However, in the church, that can become a problem. Our desire to keep from offending someone or to maintain a certain comfort or appeal can result in our straying from biblical doctrine.

We need to be careful that the truths we follow are based on Scripture, not our human desires. We need to make sure that we become the people God wants us to be, rather than making God who we want Him to be. It will not always be comfortable, and we will offend some people.

God, grant me the wisdom to seek out leaders who will lead Your way and the strength to follow them. Amen.

September 2

Make every effort to live in peace with everyone
and to be holy; without holiness no one will see
the Lord.

—Hebrews 12:14

We all know that we're going to fall short. We simply cannot be righteous and holy enough to earn eternal life on our own. So why should we even bother?

Most of us have probably also met at least one person who makes it difficult for us to remain peaceful. This person knows how to push our buttons. At some point we just lose it with this person. Again, knowing that we will fail to live in peace with everyone, why should we bother?

In both cases, the goal is not actually to succeed. Instead, the goal is to keep trying. By continuously trying to live in peace, we do our part to cultivate a nurturing environment. As someone who is very sensitive to negativity and conflict, I cannot stress enough how wonderful it is to be surrounded by people attempting to get along.

Yes, there will be times when we fail to keep the peace. That's understandable. And thanks to Jesus, it's also forgivable. But for the sake of our own inner peace, as well as the comfort of those around us, let's keep trying to live peacefully.

Lord, help me to live in peace with everyone. I cannot be peaceful or holy on my own, so let me learn from You and to reflect Your holiness. Amen.

September 3

"But what about you?" He asked. "Who do you say I am?" Peter answered, "You are the Messiah."

—Mark 8:29

"Who do you say I am?" This was Jesus' second question. His first question was to ask who other people said He was. Then He asked that question of His disciples, and Peter is the one who answers.

If Jesus were to ask you this question, how would you answer? I'd be willing to bet that most of us would say something along the lines of "You are my Savior." But that would only be partially true. Yes, faith is personal. Yet at the same time, we must be wary of making faith *too* personal.

Jesus is indeed your Savior. Jesus is also my Savior. But Jesus is also the Savior of the coworker who took credit for your hard work. Jesus is also the Savior of the driver who cut you off in traffic. And Jesus is the Savior of the congregation member with whom you do not get along.

Peter got it exactly right in his confession of Jesus. Jesus is the Messiah. Jesus is the Savior. It's okay to confess Jesus as our personal Savior, as long as we remember that Jesus also saves those people we do not like.

Jesus, thank You for being my Savior. May I always be mindful of the fact that You came to save everyone, not just those people who are important to me. Amen.

September 4

In the morning, Lord, You hear my voice; in the morning I lay my requests before You and wait expectantly.

—Psalm 5:3

What things are part of your morning routine? As a massage therapist, I can say that something too many of us fail to include is stretching. After six to eight hours of minimal movement, we really need to prepare our muscles for the day. We need to stretch more than just our arms. We should stretch our leg muscles before expecting them to carry us all day. I have lost count of the number of people I have told to stretch their neck when they get up.

We should also stretch our souls in the morning. As children, many of us were taught to say our prayers before bed. And of course, we should. That is the perfect way to wind down and bring the day to a close. However, we can start our day out on a strong note by praying in the morning.

God hears all prayers, regardless of the time of day. So try adding two new things to your mornings—a stretching routine and a praying routine. You could even do both at the same time! You might be surprised at how much better your day goes when you begin by focusing on the Lord.

Lord, remind me to turn to You in morning prayer so that I may start my day attentive to You. Amen.

September 5

Why, my soul, are you downcast? Why so
disturbed within me? Put your hope in God, for
I will yet praise Him, my Savior and my God.
—Psalm 43:5

I am an empath. That means I do more than just see other people's emotions. I actually absorb them and feel them as though they were my own.

As much as I enjoy being an empath, it does present me with challenges. For example, I can absorb emotions even when I am not aware of the person. That results in strange mood swings for me! Many times I have asked myself, "What's wrong? Why do I feel this way?"

The trick to being an empath is being able to process and let go of the emotions that belong to someone else. One way that I have found I can do that is to turn back to God. I put my hope back in my Lord, trusting that He will right whatever wrong that has caused my soul to become troubled.

I do praise God. I praise Him for making me an empath, enabling me to truly feel what others feel. And I praise Him for always responding to those who need Him.

God, when my soul is troubled, let me turn to You with hope and praise and to trust in Your saving power. Amen.

September 6

And He took the bread, gave thanks and broke
it, and gave it to them, saying, "This is My body
given for you; do this in remembrance of Me."
—Luke 22:19

Memory is a strange thing. While we usually think about memories being stored in our brains, they can also be stored in the world around us. From objects we hold in our hands to activities we do, memories can come cascading back when we least expect them.

Jesus wanted us to remember His love and His sacrifice. By giving us the sacrament of Holy Communion, Jesus gave us two ways to help us remember. He gave us an object to hold in the bread that is broken. He also gave us an activity—the actual consumption of the bread.

We should never just go through the motions of Holy Communion. There is a reason why churches tend to wait until someone is old enough to understand before allowing that person to partake in the Lord's Supper. We need to remember, not just because Jesus wants us to but because we need the peace and grace that can come only from Jesus' self-sacrificing love.

Dearest Jesus, through Holy Communion, You provided powerful reminders of Your love and grace. May I ever be mindful of Your sacrifice, even between the times I partake in Your holy meal. Amen.

September 7

On hearing this, Jesus said, "It is not the healthy who need a doctor, but the sick."

—Matthew 9:12

Jesus was responding to criticisms that He was eating with tax collectors and sinners. The Pharisees believed that righteous people should not associate themselves with sinners. It was as though they thought sin transferred the same way that dirt does, by direct contact or close proximity.

However, that is not the case. Jesus points out that the reverse is actually true. Only by association would Jesus be able to make the sinner righteous. The only way for Jesus to help sinners then and us today is to be close.

If you go back a few verses, you will read that many tax collectors and sinners came to the house where Jesus was eating already. That is a very important point to note because more often than not, doctors do not seek out the sick. They wait and let the sick come to them. Jesus was also letting the sinners come to Him, and He would have accepted the Pharisees if only they had realized how much they, too, needed Jesus. Likewise, Jesus will wait for us to come to Him and then will make us clean by association once we admit we need Him.

Jesus, I am a sinner who needs Your grace. I come to You, knowing that You will make me clean. Amen.

September 8

Your word is a lamp for my feet, a light on my path.

—Psalm 119:105

Have you ever tried negotiating your way around in the dark? That can be very challenging. Even when you think you know your way around, obstacles can surprise you. I know my way around my acreage pretty well, but I will not do chores after dark without a flashlight. I need that light so I can avoid tripping on my dark-colored barn cats.

Life is that same way. We may get fairly comfortable and confident in our ability to negotiate life on our own. But we cannot always predict when something or someone will come along and cause us to stumble. We need the light that comes from God's Holy Word.

There are times when my barn cats are not around while I am choring. However, if I am doing chores after dark, I automatically grab a flashlight. I would rather have the flashlight and not encounter my cats than to be walking in the dark and have a dozen dark cats underfoot. We need to take that same approach with the Bible. We need to keep God's light with us, whether or not we think we need it.

God, Your Word is indeed a light on my path. Teach me to keep it handy, whether or not I feel I need it. Amen.

September 9

You will look for Me, but you will not find Me;
and where I am, you cannot come.

—John 7:34

Jesus was talking about His upcoming crucifixion and ascension into heaven. Yet His words took on a whole new meaning for me when I paused to consider some of my own habits. There are occasions when I completely withdraw from all of my friends.

I have many reasons for withdrawing, and most of them somehow involve my being an introvert. Most times I will not tell anyone when I am about to withdraw, so they will continue to email or text me. I will read their messages, but I will not respond to them. At that time, they can look for me, but I am in a place where they cannot join me. When I am ready, I make myself available to my friends again and catch up on the correspondence that came during my withdrawal.

Jesus has also essentially withdrawn from us. He is still with us in spirit and will continue to help us from a distance. But when the time is right, when He is ready, Jesus will return to us. Until then, as my friends must wait for me in my introversion, we must wait for Jesus in His divinity.

Lord Jesus, thank You for being present with me in spirit, and help me wait until that time when You will be with me physically. Amen.

September 10

Balaam answered the donkey, "You have made a fool of me! If only I had a sword in my hand, I would kill you right now." The donkey said to Balaam, "Am I not your own donkey, which you have always ridden, to this day? Have I been in the habit of doing this to you?" "No," he said.
—Numbers 22:29–30

This may be a relatively unknown Bible story, so allow me to summarize. Three times Balaam's donkey sees an angel blocking the path and will not move any closer. And three times Balaam, not seeing the angel, beats the donkey for punishment. Finally God allows the donkey to speak.

I love how the donkey responded to Balaam's death threat. "Do I usually do this?" the donkey asks. With that simple question, the donkey gets Balaam to stop and think, and then Balaam is also able to see the angel.

Too often we react out of anger when we think someone has wronged us. Yet, instead of reacting abruptly, we should really pause a moment and ask ourselves the donkey's question. "Do they usually do this?" If the answer is "no," then we need to wait for our eyes to be opened to the reason behind the other person's actions.

God, teach me to look at a person's reasons for their actions, rather than reacting to the actions themselves. Amen.

September 11

I rejoiced with those who said to me, "Let us go
to the house of the Lord."

—Psalm 122:1

A friend of mine once invited me to a midweek Eucharist
service at one of the local churches. I accepted, which began a
Thursday tradition for me. Now, very few things are able to keep
me away from that Eucharist service, and, even though it takes a
good portion of my Thursday lunch break, I am always excited
when it's time for me to leave for that service.

Going to church should be a time of rejoicing. The church
does not belong to humans. It is the Lord's house. Thus, the Lord
is our host when we come. And unlike many human hosts, God
does not care how we come.

The first time I went to that midweek service, I was broken.
I have also gone to that service stressed with a substantial to-do
list, excited for an upcoming trip, and troubled by a loved one's
failing health. No matter how I am feeling at the time, I go to
the Lord's house, and I kneel at the Lord's table.

Come, let's go to the house of the Lord! Let's come as we are,
sinful and broken. And let's rejoice as we come!

Lord, all are welcome in Your house. May I always rejoice as I
accept Your invitation! Amen.

September 12

In You, Lord my God, I put my trust.
—Psalm 25:1

Trust is a delicate thing. And if you've ever had anyone betray your trust, you know how difficult it can be to trust that person again. It's even worse for people who are slower to trust in general. A betrayal in trust can result in that person being that much slower to trust everyone, not just the one who betrayed their trust to begin with.

One thing is for sure, though. Regardless of how hesitant we are to trust, we are always safe to put our trust in the Lord. God understands us better than we understand ourselves. He knows in ways we cannot how important and valued trust is. Thus, God will never betray our trust.

That's not to say there won't be times when God surprises us. But if the Lord fails to respond in the way we want, it's not because the Lord is betraying our trust. He's only saying that He has another plan, a larger plan that we just cannot see. So, remember, if God appears to be betraying your trust, He's really not. In fact, He's simply asking you to continue to trust Him. What God has in store for you is worth the wait and the trust!

Lord, help me to always trust in You, even when You seem to be responding in ways that make no sense to me. Remind me that You have a plan for me. Amen.

September 13

Then he said, "Jesus, remember me when You come into Your kingdom."

—Luke 23:42

One day after school when I was a sophomore in high school, I walked down to the middle school where my mother taught. She was going to take me to the community college library so I could do some research for one of my classes. But when I got to the middle school that afternoon, Mom was nowhere to be found. She had forgotten of our plans. I had no way of getting to the community college library, but, more importantly, I had no way of getting home to my family's acreage four miles out of town!

It never feels good to be forgotten. Even when we're not left physically stranded, being forgotten can deal a harsh blow to our self-worth. We want to be remembered. We want to know we are important to others.

The criminal being crucified with Jesus didn't ask for rescue or for any special honor. He simply asked to be remembered. And I imagine the criminal's tone was more begging than demanding. "Please, Lord, don't forget me." And in the very next verse, Jesus assured the criminal that he would indeed be remembered.

Jesus, please remember me now and forever. Amen.

September 14

When Jesus saw him lying there and learned
that he had been in this condition for a long time,
He asked him, "Do you want to get well?"

—John 5:6

Jesus was at the pool called Bethesda, a place that was said
to have healing powers for those who got into the pool when
the water was stirred. There He met an invalid who had been
beside the pool for 38 years. This man remained beside the pool
because he had no way of getting into the pool.

One might wonder why Jesus asked this man if he wanted to
get well. After all, why would this man be lying beside a pool if
he didn't want to be healed? This seems like a strange question.

However, there is a deeper meaning to Jesus' question, and
anyone who works in a healthcare field can potentially experience
this. Some people want symptoms resolved but do not care
about the underlying condition. That can be very frustrating
for healthcare providers. So really, Jesus was making sure this
man wanted full healing, which included spiritual healing. Then
Jesus didn't just enable the invalid to walk. Jesus truly made
the man well.

Great Physician, make me well. Do not simply address my
symptoms, but heal me of my underlying condition—my sinful
nature. Amen.

September 15

For where you have envy and selfish ambition,
there you find disorder and every evil practice.
—James 3:16

How many of us will open a bag of carrots, expecting to find radishes inside? Or course not! Most bags of carrots are transparent, allowing us to see the contents. Then there is the fact that the bag is labeled as being a bag of carrots. But if you ever want a laugh, look to see if the bag has a list of ingredients. Most, if not all, will. And that list will plainly say "carrots." Something is seriously wrong if there are radishes inside our carrot bags!

The same is true, though, for our spiritual life. You will not find righteousness and holiness in a person actively indulging in evil practices. Those who are envious and selfish will have nothing but evil desires and actions. And those who have truly accepted Jesus as their Lord and Savior will still make mistakes but will not actively engage in sinful behavior.

Let this verse today serve as a guideline to help you distinguish what company you keep. Avoid those who would lead you astray. Stay with those who will help you continue to be the person you want to be.

God, open my eyes to the behaviors of those around me. Keep me close to those who will help me be the person I want to be—the person that *You* want me to be! Amen.

September 16

Heaven and earth will pass away, but My words
will never pass away.

—Matthew 24:35

Whenever I go back to my hometown, I always make a
point of spending some time in my home church's cemetery.
Sometimes, I'll even step inside that small country church.
Every time I go back, there are changes. There are a few more
dates engraved on headstones. There are a few different names
on the church mailboxes in the narthex. Even the Sunday school
rooms have changed since my youth.

One thing that has never changed, though, are the stained
glass windows in the sanctuary. Those windows tell the story
of the Bible, starting with creation and ending with Jesus'
crucifixion. I find so much comfort in my home church's
sanctuary, mainly because of those windows. They are as
steadfast as the Bible stories they represent.

No matter what happens, we have Jesus' promise that His
words will remain forever. Whether we go home to find fuller
cemeteries and emptier pews or we no longer have a home to
which to return, we will always have the Bible—God's Word—
as our anchor.

Thank You, dear Lord, for providing the comfort that can only
be found in Your Holy Word. Thank You for the Bible, my
anchor in a world of change. Amen.

September 17

The Lord brings death and makes alive; He brings down to the grave and raises up. The Lord sends poverty and wealth; He humbles and He exalts.

—1 Samuel 2:6–7

This theme shows up in several places throughout the Bible. I'm sure that most people read this as God doing two different acts to two different groups of people. For example, God humbles the proud. That's one act on one group of people. God exalts the lowly. That's a different act on a different group of people.

However, these different acts can be done on the same person. It's been said that military boot camp, especially the really tough training camp of the US Marine Corps, breaks a person down and then rebuilds them. By doing so, the military destroys the person the recruit had been before turning them into the better person the recruit will become in the military.

God can do that with us, too. He can bring us to the brink of death, either literally or figuratively, in order to make us better appreciate the life He gives. God can humble us in our pride to make us the humble person He would exalt. God only tears us down to make us better.

God, destroy the sinful person I am now. Tear me down so You can recreate me to be the better person You want me to be. Amen.

September 18

I seek You with all my heart; do not let me stray
from Your commands.

—Psalm 119:10

In this day and age, it seems like many people are afraid
to set boundaries. Whether it's with children, coworkers, or
fellow church members, we seem to be more afraid of hurting
someone's feelings than setting appropriate boundaries. But
boundaries are part of a healthy, loving relationship.

The psalmist knew that. In this one verse, he talks about
seeking the Lord and asks God for boundaries. "Do not let me
stray from Your commands." The psalmist wants God to set
boundaries for his own good.

How are the boundaries in your relationships? Do your
children know without a doubt what time they are to be in bed?
Do your coworkers know how many favors they can ask of you
before they are taking advantage of you? Do your fellow church
members know that you will only agree to serve on so many
committees?

Remember boundaries are healthy. Ask God to not only
hold you within His boundaries, but also ask Him to help you
set boundaries in your other relationships.

Lord, do not let me stray from the boundaries You have set, and
help me not to let others stray from the boundaries I set. Amen.

September 19

Be merciful to those who doubt.

—Jude 1:22

A young woman once confided in a friend when she was struggling with depression and frustration caused by her grim financial situation at the time. She began to doubt her self-worth and even mentioned suicide. Her friend's response was less than merciful as he told her that such thoughts were selfish and he wouldn't listen to it anymore.

While this verse actually refers to those who doubt God, there is a much larger application for this sound advice. Be merciful to those who doubt if others care about them. Be merciful to those who doubt their importance. Be merciful to those who doubt their self-worth.

Being merciful doesn't mean chastising them for their doubts. Nor does it mean making them feel bad for having doubts. It means guiding them to the truth that they are unable to see for themselves.

If someone confides doubts in you, don't question how they can have those doubts. Rather, assure them that their doubts are not their realities. If nothing else, remind them that God loves them and that you do, too.

God, You love me even when I have my doubts. Help me to share Your love with those who confide their doubts in me. Amen.

September 20

Do not let any unwholesome talk come out of your mouths, but only what is helpful for building others up according to their needs, that it may benefit those who listen.

—Ephesians 4:29

We all know them. We can all name at least one person who seems to thrive on spreading negativity. It's especially difficult to be around those people when the negativity they spread degrades someone else.

Have you ever found out that someone has spread a lie about you? Have you ever learned that someone shared something you said or did but put such a spin on their statement that it made you look either foolish or cruel? Isn't it painful how quickly the negativity spreads?

It is indeed unfortunate that bad news spreads so much faster than good news. And it is difficult to combat the spread of lies and gossip. However, there is one thing we all can do. We can refrain from sharing any gossip we hear.

All we must do is remember the pain we feel when someone slanders us or otherwise speaks ill of us. That will put us in the other's shoes and will stop us from adding to their hurt. Let's be positive and spread it around!

Guard my mouth, dear Lord, that only good and wholesome talk passes my lips. Let me build others up as I myself would like to be built up. Amen.

September 21

To do what is right and just is more acceptable
to the Lord than sacrifice.

—Proverbs 21:3

Sacrifices were a big part of Jewish life. Even though
sacrifices were clearly lined out in the law Moses presented to
the Israelites, the law that God commanded, sacrifices are not
really what God wants. Sacrifices were the way for humans to
atone for their sins. And while God does want sinners to repent,
He would much rather we humans not sin in the first place.

Sure, it can be discouraging to know that we will never live
the perfect life. That can lead us to wonder why we should even
try. But that is where the sacrifices of the Old Testament came
in to play. The goal for the Israelites was to do what was right.
Sacrifices were meant to be the backup plan.

For Christians, the sacrifices of Mosaic law are made
unnecessary by Jesus' ultimate sacrifice. However, our goal
is still the same. We should do what is right and just. That
is what God wants from us, which is why righteousness is
more acceptable to the Lord than is sacrifice. We should not
be discouraged in doing right because we do have that backup
plan. And God knows when we try. So let's just keep trying.

God, forgive me when I sin, and encourage me to keep trying to
do what is right in Your eyes. Amen.

September 22

Whoever dwells in the shelter of the Most High
will rest in the shadow of the Almighty.
—Psalm 91:1

When I was growing up, we didn't have air conditioning in my house. So I spent a lot of time outside in the shade. There I could enjoy the breeze without taking the beating of the hot sun. Growing up in the upper Midwest meant that the shade could be as much a refuge in September as it was in July! And my favorite tree to use for shade was the big maple tree right outside my bedroom window.

Anyone who has spent any time outside in the heat of summer, or even on a warmer fall day, knows how wonderful shade can be! The thing is, shade is simply a shadow. While tree shadows may be the first thing that come to mind when we think about shade, the fact is that buildings can also provide shade with their shadows. And when a person is hot and miserable, the source of the shade isn't important.

Life can get really uncomfortable for us, too. Fortunately, we have shade for our weary souls. All we need to do is turn to God and rest in His holy shadow. There we will find comfort and rest.

Lord, when I am weary and in need of rest, draw me once again to Your shadow. Let me find my comfort when I am sheltered in You. Amen.

September 23

Jesus answered, "It is written: 'Man shall not live on bread alone, but on every word that comes from the mouth of God.'"

—Matthew 4:4

According to science, the human body can go three weeks without food but only three days without water. Therefore, according to science, Bob should not have lived as long as he did. His disease was taking its toll on his body, and he went for more than a week without eating or drinking anything before his body finally failed entirely.

Bob had been a pastor and was constantly looking for new ways to share the gospel of Christ. Bob's desire to share the Good News didn't stop when he retired. Bob was faithful right up to his death, so it seems only fitting that God gave Bob yet one more teaching method in his final week.

"Man shall not live on bread alone, but on every word that comes from the mouth of God." That was Jesus' answer to the devil's temptation, and it was Bob's answer on how to find yet another way to teach others about God.

Cherish God's Word. Not only can it save you from temptation, but it can also give you life.

God, Your words are life-giving nourishment. Teach me to treasure every word You speak. Amen.

September 24

Remain in Me, as I also remain in you. No branch can bear fruit by itself; it must remain in the vine. Neither can you bear fruit unless you remain in Me.

—John 15:4

Some translations of this Bible verse use the word *abide*, rather than *remain*. Personally, I do prefer this translation. *Abide* can mean "tolerate," and that definition brings to mind an image that just doesn't seem right when talking about relationships, especially not a relationship with Christ!

When I was a freshman in high school, one of my teachers asked me to befriend a girl who had just moved to the school district shortly before school started. I obliged my teacher, and for the rest of high school, I had a friend who I, at best, tolerated. When high school ended, so did our friendship.

But now, I am blessed to have two best friends. No matter what happens, no matter where our lives take us, these friends and I are always there for each other. Our friendships remain strong.

That is the kind of relationship Christ wants us to have with Him. He doesn't want us to merely tolerate Him. He wants our relationship to last with Him forever. He wants us to remain with Him.

Christ, help me to remain in a relationship with You that will last forever. Amen.

September 25

In peace I will lie down and sleep, for You alone,
Lord, make me dwell in safety.

—Psalm 4:8

I grew up on an acreage with a lot of animals. Consequently, my family and I did not take many vacations. In fact, most of the camping I did as a child was with my sister in our tent pitched somewhere in our yard.

If I was ever apprehensive about sleeping outside, it was not a fear that lasted long. Our faithful farm dog would always stay with my sister and me. All through the night, he would lie on the door to the tent—not beside it, but actually on it. Nobody was getting in or out of that tent without that dog knowing! He would only leave if he felt there was a threat he must face (like my dad coming home from his nightshift at work and breaking his usual routine) or once the sun came up. My sister and I could always sleep in peace, knowing that our farm dog was guarding us.

The safety our farm dog provided was nothing compared to the safety provided by the Lord. While our dog obviously had to sleep at some point, the Lord never slumbers. Thus, we can indeed lie down in peace to sleep. We are always safe under the Lord's watchful eye.

Thank You, Lord, for providing me the safety in which I sleep at night and spend my waking hours. Amen.

September 26

Jesus was in the stern, sleeping on a cushion. The disciples woke Him and said to Him, "Teacher, don't you care if we drown?"

—Mark 4:38

My house dog notices everything! And he will "sound the alarm" if he thinks there is something amiss. Sometimes my dog will think he sees something, start barking up a storm, and then come running to me. He'll then stare at me as though he were trying to say, "Well? What are you going to do about this?"

While I will make jokes with my family about the things my dog chooses to bring to my attention, there is a lesson to be learned here. More often than not, the thing that is upsetting my dog is actually nothing at all. Then I must quiet him and assure him that the rabbit in the yard is not going to kill us or that my car is fine in the driveway, rather than in the garage.

But, like the disciples, we tend to run to God anxiously, insisting that we are going to die. We need to remember that once God assesses our situation, we can to trust His judgment. Yes, we may be facing a terrible storm, but if God says we'll come through it just fine, then that is what will happen.

God, help me to trust Your judgment on the storms I face in my life. Please be patient with me when You must assure me many times that I will be okay. Amen.

September 27

Terrified at her torment, they will stand far off and cry: "Woe! Woe to you, great city, you mighty city of Babylon! In one hour your doom as come!"

—Revelation 18:10

One of my favorite books is *Alas, Babylon* by Pat Frank. In that book, the phrase "alas, Babylon" is the code a man in the military uses to warn his brother that nuclear war is imminent. Most of the book tells the story about how the brother, along with the military man's family and an entire town survive after the U.S. is hit with atomic bombs.

The book *Alas, Babylon* calls us to realize that our actions have consequences. Some of those consequences are bigger than we can even imagine. And the reference the book makes to Revelation only underscores our need to look to the future.

Our world is corrupt, and there will come a day when God wipes the slate of our sinful nature. Only those who turn to God will be spared from the torment of the end times. But do we really want to wait that long? Should we not all, here and now, fight the evil and corruption of our world? We can't stop God's final judgment, but we certainly don't need to contribute to it!

Lord God, show me the error of my ways! Let me see how my actions impact the world around me. Amen.

September 28

I will give thanks to You, Lord, with all my heart; I will tell of all Your wonderful deeds.
—Psalm 9:1

Think about a time you found yourself in a nasty predicament and someone came to your aid. Maybe you were stuck on the side of a highway with a flat tire and no jack. Or maybe the situation was much worse, like having an unexpected expense you couldn't handle.

How did you feel when that person brought you out of what seemed like a hopeless situation? My guess is that you couldn't thank that person enough for what they did for you. I would also be willing to bet that whenever the opportunity arose, you would tell others about the wonderful thing that person did for you.

If we are that thankful and that vocal about the people in our lives who have helped us, how much more thankful and vocal should we be about what the Lord has done for us? Remember that it was the Lord who caused that complete stranger to stop and help you change your car tire. Remember it was the Lord who called that friend to bail you out of your financial dilemma. The Lord is always behind you and behind those who help you.

Lord, thank You for the help You give me through others. May I never cease telling others about Your faithfulness! Amen.

September 29

When Jesus had finished saying these things, the
crowds were amazed at His teaching, because
He taught as one who had authority, and not as
their teachers of the law.

—Matthew 7:28–29

One of the most difficult things I ever did was take a college
class that used a textbook written by the class's instructor. That
professor came at that class with an approach unlike any other!
He was truly an expert in his field, which intimidated many of
us students.

I would imagine that the crowds who heard Jesus' teachings
often felt that same intimidation. Jesus was no ordinary teacher
of the law. Jesus had more authority than those other teachers.
Jesus was the expert on holy and righteous living.

Because I was so intimidated by this one college professor, I
never sought him out during his office hours. If I had a question
about an assignment or about a concept, I went to classmates for
help. I avoided the person who could help me the most.

Yet, we need not be intimidated by Jesus' authority or
expertise. Jesus is okay with our turning to Him for help; He
even encourages it. Jesus is so determined to help us succeed
that He died for us.

Jesus, may I always turn to You and seek Your help for living
an upright, righteous life. Amen.

September 30

Elijah went before the people and said, "How long will you waver between two opinions? If the Lord is God, follow Him; but if Baal is God, follow him." But the people said nothing.

—1 Kings 18:21

"Would you make up your mind?!" It can be very frustrating to be around someone who is sitting on that proverbial fence. How you interact with that person may depend on where they choose to take a stand. But what happens when that person doesn't take a stand at all?

I can just hear that same frustration in what Elijah said to the people in today's verse. Elijah knew who the true God was, but the Israelites seemed to be stuck on the fence. One day they might be following the Lord. The next day they were following Baal. Elijah could not move forward with his role as prophet until he knew where the Israelites stood. But even the people didn't seem to know where they stood!

Do you know where you stand? It may take a lot of time and prayer to reach a decision on a moral or ethical issue, but do you at least know who the ruler of your life is? If not, make up your mind. And, like Elijah, I pray you choose the Lord.

Lord, pull me from the fence to follow You alone. Then, help me to lead others back to You as well. Amen.

October 1

As they talked and discussed these things with each other, Jesus Himself came up and walked along with them; but they were kept from recognizing Him.

—Luke 24:15–16

I remember the last night of my last county fair as a 4-H exhibitor. I'd been showing horses the previous two days and had shown my dog that morning. I was sitting in the horse barn, waiting for 10:00 p.m. to come so I could finally take my horses home. Suddenly, the boss from my summer job came walking down the aisle. But between the exhaustion from showing at the fair and the knowledge that my boss was supposed to be off somewhere racing his horses that day, I did not recognize him immediately.

These two disciples on their way to Emmaus were grief-stricken. They were probably also really tired. They, too, had experienced a few late nights and early mornings over the preceding days. Plus, Jesus had died. He wasn't supposed to be walking down the road with them. Yet there He was.

Jesus was patient with the disciples when they didn't recognize Him. In fact, Jesus could use that to His advantage. Thankfully, Jesus has that same patience with us when we fail to recognize Him in our lives.

Jesus, forgive me when I fail to recognize You in my life. Patiently use my blindness to whatever advantage You see fit. Amen.

October 2

Even fools are thought wise if they keep silent,
and discerning if they hold their tongues.
—Proverbs 17:28

I'm sure we all know at least one person who never seems to stop talking—a person who apparently talks just to hear their own voice. Many times, such people end up saying things that sound foolish to the rest of us. We had no idea their brain worked that way until they spoke.

Unfortunately, there have been more times than I'd care to admit when I'm the person who should not have said something. More than once, the thought in my head did not sound so great once it came out of my mouth. Then I must try to not dig myself into a deeper hole than I am already in!

That's not to say that we shouldn't speak. There can be great wisdom shared through spoken words. What's important, though, is to make sure that the words we are about to say are worth saying. We shouldn't speak just to fill silence. Let's just make sure that the words we say are truly worth being said. Otherwise, we can prevent ourselves from looking foolish by holding our tongue.

Lord, give me the wisdom to discern between what I should say and what I should leave unsaid. Amen.

October 3

But the Lord said to me, "Do not say, 'I am too young.' You must go to everyone I send you to and say whatever I command you."

—Jeremiah 1:7

One day, I emailed a friend to check up on him after we had both endured a mutual friend's funeral. My friend never came right out and said how he was doing. Instead, he talked about how friends grieve differently than family but still grieve deeply. I sensed that he was not just explaining why he had expressed concern for me at the funeral but that he was also quietly admitting his own level of grief. I gave a short response, simply reminding him that our mutual friend had loved him. When my friend replied to that email, I realized how I had once again mimicked the prophets of old.

I could not use the excuse that I am too young to be God's prophet. I'm not old, by any means, but I could have used my grief as an excuse. I could have told God, "I can't do this. I hurt too much." But God would not have accepted my excuse any more than He accepted Jeremiah's excuse.

God doesn't accept excuses. He has jobs for each of us. We have work to do, and God wants us to do it.

God, grant me the strength to go where You send me and to say what You command of me, even when I try to make excuses. Amen.

October 4

The trumpeters and musicians joined in unison to give praise and thanks to the Lord. Accompanied by trumpets, cymbals and other instruments, the singers raised their voices in praise to the Lord and sang: "He is good; His love endures forever." Then the temple of the Lord was filled with the cloud.

—2 Chronicles 5:13

It's that time of year again. It's marching band season! That means a lot of early morning band rehearsals, musicians frantically trying to keep instruments from freezing during football games, and long bus rides to various band competitions.

For those who were never in band, marching band season may sound miserable. But for those of us who proudly bear the title "band geek," marching band was always a season to enjoy. There was a joy that could only come through the harmony of the various instruments blending their voices together in the great outdoors.

Although most band members probably don't think about it much, each instrument does indeed give praise to the Lord. Whether you are watching the band or marching in it, remember that you are part of praise and thanksgiving being raised to the Lord!

Lord, thank You for the gift of music. May my praise for You always ring out as though it was coming from the biggest marching band imaginable! Amen.

October 5

But now, this is what the Lord says—He who created you, Jacob, He who formed you, Israel; "Do not fear, for I have redeemed you; I have summoned you by name; you are Mine."

—Isaiah 43:1

My older sister and I are three years apart in age. Even though it was just the two of us and even though we never looked a lot alike, our poor parents were always calling us by each other's names. They would usually, if not always, catch their mistake. But they did have a terrible time keeping our names straight.

That's one reason why I like this verse so much. Being the younger sister, I was frequently being called by my sister's name, and not just by my parents. I've been called by my sister's name so much that even now I will answer to it without hesitation. After so many years of being called by my sister's name, the thought of God calling me by my name makes me feel special.

We all belong to God, so God has many names to know. Yet God summons each one of us by our own name. God does not make mistakes. When He calls a name, that is the person He is calling. And when God wants to call someone, He never calls out a sibling's name first by accident.

God, when You call my name, I know that You are truly calling me. May I always answer when You summon me, assured that You really do mean me. Amen.

October 6

I baptize you with water for repentance. But after me comes one who is more powerful than I, whose sandals I am not worthy to carry. He will baptize you with the Holy Spirit and fire.
—Matthew 3:11

Look at any sports team roster, and it is almost immediately obvious who the best players are. All you have to do is read the starters for each position. After all, no coach is going to put lesser players in the game first. Always start with the best. Save the inferior players for substitutions due to injuries. Don't settle for less than the best unless you have to.

However, that's not the way God works. John the Baptist made that quite clear. John was "in the game," so to speak, well before Jesus arrived on the scene. John knew he wasn't the greatest, but that didn't stop him from playing his part.

We may not feel that we are the best either. We may think we should sit out until we are the last option. Still, God is sending us into the world, assigning us a position to play in this game of life. Let's trust our "Coach." He's got Christ, His "star player," ready to bail us out.

God, grant me the courage to go out into the world to do what You ask of me, even though I know I am not the greatest. Amen.

October 7

Didn't it belong to you before it was sold? And after it was sold, wasn't the money at your disposal? What made you think of doing such a thing? You have not lied just to human beings but to God.

—Acts 5:4

Ananias and his wife had sold a piece of their land. They gave part of the money to the apostles and kept the rest for themselves. But they both lied to Peter and claimed they had given all of the money to the apostles. Peter pointed out that Ananias could have openly kept back some of the money, since it had been his land. Holding back wasn't really the sin. Rather, the lie was.

Take a look at your own life. Specifically look at your heart. How much of your heart have you given to God? Be honest. If you are holding back but refuse to admit that, there is nothing God can do for you. You are lying to yourself, and you are lying to God. And that lie will have the same deadly consequence it had for Ananias and Sapphira.

However, if you admit that you are holding back some, God can work with you. He can help you reach the point of completely giving yourself to Him. In your confession, you will find life.

Forgive me, God, when I do not give You my whole heart. Help me to recognize when I hold back and to accept Your help to be open to You and with You. Amen.

October 8

There are different kinds of gifts, but the same
Spirit distributes them. There are different
kinds of service, but the same Lord. There are
different kinds of working, but in all of them and
in everyone it is the same God at work.
—1 Corinthians 12:4–6

I am one of two massage therapists at the chiropractic
clinic where I work. There have always been some clients who
will switch back and forth between us therapists. When I first
started working at that clinic, I felt that I had to match the
pressure, if not the style, of the other therapist when massaging
the shared clients.

Eventually I stopped doing that. I realized that it was not
only okay for me to be different, but it was actually good for
me to be different. By having differing styles, we could address
more issues on the same client. All the client had to do was
decide which skill set they needed most at that time.

God has given us all different gifts. He has called us into
different forms of service and has given us different work to
do. He has done so because we are able to accomplish more by
being unique. God hasn't just made us different. He has made
us special!

Dear God, You have called me into a role made especially for
me. Remind me that You made me unique for a reason, and help
me embrace the differences You created in me. Amen.

October 9

You have taken from me friend and neighbor—
darkness is my closest friend.

—Psalm 88:18

This is a very interesting psalm. While there are many psalms that lament, Psalm 88 is the only lament that does not turn itself around. Today we read the last verse of this lament. There is no talk of hope or praise.

We don't usually like stories that leave us hanging. Even stories with sad endings still resolve issues, just not necessarily with the closure we'd like. The psalms tell stories too, and the writer of this psalm offers no closure.

However, it's good that there is this one lament that does not resolve its pain. Often in our own lives, what we suffer does not turn itself around very quickly. We can be left without closure for years, maybe even a lifetime.

When we seem stuck in our grief or sorrow, we can be comforted by Psalm 88. We aren't the only ones who have lacked closure. Yet the psalmist was not left alone forever either. This is only one chapter of a book of books. It's okay for us to feel stuck because there is more story to come, a story whose ending we already know.

Lord, when I feel stuck in my pain, assure me that I still have not reached the end of the story. My closure will come in another chapter. Amen.

October 10

When Jesus reached the spot, He looked up and said to him, "Zacchaeus, come down immediately. I must stay at your house today."
—Luke 19:5

Zacchaeus was a man of short stature and, as a tax collector, disliked by many. Yet Jesus accepted Zacchaeus. In fact, by staying in his house, Jesus embraced Zacchaeus. Jesus never forced Zacchaeus to change. Zacchaeus changed by his own choice. And Jesus never mocked Zacchaeus for what he had to do or for his lack of height.

If you've ever had someone criticize you for any of your physical or personality traits, you know how painful it can be to essentially be told you aren't good enough. However, when someone not only accepts you for who you are but fully embraces you as you are, amazing things can happen.

Zacchaeus did not remain the crooked tax collector he had been. When Jesus embraced him as he was, Zacchaeus felt compelled to better himself. In the same way, we also should embrace one another. Who knows—maybe the person you think should change will actually inspire you to make a few improvements of your own.

Jesus, You meet me where I am and inspire me to make myself better. May I embrace others as You have embraced me. Amen.

October 11

We who are strong ought to bear with the failings
of the weak and not to please ourselves.

—Romans 15:1

There is much we could learn from God's animal kingdom.
Every so often, there is a certain post that circulates around the
internet. This post tells the story of a band of wild horses on one
side of a river encountering another band on the other side of the
river. Horses in the first herd start crossing the river to meet the
other herd. While crossing the river, one young foal gets swept
up in the current and starts to drown. The herd stallion grabs
the foal by the back of the neck and pulls the young one to safety
before moving off to meet the horses of the other herd.

Even with the pictorial evidence, one might be skeptical of
this story. Would a wild stallion really care if a foal perished?
Would any animal, other than a mother, put the needs of a
weaker animal ahead of its own desires?

Well, let's find out. Let's learn a lesson from this wild stallion,
regardless of the story's truth, and care for those who are weaker
before satisfying our own desires. Remember, the stallion did
meet the horses of the other herd eventually. He just saved the
foal's life first.

God, teach me how to put the needs of the weak ahead of my
wants. Give me the strength to bear them up. Amen.

October 12

The words of the reckless pierce like swords, but
the tongue of the wise brings healing.
—Proverbs 12:18

Words have more power than most of us realize. I confess that I am as guilty as anyone of badmouthing someone behind their back. I'll figure it's okay as long as that person didn't hear what I said. Sometimes our harsh words get back to the person we were talking about; sometimes they don't.

Marge was different, though. She never said a cruel word about anybody. If she couldn't say something nice, she wouldn't say anything at all. It was always a joy to go visit Marge because her house had such a positive atmosphere. Part of that atmosphere was her actual hospitality. But most if it came from the fact that I highly doubt there was ever a mean word spoken in that house.

There are days when I miss her terribly, especially days when I have been around people criticizing other people. Harsh words, even when not spoken about me, have a way of dragging me down. To be around Marge was to experience healing from such harshness as her words were always uplifting.

Heavenly Father, make me wise enough that my tongue brings healing to those around me. Let me speak only kind words, both to others' faces and behind their backs. Amen.

October 13

Now when Daniel learned that the decree had been published, he went home to his upstairs room where the windows opened toward Jerusalem. Three times a day he got down on his knees and prayed, giving thanks to his God, just as he had done before.

—Daniel 6:10

In today's society, Christianity seems to be turning invisible. We are labeled as prejudiced or intolerant if we dare demonstrate our beliefs. We don't want to offend anyone, so we keep our faith secret.

Daniel learned that the king had made it illegal for prayers to be offered to anyone other than his royal majesty himself. The punishment for breaking this decree was death. It wouldn't be just any death either. He would be ripped apart by ravenous lions!

Yet Daniel didn't care. He had never been someone to stand on street corners and make a big deal out of his times of prayer. He just didn't keep his faith a secret. His was not an invisible faith. Daniel carried on, not afraid of anyone.

And let's not forget the rest of the story. Daniel was indeed caught and thrown into the lion's den. But God saved him. If we are also faithful, God can and will save us, too.

God, grant me the courage to not hide my faith in You, regardless of how many people I may offend. Amen.

October 14

Therefore, there is now no condemnation for those who are in Christ Jesus.

—Romans 8:1

"Be gentle with yourself. We are all flawed and fallible." These words of grace were spoken by one friend to another. The woman on the receiving end of this grace had just shared one of the many intense guilts she carried around with her. Her friend acknowledged her guilt but encouraged her to stop condemning herself for her past mistakes.

Some of us are more prone to guilt than others. It all depends on how accepting we are of actions short of perfection. This particular woman admitted to her friend that she will accept nothing less than perfection from herself. Thus, she is always riddled with guilt over her failures.

But as the apostle Paul said to the church in Rome, there is no condemnation for those who are in Christ. We may try to condemn ourselves for our mistakes, but we are the only ones assigning the condemnation. Through Christ, we are all pardoned in God's eyes. We are all flawed and fallible, but we are also all forgiven.

Thank You, dear God, for Your forgiveness through Christ. When I become burdened with guilt, remind me that in You I have pardon, not condemnation. Amen.

October 15

Then Jesus said to her, "Woman, you have great faith! Your request is granted." And her daughter was healed at that moment.

—Matthew 15:28

This is the last verse of the story about a Canaanite woman who sought Jesus' healing for her demon-possessed daughter. After a brief dialog concerning who Jesus was sent to help, He looked beyond this woman's race and healed her daughter.

I grew up in an area that could definitely be described as "cowboy country." It was most evident during the county fair where any horse that was not an American Quarter Horse was deemed inferior. The judges brought in every year were well-versed in Quarter Horse conformation only. Some breeds, like the Arabian, were shown outright hatred.

Prejudice is everywhere. We can see it among human ethnicities, as well as among preferred breeds in various pets and livestock. But prejudice is not godlike. Jesus demonstrated that it's okay to have a preference, but it is not okay to use that preference as a reason for hatred. Every animal and every human has value and deserves the best treatment.

Lord, teach me to respect all living things, regardless of their species, and to see the value in them that You see. Amen.

October 16

But the Pharisees and teachers of the law who belonged to their sect complained to His disciples, "Why do you eat and drink with tax collectors and sinners?"

—Luke 5:30

Eating is a big part of socializing. In Jesus' day, who a person dined with spoke volumes about that person's morals and values. One simply did not break bread with anyone who was less righteous.

Today, eating together is still a major part of socializing. Take any lunch room in any school. If kids are allowed to choose where they sit, they will choose to sit with their friends. The new kid frequently eats alone.

We adults may not necessarily eat meals together with friends, but we do still use eating as a way to show who we like. After all, when was the last time you invited your annoying coworker out for a cup of coffee at the end of the day?

There is nothing wrong with "wining and dining" with good friends. However, including the new person or the unpleasant person is the Christian thing to do. You might just end up with a new friend out of the deal. At the very least, you've made an effort to show you care.

Lord, You cared enough to eat and drink with those who were unworthy of Your presence. May I include others as You did. May I reflect the love and care You have for all people. Amen.

October 17

See now that I Myself am He! There is no god besides Me. I put to death and I bring to life, I have wounded and I will heal, and no one can deliver out of My hand.

—Deuteronomy 32:39

Throughout the Old Testament, the Israelites were constantly turning away from God to follow idols. I would imagine that every time the Israelites turned back to God, He would have made this same statement. "I am He!" Yet the Israelites had a terrible time remembering that from one generation to the next.

Unfortunately, we Christians today aren't any better. We give ourselves more credit than we ought, using "luck" and "skill" as the reasons for our success when things are going our way. When things don't go so well for us, we cast blame on bad luck, bad timing, or maybe even bad karma. And we think it is entirely up to us to set things right for ourselves again.

However, that was not the case in Old Testament times, and it is not the case for us now. God alone is responsible for our good times. God alone can get us out of our bad times, regardless of what caused them. Most importantly, we are never out of God's reach because no one can take us out of God's loving hand.

God, You alone are God! May I never cease to praise You! Let me turn to You with gratitude in the good times and with humility and trust in the bad times. Amen.

October 18

Go, gather together all the Jews who are in Susa, and fast for me. Do not eat or drink for three days, night or day. I and my attendants will fast as you do. When this is done, I will go to the king, even though it is against the law. And if I perish, I perish.

—Esther 4:16

One just cannot help but admire Esther. She was a meek Jewish woman chosen to become the queen of Persia. Even as queen, she knew what she was and was not allowed to do. Yet, when push came to shove, she was willing to risk her life to save her people.

Esther had bold faith. She knew that entering the king's presence without being summoned could mean her death. But she was willing to face that risk in order to prevent the deaths of all the Jews in Persia. She knew that her people would not be spared without her help. If it turned out to be God's will that the Jews should perish, then Esther was willing to perish with them. No matter what, she knew her life was in God's hands.

Such bold faith is admirable. It is also attainable. We, too, can have bold faith to place our lives in God's hands while fighting against the injustices of the world. Esther is a wonderful role model for faith!

Lord, teach me to have bold faith like Esther. Show me how to trust in You, even when the things I must do may lead to my demise. Amen.

October 19

The fool says in his heart, "There is no God."
They are corrupt, their deeds are vile; there is
no one who does good.

—Psalm 14:1

This is an absolutely amazing time of year! The trees are turning vibrant colors before they drop their leaves for winter. The skies are filled with ducks, geese, and other birds migrating with an uncanny sense of direction.

Perhaps the most amazing migration of all is that of the monarch butterfly, embarking on a flight they have never taken before and will never take again. The preceding generation migrated in the spring and died in the northern regions. These butterflies migrating in the fall will die in the southern regions over the winter. Yet, somehow these butterflies know where they are going.

It's hard to believe that there are people out there who actually think the beauties and wonders of autumn all happen by chance! I guess that's why the psalmist refers to nonbelievers as "fools." Fools may give various scientific reasons for the leaves changing colors and for all animals, even monarchs, knowing their migration paths. But the truth is that God's hand is painting on the canvas of this earth and is guiding every animal on its journey. There is a God, and He is great!

Thank You, God, for the beauty and wonder of the earth. The works of Your hand are breathtaking! Amen.

October 20

But he replied, "Truly I tell you, I don't know you."
—Matthew 25:12

I remember one Bible study when I was in college where we talked about this parable of the ten maidens. Our campus pastor presented us students with an interesting fact. He told us that the five maidens who arrived late would never have been invited to the wedding banquet if the bridegroom had not known them. It just was not customary for complete strangers to be invited to wedding feasts. Thinking about how my roommate had gone from being really nice to really hostile pretty much overnight, I made the comment, "If someone does what you don't expect them to, you might say you don't know them anymore."

Jesus expects us to heed His warning—to stay alert and be prepared for His second coming. If we fail to be ready, we will be pained to hear Jesus tell us, "I don't know you." We will be left behind.

So we need to keep tending to our lamps, making sure that the oil of faith is sufficient to keep us shining until Jesus returns. Then we can join Him in the eternal feast!

Jesus, please guide me to the faith I need to be ready to meet You when You come again. Help me to keep my lamp burning brightly. Amen.

October 21

I will not leave you as orphans; I will come to you.

—John 14:18

Whenever I leave my dog, Spock, I must tell him, "I'll be back." I am the world to him. If I leave Spock without assuring him of my return, he will get very anxious, even agitated, at my departure. He feels abandoned, perhaps even orphaned, if I do not promise him that I will come back to him.

Jesus had become the world to His disciples. But Jesus had to leave His disciples in order to accomplish His Father's will. This separation was necessary, as it sometimes can be.

Just before speaking this, Jesus had promised His disciples the Holy Spirit. Yet, just as nobody can take my place in my dog's heart, Jesus knew the Holy Spirit's arrival would not completely replace Jesus in the hearts of His disciples. So Jesus promised to return to them.

Jesus promises to return to us, too. We have no need to be anxious or agitated. Jesus did not abandon us. He gave us the Spirit to help us now, and He has promised He will come back to us.

Dear Jesus, thank You for giving us your Holy Spirit to be with us until Your promised return. Help us to believe Your promise and to wait for Your return with patience. In Your name we pray. Amen.

October 22

I will never forget Your precepts, for by them
You have preserved my life.

—Psalm 119:93

One of my favorite songs is "Hold Tight," written by Kyle Matthews. The first verse of that song tells about a mother crossing the street with her young son. The boy resents his mother for holding his hand and fights to get away from her.

Her response to him comes in the words of the chorus. She tells her son that she won't have to hold on to him so tight if he'd hold tight to her. She is trying to give him the help he needs that could save his life, all because she loves him.

Like the mother in this song, God has given us boundaries to keep us safe. The psalmist was aware of those boundaries, laid out in God's laws and precepts, and knew that those boundaries were essential for life. God wants to protect us because He loves us.

And like the boy in this song, we would be wise to follow the example of the psalmist and hold tight to God's precepts. We should accept the help that can and will save us.

Lord God, like the psalmist, may I never forget Your precepts. When I fail to hold tight to You, please hold tight to me. Through Your love, save me even when I don't realize I need saving. Amen.

October 23

Then Philip ran up to the chariot and heard the man reading Isaiah the prophet. "Do you understand what you are reading?" Philip asked. "How can I," he said, "unless someone explains it to me?" So he invited Philip to come up and sit with him.

—Acts 8:30–31

Reading Scripture can be very difficult! The Ethiopian eunuch had discovered that, and he was reading the Scripture in its original language. How much harder is it for us, who have the Bible translated into various languages!

Even in the English language, there are still many different versions. I personally have at least three different versions of the Bible—the Good News Bible, the New International Version, and the Message. All versions are well used as I have been known to switch from one version to another when meditating on a particular passage.

It's okay to have problems understanding the Bible. You should never feel ashamed of needing someone to explain it to you. In fact, feel free to have commentaries handy as you read the Bible. There are many explanations already available.

Lord, Your Holy Scripture can be very difficult to understand. Thank You for providing me with those who can explain it to me. Amen.

October 24

Do nothing out of selfish ambition or vain conceit. Rather, in humility, value others above yourselves.

—Philippians 2:3

The time was during WWII. The place was Iowa. Frank was working a munitions factory. He, his wife, and his son were quite some distance away from any other family. Frank's wife was miserable. She missed her family, and she missed South Dakota. She wanted to go home.

Frank quit his job at the factory and moved his family back to South Dakota, back among the extended family. But now he was unemployed. That meant only one thing—Frank was going to get drafted into the military. Frank was not only drafted into the army, but he was deployed to France. He was sent to war.

Frank is the perfect example of humbly valuing others above oneself. He put himself in a position to be drafted so that his wife would no longer be homesick. And, knowing that his wife and son would be safe among other family, Frank went to war so that others—including complete strangers—could have a better life. I don't know that Frank ever put himself first in anything. This world needs more people like Frank.

God, teach me how to value others above myself. Help me to serve others out of humility, rather than out of selfish ambition. Amen.

October 25

When Jesus heard what had happened, He withdrew by boat privately to a solitary place.
—Matthew 14:13a

Jesus had just heard that His cousin, John the Baptist, had been killed. At that point, Jesus needed some time to Himself. He needed to be alone.

We all have times in our lives when we need to withdraw from other people. Things happen, and we just need to be alone. Sometimes it's grief that compels us to solitude. Other times it might be stress from work or strife in a relationship.

Jesus knew when He needed His solitude. He knew when He needed to be alone. He also took that time to withdraw. Everything else could wait, at least for a little while. While off alone, Jesus undoubtedly prayed to His Father. By pulling away from everyone else, Jesus could connect to His source of strength. That solitude would then enable Jesus to resume caring for others.

We, too, need to acknowledge when we need our solitude. We should withdraw without guilt. If Jesus, the Son of God, needed time to privately reconnect with the Father, how much more do we need that time? That is the only way we can continue tending to the needs of those around us.

Father, when I am weary or otherwise burdened, let me withdraw into solitude with You. Amen.

October 26

I am the Good Shepherd; I know My sheep and
My sheep know Me.

—John 10:14

I love sheep! We had a small flock for awhile in my childhood,
and I gained a fair amount of experience with those sheep. Our
flock started out with several bottle lambs. My sister and I
named each one of our lambs. My favorite was a black-faced
ewe that had two white spots on her face. Her name was Mary.

When I would go out to our sheep, I would almost immediately
start calling Mary. The moment I called her name, I would see
that black face with those two white spots look up and turn
toward me. Then Mary would leave whatever vegetation she'd
been grazing on and come over to me. When she'd get to me, I
would pet her, scratch her, and sometimes pull branches out of
her wool.

Whenever I hear references to Jesus as the Good Shepherd,
I am reminded of my beloved Mary. Compared to humans,
sheep are stupid. Yet, compared to God, we humans are stupid!
Still, I loved Mary, just as God loves each and every one of us.
We are the sheep of God's holy flock.

Jesus, You are my Shepherd. Thank You for loving me and
caring for me, despite the foolish things I do in Your sight.
Amen.

October 27

As for me, I will always have hope; I will praise
You more and more.

—Psalm 71:14

My grandmother used to say the phrase "hope and pray" a
lot. One of the women in her ladies' aid group thought that was a
terrible thing to say. This woman insisted that if you are hoping,
then you are not truly praying. If you are praying, then you do
not need to be hoping.

Like Grandma, I have found myself using the phrase "hope
and pray" frequently. I never thought there was anything wrong
with saying that, but I would still remember that woman in
Grandma's church. So when I met a pastor who also used the
phrase "hope and pray," I told him the backstory and asked him
how he would justify that expression. The answer that pastor
gave me is echoed in this psalm. The pastor told me that for us
Christians, our hopes and prayers are the same thing. Thus, to
say "hope and pray" is essentially saying the same thing twice
for emphasis.

The psalmist says that he will always have hope. With the
very next breath, he is talking about praise. That is the ultimate
combination of hope and prayer! So go ahead. Hope and pray.
Say it—do it—twice for emphasis!

God, I praise You for the hope You have given me. Amen.

October 28

He replied, "You are talking like a foolish woman. Shall we accept good from God, and not trouble?" In all this, Job did not sin in what he said.

—Job 2:10

The book of Job has often been used to explain why bad things happen to good people. However, the book really doesn't answer "why." Basically all it does is point out that we may never know why bad things happen but that we should accept them anyway.

In this verse, Job says that exact thing to his wife. Yes bad things were happening to Job. By this time, Job had lost livestock and slaves and was presently covered in sores. Things were really going wrong for Job! Just when it would seem that things could not get any worse, something else would happen.

Accepting the bad things that happen, whether we believe God caused them or not, is an act of faith. It takes faith to acknowledge that we cannot handle our problems alone. It takes faith to trust that God will see us through the hard times. It's even an act of faith to lament to God about the troubles. Even Job did that eventually. But by accepting what is happening, we can then turn to God for the help we need.

God, when bad things happen to me, guide me to accept the troubles so that I may trust in You to bring me through my times of trouble. Amen.

October 29

The earth is the Lord's, and everything in it, the
world, and all who live in it.

—Psalm 24:1

When I hear the word "stewardship," I think about my years
in middle school and high school band. While many students
had their own instruments, those who played the more expensive
or more unique instruments used the school's instruments. I
was different in that I owned my own alto clarinet. And I could
always see the difference between the condition of my alto
clarinet, loved and properly cared for, and the condition of the
abused school-owned alto clarinets.

We do not own this earth. One might say that the way we
abuse the earth shows that we think this planet is ours to do with
as we please. But I look at our treatment of this planet and think
only of the way students treated the alto clarinets and other
instruments owned by the school. Those students had nothing
invested in those instruments and didn't care that other students
would need to play them years down the road.

However, we do need to care. Who would want their child
playing an instrument so abused that it falls apart easily? Do we
want our children to live in such an abused and fragile world?

Lord, let me be a good caretaker of this world, *Your* world, so
that it may sustain future generations. Amen.

October 30

Then Jesus said to him, "Get up! Pick up your mat and walk."

—John 5:8

There are several times when Jesus told someone that their faith has made them well. However, there are many times, like this time, when Jesus healed someone and made no reference to faith. He simply barked a command to do something that seemed impossible or pointless.

To accept Jesus' help and healing means that we must follow Jesus' commands. Jesus will never tell us to do something that we absolutely cannot do. Jesus will not give us a command just to watch us fail. John 5:9 tells us that this man did indeed pick up his mat and walk. An invalid, a man who could not physically walk, got up and walked!

Jesus has a reason for giving us whatever commands He does, and Jesus will make sure we succeed. All we have to do is have the faith to be willing to obey. Jesus will take care of the rest, and He will be proudly cheering us on as we, with His holy help, proceed to do the impossible.

Jesus, grant me the faith to obey Your commands, even those that seem impossible. Assure me that You will never let me fail. Amen.

October 31

Show me Your ways, Lord, teach me Your paths.
—Psalm 25:4

For Lutherans, this day is more than just a day of costumes and candy. Sure, it may be Halloween, but today is also Reformation Day. It was on this day in 1517 that Martin Luther nailed his 95 theses to the church door in Wittenberg, Germany. After many years of studying the Bible, Luther felt compelled to share his 95 grievances, 95 points where he believed the church had strayed from God's Word.

Even Christians of other denominations have to admit that what Martin Luther did was risky. But the Lord had revealed His ways, His truth, His life to Martin Luther. And that was something Luther just could not keep to himself.

Regardless of what denomination you choose to claim, let the words of Psalm 25:4 be as strong for you as they had apparently become for Martin Luther. With the psalmist, ask the Lord to show you His ways and to teach you His paths. And once the Lord has revealed His truth to you, go and share it with others. You don't have to nail anything to the church door like Martin Luther, but don't hesitate to share the Good News!

Lord, Your truth is the only truth anyone needs. Teach me Your ways so that I, in turn, may instruct others in Your paths. Amen.

November 1

Therefore, since we are surrounded by such a great cloud of witnesses, let us throw off everything that hinders and the sin that so easily entangles. And let us run with perseverance the race marked out for us.

—Hebrews 12:1

Today is a special day in the Roman Catholic Church as well as in some Protestant denominations. Today is All Saints' Day, sometimes also known as the Feast of All Saints. It is the day when churches all over remember and celebrate the faithful lives of those who have died.

This can be a painful day, especially if a loved one has recently died. However, it is also a day to be thankful. For without the faith of our loved ones, our own faith would not have taken the shape it has. They witnessed of Christ through their faithful lives.

So, take a moment today to stop and give thanks to God for the people in your life who have nurtured your faith along the way. Even if the rest of the world doesn't recognize your loved ones as saints, go ahead and celebrate them. If, by their faith, they showed you the way from sin to eternal life, then they were truly saints.

Thank You, dear God, for the loved ones You have given me to serve as witnesses. Each one of them was truly a saint, and I thank You for how their faith helped shape my own. Amen.

November 2

When Jesus spoke again to the people, He said, "I am the light of the world. Whoever follows Me will never walk in darkness, but will have the light of life."

—John 8:12

This is not the only passage where Jesus talks about being the light of the world. In fact, in the first chapter of John's Gospel, he refers to Jesus as the light that the darkness could not overcome. And the Gospel of John is not the only book in the Bible that references light when talking about Jesus.

In the age of electricity, we tend to take light for granted. As we walk into our homes, we reach for the light switch without even thinking. It's not until the lights don't come on that we truly experience the darkness. Ever try to find a flashlight or candle in your house when the electricity goes out? That can be difficult!

At best, darkness is a mild inconvenience. At its worst, darkness can be outright dangerous. Walking in darkness can result in injuries ranging from stubbed toes to broken bones.

Life without Jesus is also dangerous. When it comes right down to it, life without Jesus is deadly. The only way we will get to eternal life is to follow Jesus, the light of the world.

Lord Jesus, You are indeed the light of the world. May I always follow You, the light that leads to life. Amen.

November 3

The Lord is my rock, my fortress and my
deliverer; my God is my rock, in whom I take
refuge, my shield and the horn of my salvation,
my stronghold.

—Psalm 18:2

In Wyoming there is a fascinating natural monument known
as Devils Tower. It's a solid rock structure with an altitude of
over 5,000 feet at its highest point. This giant rock has some
interesting Native American folklore connected to it.

One such story tells of two Sioux boys who wandered far
away from their village only to be spotted by a giant bear with
claws the size of tipi poles. The boys prayed to Wakan Tanka, the
Creator, to help them. Then they rose up on a huge rock while
the bear tried to reach them. The bear left huge scratch marks
in the rock but was unable to reach the boys.

God may not bring towering rocks out of the ground to save
us from hungry bears, but He does deliver us from our troubles
in ways that we cannot always understand. Sometimes the
circumstances that happen to spare us may seem as unbelievable
as the rescue in Native American folklore. However, God is
indeed our rock, our protection in our time of need.

Lord, You are my rock and my refuge. Thank You for the many
miraculous ways that You deliver me from danger. Amen.

November 4

God is not unjust; He will not forget your work
and the love you have shown Him as you have
helped His people and continue to help them.
—Hebrews 6:10

It happens all too often. A person or small group of people
set out to do some wonderful project. They are going to help a
bunch of people. The dreams are big, but somehow those dreams
don't quite become realities. The projects either don't reach their
goals or never materialize at all.

Many times when a beneficial project fails to reach its full
potential, those involved will shrug and say, "Well, I tried."
Unfortunately, what people in these instances don't see is the
good that was done by their project. Maybe the project was to
raise money to help a needy family cover medical expenses. And
maybe the project didn't reach the goal set by its creators. That
doesn't mean the project was a failure. The family was still given
financial help that they would not have otherwise received.

God notices our every attempt to help those in need in our
midst. He sees the work we do and will not forget it. And God
is pleased as we continue to help others.

God, teach me to reflect Your love to those around me by
continuing to help those in need. Amen.

November 5

My eyes are ever on the Lord, for only He will
release my feet from the snare.

—Psalm 25:15

Shortly after my dad had gotten a new horse, another of our
horses got very aggressive and forced this new horse through a
fence. Since none of us saw this, we discovered she was missing
but had no idea where to find her. We split up to look for her.

I saddled up one of my horses to ride through neighboring
fields to see if I could find the missing horse. After a while with
no luck, I headed for home. Time for a new plan. As I rode on
the gravel road along our pasture, my mom neared the same
area. She'd been walking the fence line, attempting to find the
place where the horse had escaped. Upon hearing my horse's
hoofbeats on the road, our missing horse whinnied. That's when
Mom and I found her, lying in the weeds and tall grass of the
ditch with her feet snared in the fence.

There are times when we all are like Dad's poor horse. We
end up in situations from which we simply cannot free ourselves.
That's when we must turn our eyes to our Lord again and call
out for His help. He will free us.

Lord, when I find myself ensnared and in need of rescuing,
let me turn to You and wait for You to release my tangled feet.
Amen.

November 6

Am I now trying to win the approval of human beings, or of God? Or am I trying to please people? If I were still trying to please people, I would not be a servant of Christ.

—Galatians 1:10

"You can please some of the people all of the time, you can please all of the people some of the time, but you can't please all of the people all of the time." These words, first spoken by poet John Lydgate and later echoed by Abraham Lincoln, explain beautifully the folly of trying to please people. No matter what we do, eventually someone will disapprove of our actions.

So how do we decide what actions to take? Should we look at how many people we can please? Should we consider the statuses of the people and try to please those who have the most power? Should we just blow everyone else off and simply do what pleases us?

Actually, in everything we do, we should seek God's approval. His is the only opinion that should matter to us. By doing what is pleasing to God, we show that we belong to Him. He is our Lord and our Master. That becomes very evident when God's approval is all we care about.

Lord, in this world, I am constantly faced with conflicting opinions. Teach me to care only about pleasing You, not about pleasing people. Help me to be interested in Your approval alone. Amen.

November 7

For the love of money is a root of all kinds of evil. Some people, eager for money, have wandered from the faith and pierced themselves with many griefs.

—1 Timothy 6:10

This is probably one of the most misquoted Bible verses. Many people insist that the Bible says money is the root of all evil. While versions may differ on whether the love of money is "a root of all kinds of evil" or "the root of all evil," one thing remains the same. The apostle Paul did not condemn money itself, but rather the love of it.

Even Jesus had no problems with wealthy people. The only concerns Jesus had were when people would not part with their wealth to follow Him. It wasn't the money itself holding people back. It was the love people had for their money.

So, remember that it is perfectly fine to have money. You are not evil for being wealthy. You just need to make sure your wealth does not interfere with your relationship with God. You are okay as long as you are always willing to choose God over money. And one way you can do that is to be generous with a cause of your choice. Give some of your wealth away.

God, I humbly ask that You keep my heart focused on You. May You, not money, always be the one love of my life. Amen.

November 8

The fear of the Lord is the beginning of wisdom,
and knowledge of the Holy One is understanding.
—Proverbs 9:10

The book of Proverbs is full of wise sayings. Many verses have two parts, with one part describing the right thing to do and the other part describing the wrong thing. Yet, oddly enough, the entire book can be summed up in this one verse.

If we want to be wise, then we need to have a healthy fear of the Lord. We need to acknowledge His power and revere His word. Wisdom begins by respecting and honoring our God.

The second part of this proverb is a little tricky. Most of us will say we "know of" a person when we know a little about that person but haven't gotten beyond the basic information. We say that to explain that we do not understand their motives, their thought processes, or anything else that goes deeper into who that person is.

Still, there is some understanding that comes with basic knowledge. For example, knowing a person's profession might reveal something about that person's deeper interests. And even knowing of God is a start to understanding who God is and what kind of relationship He wants to have with us.

Lord, teach me to honor You and to guide me to understand You. Amen.

November 9

Nothing outside a person can defile them by going into them. Rather, it is what comes out of a person that defiles them.

—Mark 7:15

Traditions are interesting things when you stop to think about them. Traditions are things that we do habitually, frequently without even thinking about their origins. Families may have traditions for holidays. Workplaces may have traditions for celebrations of employee birthdays or work anniversaries. Churches may have traditions for many occasions!

In this verse, Jesus is throwing out the "tradition" of regarding certain foods as unclean. It was a tradition that had its roots in law, but the Jews were missing the point. God's law was established to keep the people holy and righteous. However, simply obeying the law wasn't enough. Going through the motions was not the same as remembering the reason behind the action.

The next time you find yourself participating in tradition, stop to think about the origins of that tradition. If none is known, either let go of that tradition or, even better, find a way to make that tradition honor God.

God, help me to do things that honor You, and not just because these things have always been done. Remind me that it is by my heart, not my actions, that I bring glory to Your name. Amen.

November 10

When Jesus entered the temple courts, He began
out drive to those who were selling. "It is written,"
He said to them, "'My house will be a house of
prayer;' but you have made it 'a den of robbers.'"
—Luke 19:45–46

In Jesus' day, there were people in the temple who were
selling animals and other items to be used for sacrifices.
However, the prices were not always fair. Those who wanted
to atone for their sins frequently had to pay for their wrongs in
more ways than one!

We may not have people selling livestock in our churches,
but have we fallen into a similar trap? Are church buildings
today "houses of prayer"? Are our congregations open and
welcoming to all people?

I would invite you to consider the workings of your own
congregation prayerfully. Is God at the center of every activity
at church? Are those who come through those doors accepted
as they are, or are they forced to pay for their mistakes several
times over? Are the sins of previous members held against its
current members?

If the church you attend seems to be more like a den of
thieves, robbing people of dignity and hope, then it's time to turn
some tables. Return the church to God.

God, the church is Yours to be a house of prayer. Give me the
guidance to do my part to keep the robbers out of Your holy
house. Amen.

November 11

God is our refuge and strength, an ever-present help in trouble.

—Psalm 46:1

Some of us will experience more trouble than others. Today honors a group of people who have faced more than their fair share of trouble and have done so on behalf of others. Today is Veteran's Day, when we thank our military veterans for their service.

If you have ever talked to a veteran who has been deployed, you will hear about how difficult their living conditions were. Even if they never saw combat, they had their troubles. Life on deployment is far from being a bed of roses!

Of course, not all veterans have been deployed. Some veterans have been stationed in peaceful zones overseas, while some never left the states. Yet, even those veterans have had their troubles. They have spent holidays away from family because they were denied leave. They have missed important milestones in their children's lives because of their military duty. Only God knows how these veterans were able to carry out their military service. So today, thank a veteran. And while we're at it, let's thank God for our veterans!

God, thank You for the veterans who have faced trouble to give me a better life. Continue to be their strength and help. Amen.

November 12

But when the set time had fully come, God sent His Son, born of a woman, born under the law, to redeem those under the law, that we might receive adoption to sonship.

—Galatians 4:4–5

One Sunday, while visiting another church, I found myself in an interesting conversation. I was approached by someone who was also visiting. Eventually our conversation made its way over to Christianity and the world today.

This fellow visitor made the remark that Jesus was "before His time." He went on to say that Jesus didn't have to deal with women's rights, gay rights, or any of the other issues we have today. I let the conversation move on, while I mulled over what this man had said.

But God's time isn't like ours. We measure things by the passage of time, but God creates His own time. So, not only was Jesus not "before His time," but He's not confined to any one earthly period of time. Everything Jesus said those two thousand or so years ago is just as valid today. Jesus was indeed dealing with the issues of women's rights, gay/lesbian rights, and the rights of every other minority in the world. No matter what the issue, Jesus has dealt with it.

Lord, nothing You have said or done was ever "before its time." Teach me to follow You, no matter what issue I am facing at the moment. Amen.

November 13

How beautiful on the mountains are the feet
of those who bring good news, who proclaim
peace, who bring good tidings, who proclaim
salvation, who say to Zion, "Your God reigns!"
—Isaiah 52:7

As a massage therapist, one of the most common questions I get asked is, "Do you touch feet?" Most people can't stand the thought of touching someone else's feet. But yes, I do massage feet.

While many people dislike feet, either finding them to be stinky or ugly, feet are truly amazing body parts. And I highly doubt anyone would insult the feet of someone bringing good news. However, it's not the physical appearance of the feet that make them beautiful. Rather, it is the joyous news they bring.

Wouldn't it be wonderful if such standards were used to measure the beauty of an entire person? How wonderful would it be to rate a person's beauty by what they do, instead of how they look! We can't agree on what physical traits are appealing anyway. Why don't we start measuring beauty by how a person acts? That is, after all, where true beauty lies. Love and goodness, regardless of where they are found, are always beautiful!

God, change my method of rating beauty. Help me to see that true beauty comes from within. May I recognize the beauty in myself and in those around me. Amen.

November 14

When tempted, no one should say, "God is tempting me." For God cannot be tempted by evil, nor does He tempt anyone; but each person is tempted when they are dragged away by their own evil desire and enticed.

—James 1:13–14

Temptations are everywhere, just ask anyone who is dieting. They will tell you how many times they encounter the foods they are trying to avoid. Those who are working at breaking addictions also struggle greatly with temptations.

Really, though, temptations are only those nasty little things we see when we take our eyes off our end goal. We are only tempted to eat junk food when we look away from our goal of improved health. We are only tempted to fall back into our addictions when we lose sight of the better person we are seeking to become.

We will also encounter many temptations in our spiritual lives. But again, the temptations will only have as much power as we give them. The more we look away from our heavenly goal, the stronger those temptations will become.

God is not the source of our temptations. He is our way out. When we are focused on Him, our temptations will fall by the wayside.

God, keep my eyes turned toward You so that I am not distracted by temptation. Amen.

November 15

Yours, Lord, is the greatness and the power and
the glory and the majesty and the splendor, for
everything in heaven and earth is Yours. Yours,
Lord, is the kingdom; You are exalted as head
over all.

—1 Chronicles 29:11

These words of praise can also be used as a powerful faith
statement. We humans tend to vie for all these things. We want
to be great. We want to be powerful. We want the fortune and
glory. And we don't like sharing!

How many times did your parents take away a toy that you
and your siblings were fighting over? Did you ever do that to
your own children? There's no fight when there is no prize.
Peace and tranquility is restored to the household.

We adults would be wise to follow this method for ourselves.
If we turn the greatness, power, glory, and everything else back
over to God, we humans have nothing left over which to fight.
Peace and tranquility would be restored to this world. And
in this case, this wouldn't even be punishment. After all, the
greatness, power, glory, etc. were never ours to begin with. They
always have been and always will be the Lord's only.

Lord, to You I surrender all my desires for power and greatness
and the glory that comes with them. Such honors belong to You
alone. Amen.

November 16

> Though you have not seen Him, you love Him; and even though you do not see Him now, you believe in Him and are filled with an inexpressible and glorious joy.
>
> —1 Peter 1:8

Have you ever found yourself liking someone you've never met, simply because of what you'd been told about this person? I once decided that I really liked a friend's wife because this friend told me his wife insisted that he not sleep in a chair in his office on nights he worked really late. I liked this woman simply because she would rather run the risk of her husband waking her up than to let him sleep on a piece of furniture that was not made for sleeping!

It's probably safe to say that none of us have actually seen Jesus, with the possible exception of someone who has had a near-death experience. And we certainly don't see Him standing in front of us now. Yet we love Him, simply because we have heard wonderful things about Him.

Knowing and believing in Jesus does indeed fill us with joy. We trust in Him to save us from our foolish, self-destructive ways. And we rejoice that we experience the victory over sin that Jesus has caused in our lives.

Lord Jesus, though it may be awhile yet before I see You, I cannot help but love You. Thank You for everything You have done for me! Amen.

November 17

> Now that I, your Lord and Teacher, have washed
> your feet, you also should wash one another's
> feet.
>
> —John 13:14

This verse is part of a passage that is frequently read on Maundy Thursday. Holy Week is a long ways off yet. So one might question why I chose to use this verse now.

The answer is really quite simple. Jesus never gave any restrictions as to when we were to wash one another's feet. It is not to just be a symbolic gesture done at a worship service three days before Easter. Jesus did not put any qualifications on the act of foot washing.

Before long we will start seeing the Salvation Army bell ringers, standing out in front of businesses. But the Salvation Army has a slogan that underscores the significance of what Jesus did not say: "Need knows no season." The Salvation Army will be out in full force come the holiday shopping season, but the people helped by the Salvation Army are in need year-round.

So, during this time well away from Maundy Thursday and prior to the Salvation Army's red kettles appearing, let's remember those in need. We can always serve one another. We *should* always serve one another!

Lord, You taught us that we are to serve each other. Open my eyes to those who need my help, regardless of the time of year. Amen.

November 18

"How can someone be born when they are old?" Nicodemus asked. "Surely they cannot enter a second time into their mother's womb to be born!"

—John 3:4

Oh, Nicodemus! He took Jesus' words about being born again literally. Thus, Nicodemus got hung up on trying to put an adult back inside their mother's womb. That very thought would probably have most mothers cringing!

That can be a problem with communication, especially for people who lace their talk with sarcasm. Yet, even when sarcasm is not used, people can misunderstand what the other person is trying to say. We might call it "putting words in the other person's mouth." It can be very frustrating when you are trying to say something, but the other person seems to be hearing something else. The frustration grows as we repeat ourselves, using different wording, but the other person has the wrong idea now stuck in their head.

Notice, though, that Nicodemus's narrow viewpoint did not deter Jesus. Jesus patiently clarified what He meant. When we find ourselves in miscommunication, we need to pray for patience and understanding, for all parties involved.

God, grant me the patience and understanding to get through confusing conversations. Amen.

November 19

Like clouds and wind without rain is one who
boasts of gifts never given.

—Proverbs 25:14

Living in the upper Midwest, I have experienced a number
of strong winds. I love gentle breezes. I don't mind some wind.
However, nothing will put me in a foul mood quite like fighting
a strong wind, especially if the wind is impeding my ability to
get my livestock chores done. However, if the wind is blowing
in some much-needed precipitation, I tend to be more tolerant
of the gales.

Think about the last time someone promised to give you
something or to do something for you but then failed to follow
through. How did you feel? My guess is that you were not happy
about it. And if this person is notorious for disappointing like
that, you might have even felt irritated.

Of course, we cannot necessarily stop other people from
disappointing us, but we can at least avoid disappointing other
people. We can hold to our word, delivering on promises made.
Then we are not causing others to experience the irritation we
ourselves dislike.

Lord, help me to follow through on the things I say to other
people. May my words not just be hot air, blowing without
bringing any benefit, but rather be the breezes that promise to
fulfill needs. Amen.

November 20

Lord, You are my God; I will exalt You and praise Your name, for in perfect faithfulness You have done wonderful things, things planned long ago.

—Isaiah 25:1

Have you ever been gifted with a surprise that you know took a lot of planning and effort? Maybe it was a surprise birthday party. Maybe it was a trip that you've always wanted to take but knew you couldn't afford on your own. Maybe it was a large item that you really wanted or needed but had no way to transport on your own. How did you feel when you were given that gift? Did your gratitude go deeper when you considered how much planning went into that gift?

God does that for us everyday. With each morning comes a day full of promise, where wonderful things can happen for us. And God has planned out these great things for us long before we were even born!

Therefore, we should always be filled with joyful gratitude. Sure, there will be times when the things that happen to us are far from wonderful, but we should never let the less-than-perfect days dampen our praise for the amazing things God has done for us and for the unimaginable surprises God still has in store for us.

God, You have carefully planned wonderful things for my life. I thank You and praise You for the gifts You've given me. Amen.

November 21

Thanks be to God for His indescribable gift!
—2 Corinthians 9:15

I have the rarest personality type, according to the Myers-Briggs classification. One of the more common characteristics of my rare personality type is that we tend to have a very small inner circle of friends, consisting frequently of only one or two people. But those people who are fortunate enough to be in an inner circle like mine will find themselves blessed beyond measure.

Those with my personality type hold very little back from our inner circle friends. We are willing to give of ourselves entirely to those who mean the most to us. I have left inner circle friends honored and speechless for my selflessness with them.

God treats each and every one of us as an inner circle friend. God will hold nothing back for us. He even gave His own Son for us! He sent Jesus to die for us, and what makes it even more amazing is that Jesus sacrificed Himself willingly. That is a gift that should leave us all honored and speechless. With our loss for words, we need only say one thing—thanks!

Thank You, dearest Lord, for Your gift of love and sacrifice that leaves me speechless. I cannot begin to describe what it means to me to know that You regard my soul with such high importance! Amen.

November 22

For where your treasure is, there your heart will be also.

—Luke 12:34

In this age of technology, we sure seem to love our electronic devices. We have our smart phones, our tablets, our laptops, and our gaming devices. Everything is mobile, so we can take our technology with us wherever we go. How ironic it is that Facebook is one of the most common places to find comments about families being in the same room but each member is doing something on their own electronic device?

Many people feel lost if they don't have a certain thing with them. For some people, it might be their laptop. Other people absolutely must have their tablet. But the most commonly desired thing is probably the cell phone. We will say that we are lost without this one particular item or that our life is in this thing.

As those Facebook posts point out, things can drive wedges in relationships. That's why Jesus made the statement He did. He wanted His disciples then and us today to make sure that we do not allow things to come between us in our relationship with God.

What do we treasure most? Does God have our heart? Or does our heart lie among our things?

God, I give You my heart. May I always treasure my relationship with You above all things. Amen.

November 23

"So I was afraid and went out and hid your gold
in the ground. See, here is what belongs to you."
—Matthew 25:25

Depending on what translation you read, what was given out in this parable varies. In the New International Version, this is the "Parable of the Bags of Gold." I much prefer the translations that call this the "Parable of the Talents." After all, that's really what Jesus is referencing.

Here we read the confession of the servant who refused to do anything with the talents entrusted to him. He accepted them from his master but hid them away. If we continue reading, we learn that the master is not happy.

Likewise God is not happy when we fail to use the talents He has entrusted to us. Most people will never know how nervous I get when I play my alto clarinet in church. I am incredibly talented on that instrument, which happens to be the hardest of the clarinet family to play. Still, no matter how much fear I feel, I know that God has given me this talent and wants me to share it with others. Thus, I try to play special music at church every few months.

Do you have any God-given talents that you are hiding?

God, grant me the courage to use the talents You have given me, so that with them I may glorify You. Amen.

November 24

Better a dry crust with peace and quiet than a
house full of feasting, with strife.

—Proverbs 17:1

Once, shortly after Thanksgiving, I had a client ask me how
my holiday had been. I said it was quiet, with nobody fighting.
My family doesn't actually tend to fight at holidays, or any other
time really, but I made that remark to acknowledge how many
family feasts are made miserable due to tension and strife.

As much as we enjoy grand feasts with more than our fill of
tasty foods, how many of us would rather choose a more modest
meal eaten in peace over an elaborate spread accompanied by
harsh words and hostile actions? Wouldn't we prefer the meal
we could truly enjoy, regardless of the food on which we were
dining?

When you sit down to your Thanksgiving feast, remember
this proverb. If your family functions are peaceful, take a
moment to thank God for the tranquility in which you dine. If
your family is more hostile, as a group, ask the Lord to quiet
the strife so that you may truly experience what your feast
celebrates.

Lord, I pray for families everywhere, not just mine. May all
Thanksgiving celebrations be peaceful, focused on giving You
thanks for Your gifts. Guide us all to treat our family as the gifts
they are. Amen.

November 25

> You and your sons are not to drink wine or
> other fermented drink whenever you go into the
> tent of meeting, or you will die. This is a lasting
> ordinance for the generations to come.
>
> —Leviticus 10:9

Whenever I hear this verse, I immediately think about one episode of the TV show *M*A*S*H*. This is the verse that Father Mulcahy quotes when he must give a temperance lecture to the camp. But Father Mulcahy is so nervous about that lecture that he drinks enough alcohol to become intoxicated himself.

However, God did not give this command to Aaron because alcohol was evil. This was not a divine temperance lecture at all. The next verse explains that the abstinence from fermented drink was to distinguish between the holy and the common.

Wine consumption is one way that some still choose to distinguish between that which is holy and that which is common. Of course, there are other ways as well. For example, most people will say that a church sanctuary is holy but the social hall is common. Ultimately, the important thing is that we all realize there is a difference between holy and common. What is holy needs to be approached with the utmost respect and reverence, just as we must approach the Lord.

Lord, help me to treat that which You have deemed holy with the same reverence I hold for You. Amen.

November 26

Lord Almighty, blessed is the one who trusts in You.

—Psalm 84:12

On my bedroom wall hangs a very special plaque. It has a horseshoe in the background, and a strand of thorns separates the two parts of the wording. The words on the plaque read, "I'm not lucky. I am blessed." My uncle gave that to me for Christmas one year. After I read it aloud so everyone would know what the plaque said, my uncle told me, "You need to remember that."

Yes, I do indeed need to remember that. I hung the plaque where I could see it from my bed, so it would be one of the first things I would see each morning. Those words have become my daily affirmation.

There is a big difference between luck and blessing. Luck can change in a moment's notice. Many believe that inanimate objects or certain rituals can control luck. Yet, there's nothing lucky about a four-leaf clover, and there is nothing unlucky about a black cat.

Being blessed is entirely outside our control. No charms or rituals are needed. There is nothing we can do to make things better or worse for ourselves. God's blessing is the gift God bestows upon those who trust in Him.

God, thank You for the many blessings You have given me. I know luck has nothing to do with it. Amen.

November 27

But Moses said to God, "Who am I that I should go to Pharaoh and bring the Israelites out of Egypt?"

—Exodus 3:11

One Friday evening when I was in college, I found myself feeling lonely and depressed. So I decided to go for a walk. I ended up in the football field parking lot and near a gate into the concession area.

From behind this particular gate, a woman called out to me. She was a new employee who did not yet have keys. She was locked inside the gate but outside all buildings. She wondered if I had a cell phone. No, it was back at my apartment. She then asked if I was going home soon. No, I was out for a leisurely stroll. Could I come back by before heading home to see if she had been helped? Yes, I could do that.

When I left her, I couldn't stop thinking about her. So I immediately walked home as quickly as I could, got my cell phone, and drove back to the stadium to help the woman still trapped there. She was most grateful!

There are times when we all can sound like Moses. We question our calling to help, and we give many excuses. However, we should remember that Moses did rescue the Israelites. We, too, should do what God calls us to do.

God, when You call me into Your service, give me a willing heart to immediately answer Your call. Amen.

November 28

I have hidden Your word in my heart that I might
not sin against You.

—Psalm 119:11

Do you have a special place where you keep items of extreme
emotional value? I myself have a "memory box." Among the
many things in that box are emails I have printed off and cards
people have sent me. In those messages are things people have
said that I do not ever want to forget, such as friend expressing
appreciation for my friendship or a former boss's mass email
complimenting me on my flexibility and work ethic.

Even if we don't have something like my memory box, we do
have a place where we can keep special words that we should not
forget. Like the psalmist, we can keep God's Word tucked away
in our heart. That way we never forget what God has said to us.
By remembering His Holy Word, we better equip ourselves not
to sin against our Lord.

Periodically I pull things out of my memory box to read
those messages again. I need that extra help remembering. In
the same way, we need to periodically pull out God's Word and
reread it, also. We need those reminders of what all the Lord
has said to us.

Lord, teach me to tuck Your Holy Word away in my heart but
also to reread Your words regularly, lest I forget Your love for
me. Amen.

November 29

> Now all has been heard; here is the conclusion of the matter: Fear God and keep His commandments, for this is the duty of all mankind.
>
> —Ecclesiastes 12:13

One of my massage school classmates was a practicing Buddhist. He once shared with me the answer he gives when someone asks him if he believes in God. "It's not my job to believe in God." He went on to explain the philosophy of "leaving to deities the work of deities and leaving the work of humans to humans."

That may work for Buddhists, but for those of us who follow God, we simply cannot abide by such laid-back rules. Actually, it *is* our job to believe in God. And with that comes the responsibility of doing God's work on earth.

In all honesty, though, our job is not all that difficult. We have the duty to fear and respect God and to keep His commandments. His commandments all center around love for God and for our neighbors. In fact, that's how Jesus summarized the two greatest commandments. We are to love the Lord with our entire being and to love our neighbors as ourselves. That is God's work, and it is our work.

God, help me to have the love I should for You and for my neighbor, that I may do Your work on here on earth. Amen.

November 30

Fear of man will prove to be a snare, but whoever trusts in the Lord is kept safe.

—Proverbs 29:25

When we talk about fearing the Lord, we are not referring to the type of fear that causes trembling or worry about receiving an unreasonably harsh punishment. Rather, we should have a reverent fear of God. We know what He is capable of, and we should respect Him for His power.

So what type of fear are we talking about here when talking about the fear of man? Shouldn't we also respect our fellow humans? How does that prove a snare?

While every human is due a certain amount of respect, simply for being a child of God, we need to be careful that we do not revere any human too much. Some humans will use the reverence to manipulate those around them. They will have the mentality of "I'm good; you need me. So you will do whatever I want." Not all are like that, but it's difficult to know who will act that way until it's too late.

When it comes right down to it, God is all we truly need. So love, fear, respect, revere, and trust in the Lord. He will keep us safe.

Lord, keep me from giving my fellow man too much respect and power. In You alone should I place my trust. Amen.

December 1

Comfort, comfort My people, says your God.
—Isaiah 40:1

December is now upon us. No matter how you feel about Christmas, you can't help but be bombarded with its impending arrival. With the demands of Christmas presents to buy and wrap, Christmas parties to attend, Christmas decorations to hang, and possibly even Christmas travel plans to make, this can be a very stressful time of year.

In this verse, which is part of a passage frequently read during Advent, the prophet Isaiah calls for comfort for God's people. That doesn't just mean we need to comfort ourselves by not allowing the stress of the holiday to drag us down. It means we also need to remember those for whom winter is difficult.

Comfort those who are cold by providing them with a coat. Comfort those who are hungry by giving them some food. Comfort those who are lonely by going to visit them.

This should not be a time of stress. It should be a time of comfort. And comfort is not a difficult thing to provide to others.

God, show me ways to comfort Your people, not just during this time of Advent but throughout the entire year. Amen.

December 2

A voice of one calling: "In the wilderness prepare the way for the Lord; make straight in the desert a highway for our God."

—Isaiah 40:3

Interstate highways are great for connecting countless cities with relatively straight lines. Drivers can avoid the delays of going around farms, smaller towns, etc. But have you ever thought about what constitutes a straight line in a relationship?

I can name a number of times when people have failed to be honest and upfront with me. One of those times, it took me over a month to get the truth, the whole truth, and nothing but the truth from a friend. That month he spent "beating around the bush" negatively impacted our relationship. He had to earn my trust all over again.

We do not need to take Isaiah's words in this verse literally. We are not being called to road construction on our nation's interstate highway system. But we are being called to give God the shortest distance to our hearts, and we do so by being honest and upfront with Him. When we confess our sin, we give ourselves a straight line to the Lord, and we grow in our relationship with Him.

Heavenly Father, I confess all of my sins and shortcomings to You. Forgive me, and put me in a right relationship with You. Amen.

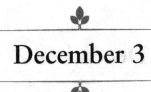

December 3

Every valley shall be raised up, every mountain and hill made low; the rough ground shall become level, the rugged places a plain.

—Isaiah 40:4

I grew up in southwest Iowa, an area of the Midwest that is very hilly. One gravel road in particular, known as "Ferguson Road," was like riding a roller coaster! Mom and Dad knew not to drive on Ferguson Road too fast, especially if I was in the backseat. I could get carsick on those hills!

Isaiah has been talking about preparing for the coming of the Lord. Again, we do not need to take Isaiah's words literally. Southwest Iowa and her beautiful rolling hills are not going to be flattened to look like Kansas. This is more figurative talk of preparing for the Lord's arrival.

The good news is that we don't have to do anything. Isaiah isn't saying WE have to level the ground. God will take care of that. All we have to do is let Him. We just have to turn our lives over to the Lord, and He will do the rest. God will eliminate the roller coaster ride, saving us from the agony of the ups and downs that make us spiritually sick.

Lord, raise the valleys and lower the hills in my life. You know how hard the ups and downs of life can be on me. Come and save me from my spiritual sickness. Amen.

December 4

The light shines in the darkness, and the darkness
has not overcome it.

—John 1:5

December is the darkest month of the year, at least for us
in the northern hemisphere. Right now, the days are getting
shorter and shorter. Just before Christmas will be the winter
solstice—the day with the shortest amount of sunlight all year.

Lights are a very common form of decorating for Christmas.
On our eaves and railings, they illuminate the dark nights. On
our trees inside, they keep the winter darkness at bay.

However, I'm sure most, if not all, of us will admit that our
world dwells in a darkness that cannot be conquered by our
manmade lights. As wonderful as LED bulbs are, they just
cannot eliminate the darkness caused by the evil and hatred in
the world.

Thankfully, there is one light that can hold back the darkness
of this world. Jesus, the one true Light, shines brighter than a
million twinkling Christmas lights! He is a light that will never
burn out, never fade. This world's dark evil has not overcome
Christ's light because it *cannot* overcome the Light!

Lord, thank You for sending the light of Christ into this dark
world. May it illuminate my way today and always. Amen.

December 5

But He was pierced for our transgressions, He was crushed for our iniquities; the punishment that brought us peace was on Him, and by His wounds we are healed.

—Isaiah 53:5

I remember hearing my campus pastor once make the comment that we do not celebrate Easter because of Christmas. Rather, we celebrate Christmas because of Easter. Yes, Christ had to be born before He could die for us. However, it is His sacrifice that makes His birth so meaningful.

"What Child Is This" is my favorite Christmas song for many reasons. One reason comes in the lyrics of the second verse: "Nails, spear shall pierce Him through; the cross be borne for me, for you." The Son was born to die. Jesus has the birthday, but we are the ones who receive the gift.

While it's fine to enjoy the baby's birth in Bethlehem, we do need to remain mindful of the man's death on Calvary. One way you can do that is to hang a nail on your Christmas tree. You can also belt out the Christmas songs like "What Child Is This" and "I Wonder as I Wander."

Father, You gave the very first Christmas gift in Your Son. In all of my Christmas celebrations, keep me mindful of the sacrifice Jesus made. Help me remember that His death is as important as His birth. Amen.

December 6

Wait for the Lord; be strong and take heart and wait for the Lord.

—Psalm 27:14

Today is St. Nicholas Day, a day that we celebrated when I was growing up. My sister and I would each get one gift on St. Nicholas Day, which helped me wait for Christmas and the many gifts that would come then.

Waiting is difficult, even for adults. I have seen people waiting impatiently for grandchildren to be born. We wait for everything from the mundane stoplights of our daily commutes to a highly-anticipated and much-needed vacation. Things just don't happen fast enough.

Perhaps the hardest waiting of all is waiting for the Lord. We must wait for the Lord to answer our prayers, and we must wait for the Lord to return to us once again. Unlike holidays, children's births, and even stoplights, waiting for the Lord has no clear end. We can't cross dates off a calendar. Even with births, there is the due date to give us a pretty good idea of how long we will have to wait. Instead, when waiting for the Lord, we must simply wait.

But take heart! We are all waiting together!

Lord, as we wait for You, grant us the strength and endurance to patiently await Your arrival. Amen.

December 7

For to us a child is born, to us a son is given, and the government will be on His shoulders. And He will be called Wonderful Counselor, Mighty God, Everlasting Father, Prince of Peace.

—Isaiah 9:6

What's in a name? Is it really so important?

I have learned to share the view of one of my uncles when it comes to the importance of spelling names correctly. So now when someone misspells my name, I see that as a sign that the other person really doesn't care that much about me. If I really mattered to that person, they would make the effort to learn how to spell my name correctly.

In this verse, Isaiah gives several names to Jesus. These names say a lot about who Jesus would be. And He still is all of these things.

Jesus is our counselor, helping and guiding us through life. He is God, divine and holy. Jesus would say that He and the Father are one, so Jesus is as much our Father as He is our brother. And to know Jesus is to know peace.

What's in a name? Everything!

God, You gave Your Son the name above all other names. Thank You for caring enough to send Jesus to be my Shepherd, who knows me by name. Amen.

December 8

"You are My witnesses," declares the Lord, "and My servant whom I have chosen, so that you may know and believe Me and understand that I am He. Before Me no god was formed, nor will there be one after Me."

—Isaiah 43:10

Many of us will, at some point in our lives, wrestle with feelings of inadequacy. Unfortunately, some of us will experience those feelings as we join family for holiday gatherings. Others of us may feel inadequate more often than just this time of year and not just because of our families.

The good news is, though, that no matter how incompetent or insufficient we feel, our views of our abilities—or lack thereof—are not God's views of us. God has chosen each one of us and has called us into a fellowship with Him. And He has not given us more than we can handle. He knows, better than we do, what our abilities are.

The great news is that, through Christ, God has given us a way out of our feelings of inadequacy. God has shown us that He does indeed know how we feel. After all, Jesus came and lived with us, as a human, just like us. Therefore, we can come to Him for the assurance that He loves us and has chosen us.

God, when I am burdened with feelings of inadequacy, remind me that You have chosen me. I am Yours. Amen.

December 9

Even Elizabeth your relative is going to have a child in her old age, and she who was said to be unable to conceive is in her sixth month.
—Luke 1:36

These words were spoken by the angel Gabriel to Mary, explaining how a virgin could conceive a child. One barren woman was already over halfway through her pregnancy. For Elizabeth, that pregnancy was a miracle. And, of course, Mary's pregnancy was also a miracle.

It's said that Christmas is the season for miracles. Many Christmas movies are centered on the premise that wonderful things happen at the end of December. All you need is hope and a little Christmas magic.

Are you in need of a miracle in your life? I once heard a pastor remark that one of the biggest miracles in the Christmas story is that Mary believed what the angel told her. Maybe the miracle you need will come by believing in God's plan for you.

Take a moment to learn a lesson from Mary. Believe in miracles. Have faith in God. Believe that God can do anything. And maybe this year you will be blessed with the miracle you need.

Dearest Lord, there are times when I need a miracle in my life. Whether I find myself in need of big miracles or small ones, give me faith in You to fulfill my needs. Amen.

December 10

Because Joseph her husband was faithful to the
law, and yet did not want to expose her to public
disgrace, he had in mind to divorce her quietly.
—Matthew 1:19

Have you ever wondered why Joseph did not want to see
Mary punished? If he loved her enough to spare her the disgrace,
why did he not love her enough to take her as his wife anyway?
Of course, the story ends with Joseph doing just that, but only
because he learned that Mary was pregnant by the Holy Spirit
not another man.

Whatever his reason, Joseph had compassion for someone
he thought had wronged him. And this compassion was not the
norm in his time. Actually, such compassion is not even the norm
in our time.

This Advent, we could each honor Joseph by following his
example. Let's show compassion to those who we think have
wronged us. And maybe, like Joseph, we will learn that we
were, in fact, never wronged in the first place. However, even
if the offense against us was real, Joseph's compassion is the
Christlike thing to have.

Jesus, Joseph showed Mary compassion before Your birth.
Remind me of his example, which preceded Your own examples
of compassion and forgiveness. Help me to extend compassion
to those who have wronged me. Amen.

December 11

Give thanks to the Lord, for He is good; His love endures forever.

—Psalm 107:1

No, I am not confused. I realize that this is the season of Advent, that Thanksgiving is over. And no, I am not protesting the fact that stores had Christmas decorations out as soon as Halloween was over.

Advent is full of preparations. Should it not also be full of thanksgiving? As we are preparing for Christmas dinner, we can be thankful for the feasts in which we will partake. As we are preparing for countless Christmas pageants and concerts, we should thank God for the children in our lives. As we are out shopping for Christmas presents, we should be thankful for the friends and family we have in our lives.

We have so much for which we should be thankful, and our gratitude for God's generosity should extend well beyond that fourth Thursday in November. God is indeed good, and He gave us the best Christmas present ever—His Son! And God's love most certainly does endure forever. Thus there is no reason that our praises and thanksgiving to God should not also endure forever!

Lord God, Your love truly endures forever. Thank You for the many blessings in my life. Thank You especially for the gift of Jesus, the best Christmas present ever! Amen.

December 12

But the angel said to them, "Do not be afraid. I bring you good news that will cause great joy for all the people."

—Luke 2:10

Have you ever watched *A Charlie Brown Christmas*? I grew up watching it. Like so many people, I could recite right along with Linus the monologue that tells Charlie Brown "what Christmas is all about." But not long ago, there was an interesting detail that was mentioned in someone's blog.

When Linus, who was so attached to his blanket that he insisted on making it part of his costume, got to this verse, he seems to drop his blanket! As I watched that clip included in the blog, I couldn't tell if the animators did that on purpose or not. Due to the closeup nature of the drawing, his blanket is essentially "off camera" when Linus says, "Fear not!" Yet, he has his blanket before that line, and when the view is more widespread moments later, his blanket is on the floor.

Whether or not the timing of the blanket drop was intentional, the blogger pointed out one very important point. Linus kept that blanket for security. And, when reciting the news of Christ's birth, Linus no longer needed that security. And neither do we. Jesus is the only source of security we need!

Christ, help me to drop the comforts to which I cling, as You alone are all the security I need. Amen.

December 13

The wolf will live with the lamb, the leopard
will lie down with the goat, the calf and the lion
and the yearling together; and a little child will
lead them.

—Isaiah 11:6

This is another verse commonly read during Advent. It
speaks of a wondrous utopia where all of creation is at peace.
Predator and prey will live together without fear or conflict.
And all this tranquility will come under the leadership of a child.

Children are absolutely amazing! They look at the world
through eyes of innocence. How many times have you stopped to
question something yourself, simply because a child asked you,
"Why?" Why is it, really, that we are allowed to make right turns
on red lights? Why do we have the school year schedules that
we do? And why do we have to eat the vegetables we don't like?

Perhaps the best question children have ever asked is, "Why
can't this person be my friend?" Children don't care about skin
color or age. We adults see the way things are in this world. But
children see the way things could be. We should let our children
lead us. Following their Christlike example will certainly yield
us many more friends!

Lord, please give me the eyes and heart of a child. Let me see
the world as You want it to be—full of peace where enemies can
truly be friends. Amen.

December 14

Therefore keep watch, because you do not know
on what day your Lord will come.
—Matthew 24:42

Advent calendars will count down the days until Christmas,
but this season is not just about preparing for the birth of Christ.
Advent is also about preparing our hearts for Christ's return.
We really don't want to be caught off-guard when Christ comes
back!

Jesus warned His disciples, and warns us also, about the
need to be alert. We know when Christmas is. We know what
day we celebrate our Lord coming to us the first time. Yet Jesus
Himself doesn't even know when He will return. He told His
disciples that much.

With all the craziness of the Christmas season, let's not
forget about Advent. Remember that Advent doesn't truly end
upon the arrival of Christmas. We still need to be watching and
waiting for Christ. He will return, and we need to be ready.

So, how do we make sure we're ready for Jesus' return? Just
as we want our houses to be neat and tidy when our Christmas
guests arrive, we need to make sure our lives are clean when
Jesus arrives. We need to get rid of the hatred and indifference
that dirty our hearts. By living lives of love, we will properly
prepare for our Lord.

Lord, help me clean up my life and my heart. Make me prepared
for Your return. Amen.

December 15

Sing to the Lord, praise His name; proclaim His salvation day after day.

—Psalm 96:2

My dad is not much of a singer. He never has been. But when I was growing up, there were two hymns I can remember hearing him actually sing during church. One of those hymns was "O Come, All Ye Faithful." Dad would not exactly belt it out, but I could quite clearly hear those familiar lines: "O come, let us adore Him! O come, let us adore Him! O come, let us adore Him, Christ the Lord!"

Not everyone can sing well. Yet, the psalmist is not telling just those with musical ability to sing. He didn't say, "All professional singers need to raise their voices in praise!" Nor did he say, "All choir members join together now!" Rather, the psalmist calls everyone to join in singing praise to the Lord. And why shouldn't we? He sent His Son for our salvation!

So whether you are the star of your church choir or someone unable to carry a tune in a bucket, heed the call of the psalmist this Advent. Sing out to the Lord! Every single one of our beloved Christmas hymns do indeed proclaim God's salvation!

God, teach me to sing Your praises every day of my life. Help me to proclaim Your salvation to all the world. Amen.

December 16

But Mary treasured up all these things and pondered them in her heart.

—Luke 2:19

Have you ever had an experience that you thought about over and over again? Has someone said or done something that made an impression on your life? I have had many treasured moments that I have pondered later.

One such time came as I was sitting down to lead a children's sermon at church. It was Easter Sunday, and there were many kids coming up to join me. As one of the younger girls sat down, she a made a point of telling me that she was going to sit beside me. A couple adults had already expressed their displeasure with me that morning, so I can't help but wonder if that girl had any idea that she melted my heart with her loving gesture.

Mary knew that her baby was going to be special. After all, she'd been told just that by the angel Gabriel. So what the shepherds said in the stable that night was not news. It should have been just a little thing. Yet she pondered it in her heart.

It is my hope that, during this Advent and throughout our lives, we never lose the sense of wonder and never stop treasuring the little things.

Lord, life is full of little things. Help me to treasure all of life's moments and, like Mary, ponder them in my heart. Amen.

December 17

We wait in hope for the Lord; He is our help and our shield.

—Psalm 33:20

There is a lot of hoping done during Advent. We may hope that we get something particular for Christmas. We may hope that we will get to see certain family members over the holidays. We may hope that the weather holds for our own Christmas travels.

Hope is symbolized on the Advent wreath by the first candle we light. And it is very fitting that we start out this season with hope. To quote the movie *Shawshank Redemption*, "Hope is a good thing, maybe the best of things." The character who said this pointed out that hope was most needed within those prison walls, where hope seemed pointless.

By now, we are well into Advent, but let's not lose the hope we started with. We lit the candle for hope first, but we are still lighting that candle. Whatever specific thing you are hoping for this season, let that hope continue to burn in you as the candle continues to burn on our Advent wreaths. The Lord will deliver. We just need to keep hoping.

God, You know how hard it can be sometimes to keep hope alive, especially when the wait has been long and hope seems pointless. Help me. Keep me hoping. Amen.

December 18

And everyone went to their own town to register.
—Luke 2:3

The first Christmas was full of traveling! Everyone had to go home. It was ordered by the emperor. I wonder what it was like for all of those people heading to "their towns" again, especially for those who had long since moved on with their lives.

Once I had graduated from college and embarked on a new life, I really experienced the concept of "leaving home to go home." I was always anxious to go home for Christmas. But, at the same time, I was always ready to come back home after Christmas.

One thing I never really enjoyed was the actual drive between "homes." I remember more than one time that the drive was more than just a little hair-raising. Winter storms, or even the threat of them, can put quite the damper on holiday travels! Of course, even when the weather is good, we must contend with the other holiday travelers.

Wherever you end up spending Christmas, even if it's not where you wanted to be, remember that any place can be home. It's not about the location. It's about the love.

Thank You, God, for the many homes I have had in my life. Please protect all who are traveling, that they may arrive safely with their loved ones for Christmas. Amen.

December 19

Therefore the Lord Himself will give you a sign:
The virgin will conceive and give birth to a son,
and will call Him Immanuel.

—Isaiah 7:14

The prophet Isaiah spoke many times of Christ's coming among us. And this is not the only place where Jesus is given a name. Here He is called Immanuel, or God With Us.

Have you ever stopped to think about the name Immanuel, or Emmanuel as it can also be spelled? We sing it in the popular Advent song, "O Come, O Come Emmanuel." Yet, how many of us have actually given any thought to what it is that we are asking in that song? We are asking the Lord to come among us.

Many children are notorious for misbehaving when they are left home alone. When left unsupervised, kids can have so much fun that they can make a terrible mess out of their homes. Parents have often kidded that they must get home to see if they still have a house standing!

And now, we are asking our heavenly Father to come back among us. We have indeed made a mess of our lives. We need God's supervision that comes from His being with us.

Father, please come back to me. I need Your watchful eye to keep me out of trouble. Amen.

December 20

Glory to God in the highest heaven, and on earth
peace to those on whom His favor rests.

—Luke 2:14

In the movie *I'll Be Home for Christmas*, a boy asks his father
why everyone keeps talking about peace on earth when there
isn't any. This movie takes place during WWII, and this boy's
oldest brother was killed trying to come home from the war for
Christmas. The father answers his son by saying that peace on
earth is a hope that everyone wishes for.

Even when our country is not engaged in war, there are
always people who cannot be home for Christmas. There are
always members of the military who must carry on their service.
Some are simply stationed overseas. Others are deployed to
hostile areas, places in the world where a strong military
presence is needed. There is never complete peace on earth.

Christmas is now five days away. Let's take a moment now
to pray for those whose holiday celebrations are not what they'd
like due to a lack of peace on earth. Let's all keep hoping that
someday everyone will be able to be home for Christmas.

Lord, I pray for peace on earth. Please end all hostilities between
nations and peoples. But until that peace is achieved, be with
those whose lives have been turned upside down because of
hostilities. Amen.

December 21

"Martha, Martha," the Lord answered, "you are worried and upset about many things, but few things are needed—or indeed only one. Mary has chosen what is better, and it will not be taken away from her."

—Luke 10:41-42

This was about the time every December in my childhood when things would just get crazy, especially when we were hosting the family Christmas. The house had to be cleaned. The turkey and all the fixings for Christmas dinner needed to be purchased. And where on earth did all the Christmas presents get hidden? They must be wrapped!

Martha was trying to be a good hostess, but, as most of us know, that takes a lot of work! Mary wasn't helping. However, Jesus reminded Martha about what was important, about *who* was important. The only thing that matters is Jesus.

As Christmas nears and our lives get more hectic with preparations, let's remember what is needed. Christmas isn't about clean homes, stuffed turkeys, or presents under the tree. Christmas is about Jesus. Indeed, Jesus is all we need.

Jesus, during this time of year, I can become worried and upset about many things. Gently remind me, as You did Martha, that all I need is You. I pray in Your holy name. Amen.

December 22

When the angels had left them and gone into heaven, the shepherds said to one another, "Let's go to Bethlehem and see this thing that has happened, which the Lord has told us about."
—Luke 2:15

One of the worst interruptions I have had while working was to have a fire alarm go off during a massage, which actually happened more than once when I was a massage therapist in a hospital. When those pesky alarms sounded, I had to listen to the message over the PA system to find out what part of the hospital was affected. Thanks to those messages, I knew how to respond.

The shepherds were working that night in the field. They had chosen to stay out with their sheep, rather than penning their flocks up for the night. Then they were interrupted by the angels. They listened to the message and also knew how to respond. They had to go see the baby Jesus.

This time of year can feel full of interruptions, especially as we prepare for Christmas festivities. But whenever an interruption comes, we need to stop and take heed of the message that is being brought to us. We might need to shift our priorities.

Thank You, God, for interrupting me with Your important messages. Keep me mindful of what You tell me, and help me shift my priorities to match Yours. Amen.

December 23

However, I consider my life worth nothing to me;
my only aim is to finish the race and complete
the task the Lord Jesus has given me—the task
of testifying to the good news of God's grace.
—Acts 20:24

Christmas is almost upon us. Soon we shall enjoy all the fruits of our labors. After that, things change. The feast we worked so hard to prepare will be leftovers we shove in the refrigerator. The pieces of wrapping paper that were so delicately folded around presents will be chunks of discarded trash. Even the presents themselves, while celebrated at first, will be casually set aside.

It can actually be a little depressing to think that what we are currently working so hard to do will be nothing in a few days. But in this speech, the apostle Paul shares his priorities with the Ephesian elders. Paul's priorities should also be our priorities.

We should focus on the task of spreading the news about God's grace. In essence, let's keep Christmas about Christ. Then we won't experience any depression when food and presents lose their allure. They won't turn into "nothing" because they truly were nothing to begin with. Christ is everything!

Lord, help me keep You as the focus of Christmas. May I be diligent about sharing the news of Your grace. Amen.

December 24

And she gave birth to her firstborn, a son.
—Luke 2:7a

In that one sentence is an ending and a beginning. Mary's pregnancy had ended. With those nine words, nine months of planning and waiting came to a close. Her journey in motherhood was just beginning. There was a new life for her to nurture, and there was someone depending on her.

That sentence still presents an ending and a beginning for us today. It ends mankind's responsibility to take punishment for sin. Instead, salvation and grace begin. There is a new life to be given for our sin, and there is someone new on whom we can depend.

And, of course, the season of Advent now ends. Christmas has begun. The joy and excitement of the holiday brings new life to each of us, and we celebrate with our family and friends, those who depend on us and those on whom we depend.

The second verse of "Silent Night" proclaims it well: "Christ the Savior is born!" Our darkness has ended. The Light has come and gives us a new beginning. Let's celebrate! Merry Christmas, everyone!

Heavenly Father, thank You for the sending Your Son to end our misery and death and to give us a new beginning with Him. May my life always proclaim His glory, and may the celebrating never end! Amen.

December 25

Let the rivers clap their hands, let the mountains sing together for joy.

—Psalm 98:8

Living in the upper Midwest, I have seen a lot of different weather for Christmas Day. I've seen sunny skies. I've seen snow gently falling. I have also seen sleet and blizzards. The strangest weather I have ever witnessed on Christmas Day came in 2016. My area of South Dakota experienced a full-blown thunderstorm!

As I exited the church after Christmas Day worship, I was disconcerted by the unseasonal thunder and lightning. However, as I waited at a stoplight, I found my apprehension shifting to awe. A smile crept across my face. I began to feel that the earth itself was rejoicing in the holiday with thunderclaps and a light display of its own!

Today is Christmas! Like the angels, let us sing. Like the shepherds, let us proclaim glad tidings. Like the earth itself, let us rejoice in whatever ways we can, even if that means we respond in ways that are unconventional.

Christ is with us. Christ has saved us. We have nothing to fear. Let go of any and all apprehensions. Embrace the excitement and the awe of the holiday.

Happy birthday, dear Jesus! Today I celebrate Your coming into the world and into my life! Amen.

December 26

When He had received the drink, Jesus said, "It is finished." With that, He bowed His head and gave up His spirit.

—John 19:30

"It is finished." Many people have that sentiment on the day after Christmas. It's done, finished, over. Throw out the Christmas tree. Take down the Christmas decorations. And, by all means, stop playing the Christmas music!

When Jesus said, "It is finished" from the cross, He was marking an end. His suffering was done. His life was over. However, even Jesus knew that His death wasn't the end of everything.

If anything, Jesus' words simply marked the end of a chapter. The story of our salvation continues. Nothing is truly finished until Jesus comes back to us again and brings us all to live with Him.

In the same way, Christmas is never truly finished. Sure, we put away the lights and decorations. Real Christmas trees are thrown out, and artificial trees are stored away for another year. Christmas albums are removed from our playlists. But the joy of Christmas never ends. So let's embrace that joy this day after Christmas, into the new year, and throughout however many years pass before Christ returns.

Lord, help me to carry the joy of Christmas throughout the entire year and throughout my whole life. Amen.

December 27

The lion has roared—who will not fear? The Sovereign Lord has spoken—who can but prophesy?

—Amos 3:8

By observing the world around us, most of us have become fairly good at anticipating what is going to happen based on what has just happened. For example, while we don't usually come face to face with lions, we are still pretty familiar with the warning signs animals give us that they are unhappy. If a dog growls or a cat hisses, we know we should approach with caution or not approach at all. And we will certainly warn those around us who are unaware of the danger the animal poses.

When God speaks, not everyone will understand. Some of us have more experience with hearing God's voice than others. Some of us are more comfortable in knowing what to listen for when listening for God's voice.

When those of us who hear and understand God's voice receive His spoken word, we can't help but pass it on. Whether we are interpreting a dog's growl or a cat's purr, we share our understanding with others. Likewise we must share our understanding of God's Word whenever we hear Him speak. We just can't help it. We have been called.

God, give me the courage to share what I hear when You speak to me. Use me as Your prophet. Amen.

December 28

A voice is heard in Ramah, weeping and great mourning, Rachel weeping for her children and refusing to be comforted, because they are no more.

—Matthew 2:18

These words are also found in the book of Jeremiah. They are mentioned in Matthew as King Herod's slaughter of the innocent children of Bethlehem fulfilled the prophet's words. Today we remember the "Slaughter of the Innocents."

There is no historical evidence that such a slaughter ever took place. But why would there be? Bethlehem was such a small town that the number of children killed may have only been somewhere between two and twenty. That is a minuscule number in the eyes of most historians. Besides, Herod was one of the bloodiest kings who ever lived! He killed his own children whenever he felt they were threatening him!

It is still important that we remember the children of Bethlehem, if for no other reason than it helps us be more aware of the slaughters that happen today. As Christians, we simply cannot turn a blind eye to people who are being persecuted and killed simply for being who they are, who have done absolutely nothing. We must stand up to genocides, wherever they occur.

Lord, protect those who are being persecuted for who they are. Help me to fight on their behalf. Amen.

December 29

[B]ut those who hope in the Lord will renew their strength. They will soar on wings like eagles; they will run and not grow weary, they will walk and not be faint.

—Isaiah 40:31

The end of the year approaches. It seems to be common practice to review the year as it draws to a close. We remember the good times—the trips, the parties, the events. And we remember the bad times—the deaths, the fights, the natural disasters. Some years are better than others. Some years leave us feeling satisfied. Other years can leave us feeling exhausted and ready for it to be over.

Regardless of what type of year we have had, we should continue to hope in our Lord. If we place our hope in God, we will find that our strength is indeed renewed. If we trust in God to bring us through the upcoming year, we will soar into the new year with the determination to tackle every obstacle.

As our new year progresses, we need to keep our hope strong. That is how God will give us the endurance to keep going strong, no matter what the year throws at us. And then, this time next year, we can reflect on a year that was full of hope.

God, in You I place my hope. You have brought me through this year, and I trust You to be with me this coming year. Amen.

December 30

Let us then approach God's throne of grace with confidence, so that we may receive mercy and find grace to help us in our time of need.
—Hebrews 4:16

I tend to be fairly confident in what I do. Sometimes I am very confident. Yet I must confess that there are times when I find my confidence lacking. In fact, the times when my confidence is the weakest tend to be when I need to ask for help.

I do have close friends to whom I know I can turn when I need that help. In one way or another, they have told me so. Still, I hesitate to ask for help. I hear a voice in my head telling me that I do not deserve any help and that my friends will not be gracious.

However, that voice in my head, no matter how loud, is wrong. These friends aren't willing to help me out of my tight spots because I deserve their assistance. Rather, they help me because they care about me. Thus, I can approach them with confidence.

The same is true of God. We don't deserve God's grace, but God cares about us. God will show us grace and mercy. All we have to do is ask. So, knowing how much God loves us, let's ask for His mercy confidently.

God, I do not deserve Your grace, but I know that You care deeply for me. I confidently ask for Your mercy. Amen.

December 31

He who was seated on the throne said, "I am making everything new!" Then He said, "Write this down, for these words are trustworthy and true."

—Revelation 21:5

Well, this is it. This is the last day of this year. Tonight many people will throw parties to usher out the old year and ring the new year in with style.

Tomorrow many people will begin new commitments, their New Year's resolutions. And the vast majority of those people won't stick with their newfound commitments for more than a few months. After awhile of struggling, they will just give up.

As we near the start of a new year, let's remember the one who makes all things new. God was with us when this year began. He gave us a year of blessings, amid the trials we faced. Throughout the course of this year, God granted us many new beginnings.

If you decide to make a New Year's resolution, make sure God is included in it. If a few months down the road you find yourself ready to give up on any commitment, turn to God and ask Him to again make your life new. Remember, God's words are trustworthy and true!

God, Alpha and Omega, You do indeed make all things new. As this year ends, grant me a year full of new beginnings in You. Amen.

Printed in the United States
By Bookmasters